# WRESTLING WITH
# THE ANGEL

# WRESTLING WITH THE ANGEL

## FAITH AND RELIGION IN THE LIVES OF GAY MEN

EDITED BY

BRIAN BOULDREY

RIVERHEAD BOOKS

NEW YORK

1995

Riverhead Books
a division of G. P. Putnam's Sons
Publishers Since 1838
200 Madison Avenue
New York, NY 10016

The editor gratefully acknowledges permission from the estate
of Jack Spicer to quote "He had sent his family across the river...";
and from Alamo Square Press to reprint "Personal Dichotomies,"
from Out of the Bishop's Closet by Antonio Feliz.

Library of Congress Cataloging-in-Publication Data

Wrestling with the angel : faith and religion in the lives of gay men
/ edited by Brian Bouldrey.
p.    cm.
ISBN 1-57322-003-5
1. Homosexuality—Religious aspects—Christianity.
2. Homosexuality—Religious aspects—Judaism.    3. Homosexuality—
Religious aspects.    4. Gay men—United States—Religious life.
I. Bouldrey, Brian.
BR115.H6W74    1995                    94-44307 CIP
277.3'082'086642—dc20

Designed by Ann Gold

Printed in the United States of America
1   3   5   7   9   10   8   6   4   2

This book is printed on acid-free paper. ∞

# ACKNOWLEDGMENTS

Several people have been instrumental in helping find the diverse voices that fill this book. Others have advised me to make the book stronger. Special thanks go to Wendy Lesser, Brad Craft, Ira Silverberg, Phil Gambone, John Skoyles, Jonathan Strong, Don Osborne, Charles Baxter, Anthony Veerkamp, Steve Sprowles, Mary South, Bernard Shir-Cliff, Jerry Thompson, Reginald Gibbons, Gwenan Wilbur, Hugh Rowland, Peter Ginsberg, Bert Herrman, Robin Blaser, Sanford Sylvan and the laboring fax machine at Jossey-Bass.

# Contents

# INTRODUCTION

It has been almost a year and a half since I woke up that morning—it was Memorial Day, of all days!—to find Jeff gone. He was still warm where he fell, and even now it occurs to me that after death, certain bodily functions continue. Nails grow, muscles tense. It makes sense to me, then, that the little hammer and anvil process in his ear vibrated so that he might have heard me mutter, "Finally." The memory of saying that makes me, at turns, ashamed and assured.

This book was inspired by the pondering of the "finally" of Jeff's existence, and his passing. Watching Jeff die led to thoughts of my own mortality and, inevitably, my own spirituality. I wanted a book that would help me piece together all that was meant by my last word to him.

Right to the end, Jeff dismissed the Catholicism we were both raised in, while I—well. Let all secrets be out now, when they matter less. I would pray at night the Prayer of St. Francis in our bedroom upstairs, while he slept on the bed downstairs, too weak to make the trip up to the top any more.

I had always wondered why Catholics are fond of praying to everybody but God—the Virgin Mary, the angels and saints, the Sacred Heart of Jesus—but since Jeff died, I have found myself praying to him, at times.

Where does Jeff fit into the hierarchy of the Catholic cosmology? He was a classic saint. He was a carpenter, and a good cook, too, and he knew the pleasures of the flesh and mind as well as anyone. Missing him made me discover why the Catholic church has constructed a vast network of flesh-and-blood intermediaries, messengers to God. I imagine that in those early days of the Church there must have been in every village an especially wonderful person, a person like Jeff, who helped others, maybe led the community, would fix my ox-cart and wouldn't accept payment, gave extra tomatoes from his garden, told a good story. Then he would die, and he'd leave a huge, gaping hole in the fabric of the village, and the people would miss him so keenly that they just knew he was close to God.

God, for those early Christians, was too vast for the imagination. God kept spilling out of the mind's frame, denying His faithful a sense of perfection, of wholeness, by putting it in heaven. But as Browning's Andrea del Sarto mused, ". . . a man's reach should exceed his grasp, or what's a heaven for?" What makeshift mosaic one could construct of God's heaven came in the form of the good people they all missed. People like Jeff, I figure. Little bits of heaven. It has always been more consoling to make saints, in order to better imagine heaven—in order to encourage the imagination and faith.

Reading, too, encourages imagination and faith, and it has always struck me as a form of prayer. My head is bent, my body is still; it is a familiar and comforting position. I have always read as much as I could—on commuter trains, in elevators. But after Jeff's death, I read insatiably, and I read out of need. I was prayerful. And I began to wonder how many men like me were discovering this same paradoxical devoutness—or rediscovering their own faith. So I asked all the writers I admired, and this book was born.

One response I received might have come directly from Jeff. It was, in fact, from the late, great John Preston, who wrote me weeks before *his* death: "Alas, I'd have nothing to say in your anthology. As an atheist I have no angels with which to wrestle and, to be honest, I think adults who worry about such a decrepit institution as organized religion should drink plenty of liquids, pop an aspirin, and take a nap, in hopes the malady would pass." He—and Jeff—those two certainly disprove that observation about the lack of atheists in foxholes.

But what I received many more of are powerful essays by writers who don't care to dwell long on the broken laws or the retracted invitations of their religions. They instead reproach the rulemakers and turn to examine the tradition and the depths of the faith in which they were raised. These essays proved to me that gays, more than ever before, are learning to embrace their whole lives.

I know that for Jeff, coming out of the closet meant jettisoning his entire past life: the farm he grew up on, his family, his friends, the girl he took to the prom and thought he might marry. It also meant abandoning his religion. Jeff came to San Francisco to make a new life in a place that would allow his natural desire.

Of course, it is human nature and good common sense to not pursue what spurns us—and the Church had to go. But Jeff lived to see his parents come around. They accepted Jeff, his homosexuality, his boyfriend, and even his illness and death. At the funeral, it seemed that an Illinois town of two thousand people accepted Jeff—and last but not least, the priest. At the wake, he asked, over our three-bean salad combination, "Did he suffer?"

I think it scared him to ask me, and I answered, "Yes," very quickly and firmly. I think I meant to wound him, stick him with the word like a knife. And I think it worked—but it did him some good. Who knows better than we do that wounds open us up?

As for me, I sometimes wonder, half-jokingly, if being argumentative with my own religion led me to my sexual identity. Was my desire to launch into a critical examination of the fine points of Catholic dogma linked in some secret way to my desire for men? I know I made my parents nervous during a lenten service I attended in prepubescence, in which I discussed, in the car ride home, how I felt sorry for the Pharisees. The Pharisees, according to the day's homily, were more interested in adherence to the Law than the presence of God among them. When Christ came among them and his followers claimed he was the Son of God, the Pharisees spent a good deal of time trying to trip him up with semantics, proving that he was breaking the laws of the Synagogue. "Do you say that you are the Son of God?" Jesus, indulging in the same antics with semantics, responded, "I didn't say that. You said that."

"Weren't the Pharisees just doing their job?" I asked.

Good Lord, my mother probably thought, this and the paper dolls! My son is a heretic—he must be a homosexual.

Being raised Catholic forced upon me a lot of stupid semantic arguments, but it also offered me centuries of good, hard thinking, even if I don't always agree with it. Pope Gregory XI, crabby jerk that he was, consented to having the priests of his time write down the medieval drinking songs of Europe in Latin because it was good practice for wandering scholars. He justified such tomfoolery by quoting the Bible: "And the Israelites went down among the Philistines to sharpen their swords." So it is with me and the Catholic dogmatists. Nowadays, I see myself grappling with Catholic dogma and think of this wrestling as an integral part of my spiritual life, as a kind of rambunctious prayer.

And I have strived, I admit. Like a boy with an incredibly complex model kit and the wrong kind of glue, I've studied the instruction book, argued with it, hammered out my own version of it, broke it, bent it, ignored it. But over the years, it's safe to say that this struggling has made me a better Catholic than I am a model-maker.

As these essays arrived, I wondered at the passion of these pieces. Clearly, now more than ever before, the issues religion takes up are those most important to gay men: the conditions and relations of the mind, body, and soul, how we live, how we love, how we die.

And finally, how we let others die—the difference between detaching oneself and giving in to despair. These essays highlight one thing the Catholic church *did* get right: despair is considered the gravest of sins. It is easy and comfortable. It is the absence of faith and a failure of the imagination. And in these times, it is awfully tempting.

My last word to Jeff was the hardest thing I have ever said. That "finally" was an act of detachment, not despair. And detachment is a painful, human act of faith.

In each of these essays there is an effort, a questioning, a wrestling with faith, but there is no despair. I hope you will feel, as I do, that the contributors to this collection have started a fight no one can lose and built something inspiring from their struggle.

—Brian Bouldrey
San Francisco
October 1994

*He had sent his family across the river.*
*The wives, the heavy oxen—paraphernalia*
*Of many years of clever living.*
*The water flowed past them. All that evening*
*Jacob was wrestling in the arms of a stranger.*
*It was not unexpected. By midnight*
*They had explored each other's strength and every hour*
*was a tender repetition.*
*At dawn the angel tried to free himself and Jacob*
*Held him with one last burst of strength, screaming.*
*After that there had never been an angel. Lucky Jacob*
*Limped across the river, thinking of his wives and oxen.*

—Jack Spicer, 1959

# WRESTLING WITH THE ANGEL

# Sweet Chariot

I grew up in two religions.

The first one—comforting, strange, rigorous, in its way— was comprised of an astonishing and lovely set of images. It was a religion given to me primarily by my grandmother, a fundamentalist Christian from East Tennessee whose faith had the kind of solidity and rock-depth upon which Jesus must have intended to found his church. *She* was Peter's rock, unshakable, holding us all up—or at least holding me up; I was too small to have much of a sense of what she meant to my parents or to her husband, my cantankerous and difficult grandfather who outlived her by twenty years. My memories of her are very particular ones: a day out behind our house when she and I picked dandelion and poke greens, and the sunlight filtered through the thin flowered rayon dress she wore—this would have been 1957 or '58— and she showed me the right leaves to pick for the greens she'd boil with fatback to serve with the chicken she'd plucked and set to roast in a black graniteware pan sparked with a whole firmament of stars. In that house, where she and my grandfather lived with us, their room was a secret source of depth and meaning. (I didn't like him much, but I liked his things: a drawerful of beautiful, useless old fountain pens with marbled cases, cigar boxes full of rubber bands, stuff saved for the day it would surely be needed.)

I loved *her* with all my heart, and everything that was hers: the green rocking chair, a fruitcake tin filled with swirled peppermint candies, the Bible with the words of Jesus printed in red, like holidays on a calendar. She would set me up on her lap and, rocking all the while, read Bible verses to me. I'm not sure if I remember especially her readings from Revelations, but it simply feels to me now, whenever I hear someone mention a phrase like "last days" or "apocalypse," that the scent of her—lavender and peppermint and clean old dresses—and the texture of her clothes and the Bible's leatherette cover and onionskin pages are forever commingled with those words; some essence of her imbues them. It was she who presented me with my first religion, which was the religion of images, and they were given to me in Bible verses and in the songs we'd sing on the porch swing, summer nights: the sweet chariot coming to carry us home, the moon turning to blood, the angels sounding the trump so that all the dead would clap hands and arise, the thin veil of this world—thin as her sprig-scattered skirt!—parting at last and opening into a world we need not fear, though it would be awesome, a world made true and just and bright and eternally resonant as the songs we sang.

I loved the word *chariot*. I couldn't sing it without thinking of the cherries in my uncle's orchard, which I'd seen once, and where my father had lifted me up into the branches so that I could pick the half-ripe fruit. Sweet chariot, sweet cherries, gold and red and green, a kind of glowing flush like heat on the skin of the little fruit, which was smooth and cleft and satisfying on the tongue as the word: *chariot*. This was the way the images invited us to dream into them.

I don't think I had any awareness of the second religion, the codes of explanation and prohibition, until after her death. I was five. She died of a heart attack, throwing her bedroom window open and gasping for air. I remember most vividly being wrapped in a quilt, one she'd made, I imagine. I watched TV very early in the morning, at an hour when I wasn't usually awake, and saw the minister come in his black jacket and collar, his odd flowery scent. And then gladiolas around her coffin, and again that sweet essence of peppermint and lavender, and little ribbons decorating the flowers on her grave. I dreamed that she came to see me, in the night, and stood beside a cane chair in a circle of lamplight to speak to me—very softly and intimately and comfortingly, and importantly, though I haven't any memory at all of what she said.

My understanding of a more worldly religion began after that. One Sunday there was a sermon especially for children—I believe this was in a Presbyterian church in Nashville, or perhaps in Memphis, that we attended then— instead of the usual Sunday school Bible stories accompanied by big colored pictures. (What were they? I want to say chromolithographs, or engravings, perhaps because the pictures and their sense of the world, an ancient and quaint exoticism they portrayed, seems so firmly of the nineteenth century.) This Sunday, no Baby Moses in the bulrushes or Joseph in his Coat of Many Colors. Instead, the minister told us a story about the terrible dangers of desire.

A little girl's mother had baked a particularly beautiful pie and set the pie on the dining table to cool, saying to her daughter, "Make sure that you do not touch this pie." The girl thought about this and tried not to touch the impossibly attractive pie. But after a time, overcome by her longing, she simply could not resist anymore, and she decided that if she snitched—that was the word the minister used, *snitched* (a particularly pinched, ratlike little word, it seems to me now, full of disdain and pettiness)—just one little piece it would be all right. So she did, taking the little bit of pie into the closet and eating it in the dark, where no one could see her. The morsel eaten, she was still filled with hunger; the pie was so good, she wanted it so badly. So she would snitch just one more little piece, and eat it in the dark, surrounded by the scratchy and comforting wool of her parents' coats. But, of course, that didn't satisfy her either; once a contract with appetite had been entered into, there wasn't any turning back. And standing in the dark, her hands and lips covered with the evidence of her need, the little girl felt, suddenly, seen. She was watched and she knew it, and so she turned her face upwards into the dark from which that sense of witness came, and there, floating above her, was the eye of God: enormous, missing nothing, utterly implacable.

My parents told me that when we came home after this sermon, I hid under my bed and wouldn't come out. I don't remember that now, but I do remember inventing a new game, which I used to play alone, since my sister was ten years older and I was, practically, an only child. We lived that year in a big old house on a horse farm we rented. The horses used to wander around about their own business— nameless, cared for by others. In my new game, I marked off some portion of the yard by the abandoned chicken coop and named it Hell, and I'd play devil, racing about the perimeter with my pitchfork, poking at souls, meting out punishments, keeping them in line. With a girl who lived down our road, I'd play a game in which we took turns dying and going to heaven, which I imagined as a kind of garden with a maze, a rose garden, in which I would meet a blond and milky Jesus. *I come to the garden alone, while the dew is still on the roses* . . . But that game, which was soon forbidden to us by a relative who said, "You mustn't play that, it might come true," was a game of images, of peace and stillness. My game of Hell was an enactment of energy and ferocity, of power and defiance. I think I have responded to the religion of prohibition in this way ever since.

Perhaps if my grandmother had lived, and if we'd stayed in Tennessee, my two religions would have merged, and I would have grown away from the images I was originally given, or felt oppressed by them. But because I was split off from that world, the landscape of my childhood and of the songs seems permanent to me, sealed, untouchable, a mythic landscape of hymns, with their rivers and flowers, their cherry trees and blood and moons. We moved away from my parents' families, on to suburbs in Arizona and Southern California and Florida, and into a succession of increasingly polite Protestant churches, which finally sort of evaporated into a bland social gesture, which was easily set aside. My mother, late in her life, found a religion of imagery again in an Anglican church so high and so influenced by the architecture and pageantry of Mexican Catholicism as to be a kind of spiritual theater. I came, after a while, to seek images of comfort and challenge and transformation in art. My mother, with her love of painting and music and beauty, had helped me to look there, but I think I understand intuitively that there was no sustenance for me in the religion of explanation and prohibition.

The explanations were never good ones—the world as trial by fire, proving ground to earn God's love or His forgiveness for having been human—and it was apparent to me even at an early age that the notion that anyone around me actually *understood* God's will or could articulate it was patently ridiculous. There's a wonderful line in Charles

Finney's quirky book *The Circus of Dr. Lao,* which I read as a kid, a kind of Americanized version of a speech of Hamlet's: "There are more things in heaven and earth, madam, than even a lifetime of experience in Abalone, Arizona, could avail you of."

The prohibitions were worse than the explanations. They suggested that the divinity had constructed the earth as a kind of spiritual minefield, a chutes-and-ladders game of snares and traps and seductions, all of them fueled by the engines of our longing; the flames of hell were stoked by human heats. As if desire were our enemy, instead of the eradicable force that binds us to the world.

❧ I cannot be queer in church, though I've tried, and though I live now in a place where this seems to be perfectly possible for a great many people. Here in Provincetown we have a wonderful Unitarian church, with a congregation largely gay and lesbian, and it pains me a bit to have to admit that when I have gone to services there I have been utterly, hopelessly bored. There's something about the absence of imagery, an oddly flaccid quality of neutrality in the language of worship. I long for a kind of spiritual intensity, a passion, though I can certainly see all the errors and horrors spiritual passions have wrought. I don't know what I want in a church, finally; I think the truth is that I *don't* want a church. My friend Phil has sweetly and politely informed me that it's a spiritual experience for him to be in the company of his fellows, worshipping together at the U.U., and that my resistance to it is really a sort of aesthetic snobbery, a resistance to its public language and marriage of spirituality and social life. I don't want to judge anyone's way of finding a soulful commonality, but nothing puts me less in mind of ultimate things than the friendly meetings held within my local church's square-jawboned New England architecture and flourishes of *trompe l'oeil*.

Perhaps my discomfort has to do, still, with issues of desire. Our wind, our glimmering watery horizon and sun, the watchful seals and a face full of snow seem to me to have far more to do with the life of my spirit. And there is somehow in the grand scale of dune and marsh and sea room for all of human longing, placed firmly in context by the larger world: small, our flames are, though to us raging, essential. There is something so *polite* about our Sunday gatherings of tolerant Unitarians that I feel like longing and need must be set aside. I am certain that the part of us that desires, that loves, that longs for encounter and connection—physical and psychic and every other way—is also the part of us that knows something about God. The divine, in this world, is all dressed up in mortal clothes, and longing and mortality are so profoundly intertwined as to be, finally, entirely inseparable.

My lover of twelve years died just last month. It astonishes me to write that sentence. It astonishes me that I am writing at all; I have not, till now, and I didn't know when the ability to focus might come back to me. I haven't yet been able to read, and there are many other things I haven't even begun to approach yet, in the face of this still unbelievable absence. I will be sorting out and naming the things I learned from Wally for years to come, probably for the rest of my life, but here is one thing I know now.

All the last year of Wally's life, he didn't stop wanting. He was unable to walk, since some kind of insidious viral infection, which his useless doctors didn't seem to know the first thing about, gradually took away his ability to control his body. But he wasn't ever one of those people who let go. Oh he did, in the sense of accepting what was happening to him, in the sense of not grasping on to what he couldn't have, but he lived so firmly in his desires. From the bed where he lived all that year he'd look out onto the street at anything in pants walking by and be fully, appreciatively *interested.* I never for a minute felt hurt by this or left out; it wasn't about me. It was about Wally's way of loving the world. I think in his situation I would have been consumed by frustration and a sense of thwarted desire, but he wasn't. Because his desire wasn't about possession, and his inability to fulfill it wasn't an issue; it was to be in a state of wanting, to be still desiring beauty and grace and sexiness and joy. It was the wanting itself that mattered.

A couple of months before Wally died, we heard about a couple in the city, one of whom was ill, who needed to give up their little dog, since they felt they couldn't take care of him. Wally talked and talked about this and it became clear, in a bit, that what he really wanted was for Dino to come to live with us. The day that I went to Manhattan to pick him up, Jimmy and Tony changed their minds; they weren't ready to let him go. Wally was so disappointed that I went to the animal shelter with the intention of finding a cuddly little dog who'd sleep with him and lick his face. What I found was a three-year-old golden retriever with enormous energy, a huge tongue, and a phenomenal spirit of pleasure and enjoyment. He didn't just lick Wally's face, he bathed his head, and Wally would scrinch up his face and then grin like he'd been given the earth's brightest treasure.

Sometimes late at night he'd tell me about other animals he wanted to adopt: some lizard, a talking bird, a little rat, fish.

I don't know many men who'd want a new dog, a new pact with domestic life, with responsibility, with caring for the abandoned, in the final weeks of their lives. There's a Polaroid I took of Wally, with golden Beau curled up and sleeping in our rented hospital bed beside him. He could barely use his hands then—our friend Darren and I would feed him and give him drinks to sip through a straw—but he's reaching over with his beautiful, hardly functional hand to stroke Beau's neck. That is how I will always see my love: reaching toward a world he cannot hold and loving it no less, not a stroke less.

Desire, I think, has less to do with possession than with participation, the will to involve oneself in the body of the world, in the principle of things expressing itself in splendid specificity, a handful of images: a lover's irreplaceable body, the roil and shimmer of sea overshot with sunlight, a handful of cherries, the texture and weight of a word. The word that seems most apt is *partake;* it comes from Middle English, literally from the notion of being a part-taker, one who participates. We can say we take a part *of* something, but we may just as accurately say we take part *in* something; we are implicated in another being, which is always the beginning of wisdom, isn't it—that involvement which enlarges us, which engages the heart, which takes us out of the routine limitations of self?

The codes and laws fall away, useless, foolish, finally, hollow little husks of vanity.

The images sustain.

The images allow for desire, allow room for us—even require us—to complete them, to dream our way into them.

I believe with all my heart that when the chariot came for him, green and gold and rose, a band of angels swung wide out over the great flanks of the sea, bearing him up over the path of light the sun makes on the face of the waters.

I believe my love is in the Jordan, which is deep and wide

and welcoming, though it scours us oh so deeply. And when he gets to the other side, I know he will be dressed in the robes of comfort and gladness, his forehead will be anointed with spices, and he will sing—joyful—into the future, and back toward the darkness of this world.

# My FATHER'S HOUSE

As far back as I can remember, back to my earliest child-hood, I have been pulled by the power of homoeroticism, perceived as a kind of life of the body, and pulled as well by the life of the spirit. Both have been mystical forces for me, alluring as fate, calling me to bear witness to something larger than time. Religion was, in my early life, the flaming sword that lay stretched between these two attractions, col-onizing desire and reproducing man's fall from pleasure.

When I was a child everything in my father's house had a name and everything had a place. If something wasn't given a place or a name in my father's house, it didn't exist. I grew up yearning for the unnameable, the unplaceable. Later, I would learn names for what was missing, but back then I lived in a hard Eden, sensing something was buried in the kingdom of my father's house, something hot and unspeak-able.

There was a way to speak to adults, my father taught me. A way to ask. A way to speak on the telephone. A way to eat. To be excused from the table. To stand. To sit. To behave when company came. A way to play so as not to disrupt the entire house. So as not to get my clothes dirty. Not a right and wrong way. There was one way: the way my father taught me. I was constantly corrected and reproved. I was rehearsed in his rules. I was policed and inspected. This color socks only goes with that color trousers. Use this fork for salad and that fork for meat. Only girls laugh: tee hee. Boys must laugh: ha ha. I took my rest at my precise bedtime, and my day began at exactly the same hour each morning. My evening and morning prayers were meticulously recited like incantations for an easy sentence in the prison of my father's house. I was not allowed to break a rule—ever. There was always something to say I was sorry for, something for which I knew I would never be entirely forgiven. Even at an early age, I learned to keep my sins a secret.

My father's Bible sat, big as the Book of Life in a DeMille epic, on the glass-topped coffee table in our living room. His Bible was bigger than the TV screen in the cabinet Magnavox he owned until the late '60s (when the civil rights movement, riots, and the murder of Martin Luther King, Jr., had won consumer credit in giant downtown appliance stores for upstanding members of the negro middle class like my father. It took all that before a nineteen-inch color television set, full of the mass cultural phantasmagoria, was installed in our North Philadelphia row home). But back in the late '50s and early '60s, when I was a baby and toddler, the Bible lay, as if in state, as the presiding shrine and oracle of my father's house.

As far back as I can remember, I was carried back and forth to church, by my father and various other relatives. I was taken back and forth as though I were receiving treatments for a persistent ailment. During my childhood, we attended various churches, all of them Black and all of them Sanctified Holiness. Although there were often prayer meetings in our home, where the Black saints would gather, transforming themselves as they sang and spoke their quiet supplications to God, church provided a mode of expression that was forbidden in my father's house. Church was a spectacle. The members of the congregation not only prayed and sang. They "shouted." They danced the holy dance and walked the floor of the church in otherworldly syncopation. They beat their hands and jangled tambourines in double time. They screamed and cried. They fainted. The services at these churches were emotional extravaganzas so feverish that a small battalion of white-gloved ushers were dispatched to administer fanning, blankets, and smelling salts to soul-struck worshipers.

I learned about the Bible in the churches we attended. When I was two or three years old I started Sunday school, where I was indelibly imprinted with religion, indoctrinated through songs and stories. I sang with the children's Sunday school choir: "The B-I-B-L-E/That is the book for me/I'll stand alone/on the word of God/the B-I-B-L-E." My favorite song, however, was "Jesus loves me/this I know/for the Bible/tells me so." I sang it in and out of church. I sang it with the plaintive sincerity and hunger to be transported that children possess.

Perhaps I was so wrapped up in this song because even then it seemed to offer a paradigm that could subvert the power of my father's religion, his house, even as I used it to make a show of submitting to its power.

I was obsessed with Jesus, though, truly, I had no idea who or what Jesus was. Perhaps my obsession stemmed from my early recognition that Jesus was a sign of ambiguity in a house where everything else seemed hard and fast. The images of Jesus available to me were of a beautiful young white man, adapted, I now realize, from the Christ images of Italian Renaissance paintings. Recently I made a brief tour of museums and cathedrals in Italy. I was struck by the homoerotic force of the Christs painted by Giotto, Michelangelo and da Vinci. The images of Christ that emerged during the Renaissance celebrated spiritual principles at the same time that they celebrated the male body.

The Christ images of *my* early childhood were the earliest images I can remember where there was the clear association of maleness with beauty. The depictions were from a standard repertoire and many quoted one another: Christ crucified, the Last Supper, the Good Shepherd, Christ praying in the Garden, Christ expelling the money lenders from the Temple, Christ with the bleeding heart. Of course the Christs of my early childhood, unlike the Christs from the Italian Renaissance, were two-dimensional, for the most part; the work of hack colorists and copyists. Still, they retained some of the flavor of their sources and passed along intimations of the power of those sources to me. I recall, very early, being fascinated by a drawing in a book my father owned of Samson straining his perfect body between two pillars, toppling the palace of the Philistines. This picture was like a door for me into which I escaped for hours from the resoluteness of my father's house. I lived in a suspended state of enchantment, poring over that picture, captivated by its tricks of proportion and light, its representation of the beauty of harmony in the male body. I assumed, until I learned to read well enough, that this was merely another picture of Jesus.

What these pictures of Jesus bore in common was the picture of an at once consequential and pregnable male youth—a god—wearing scant, diaphanous clothes, clothing that parted strategically to provide voyeuristic focus on beautiful limbs, a naked heart. The only thing I had to compare these pictures to back then was the provocative,

but by today's standards tame, pinup girl calendar photos hanging in the office of an uncle's gas station and the
neighborhood barber shop, where my father and I went for
our weekly haircuts—both aggressively male and secular
spaces.

The calendar pictures of thinly clothed young women
were profane, not sacred. They were visual confections. But
so, in a sense, were the pictures of Jesus I knew from my
Sunday school textbooks, the illustrations in my father's
Bible, funeral parlor fans, and decorative household no-
tions. This seemed especially true of pictures of the crucified
Christ wearing nothing more than a loin covering. Even as a
child, the image of the exposed, undressed Christ made
these pictures available to me for erotic readings. Both the
image of the pinup girl and the image of Jesus were sentimental, populist cultural productions. Both were idealized
and eroticized through their vulnerability to the gaze of the
viewer.

I remember once looking at a picture of Jesus, painted on
a plate, that hung on the wall in our kitchen and asking my
father, "Is Jesus a man or a woman?" The picture showed Jesus standing outside a small house knocking at the door. He
was holding a shepherd's hook, which I recognized since it
had been identified for me by my father in another picture
where Jesus was among the lambs, The Good Shepherd. If
he was a man, I had no idea what sort of man. Certainly, no
man I knew had long hair. My father had told me many
times that the Bible maintained that it was a shame for a
man to wear his hair long, and so he and I went ritualisti-
cally to the barber each week to have our heads shorn and
sprinkled with bay rum. It was not only the hair, however,
that made me suspect Jesus might be a woman. It seemed he
was always doing something a woman rather than a man

did in terms of the gender vocabulary I understood then. He suffered. He healed. He wept. He provided care. He was a kind of male mother, I thought.

In the picture in our kitchen, I was told in response to my questions, Jesus was knocking at the door of my heart, asking to come in. But I could plainly see Jesus was *not* knocking at the door of a heart. He was knocking at the door of a house, my father's house. This was even stranger, because Jesus was white.

In the neighborhood where I lived, whites did not socialize with blacks, though we had one or two white neighbors and there were several white merchants along our avenue. No white person ever entered our home when I was very young. When a caterer came, or a carpenter, or the florist or a furniture delivery man, these were negro men. In those days, we lived and socialized in an authentic black community. Moreover, images of white men in my father's house were rare and exotic. Television, newspapers, and magazines had not yet come to dominate our virtual lives. And we didn't know any white men, though at the family New Year's Eve party held annually in our home the gathered men told white man stories. In these stories, white men embodied evil and power. The white man was worse than the Devil, because, according to my father's religion, the Devil had been put under the subjection of God. The white man was godless and was subject to nothing and no one. The white man lied and seduced, jailed, ravaged, and lynched.

Yet, for all the white man's evil deeds since time immemorial, I knew that my uncles and my father smiled in the faces of white merchants and white policemen. They were gracious when a white man summoned them to a counter or a desk in a downtown bank. They deferred to white men on the sidewalk, especially at night on dark streets far from home, and spoke to no negro or family person in the same tones of high regard reserved for a white man: "Yes, sir," and "No, sir," and "Thank you, sir." My mother bore my father's children, kept his house, cooked for him, and he never once thanked *her*. These black men loved their wives and children. I knew this. I knew they were good men. They dreamed, worked, and sacrificed. Through my childhood and adolescence, each of them exhausted themselves to build a legacy out of their bodies in factories, shipyards, metal yards and, rarely, office buildings—selling second-hand, driving trucks, shining shoes, hauling, hammering, and serving. Many of them worked two or three jobs concurrently. In their time, each would destroy his body with work and strain. Once or twice a year, he might seem to weep as he prayed a desperate prayer in church. Or take down a guitar in a living room and sing a song that was like a letter from "down home." Or sit among each other in a kitchen laughing, telling drawn-out, mercurial stories. I always suspected their public deference and private hatred for white men belied a preoccupation with a white man's power to subvert or corroborate their own claim to Western manhood.

And there were the pictures of Jesus, white, lordly, and ravishing, on the walls of my father's house. It is a simple matter to say that my father, in his persistence in "white" Christianity, was only a victim of the histories of colonialism and slavery. But that version denies my father's agency and his subjectivity. After all, my father was a man, thinking and willing. *He* put that Bible in a place of prominence in his house. *He* framed and hammered those pictures to his walls.

I never asked why Jesus was white. Perhaps his "shameful" hair balanced out the social currency of his racial whiteness. I *wanted* him to be white. He needed to be white. I read Jesus' whiteness as a queerness, like the whiteness of a ghost or the queerness of the white peacock I'd once seen at the Philadelphia Zoo—a manifestation of the world's erratic side that had not yet been spoken. This whiteness was strange, not hateful. Something strange was at the gate of my father's house, knocking.

I had to wait to become a man myself to understand that my father's coldness was his gift to me. By teaching me to become regimental and unbreakable, my father taught me to safeguard my heart from the same world that would, so shortly after the announcement of President Johnson's New Society, mock my father's dreams and destroy the neighborhood that had been his Canaan, the son of Georgia peasants. My father would work himself to death by the time I reached the age at which he fathered me.

Jesus was a queer token between my father and me, a sign of paradox. The paradox, I now understand, is that love is its own safeguard. When I reached adolescence, our house had grown noisy with phantom TV, stereo, and radio voices. My father's house was heavy with things. Fine, second-hand furniture and the carpenter's handiwork were replaced by plastic-covered creations from giant factories. We hid away from one another inside that house. I, in my room, listening to music and reading books. He, in the basement, alone down there for hours, when he wasn't hiding in sleep on the living room sofa before the ghoulish light of the TV. The community outside my father's house was no longer the model black community of the late '50s that had been his pride. The neighborhood was under siege. A chapter of the Black Panther Party had moved in down the street from us in 1969, and with the Panther headquarters had come a heavy and menacing police presence on our avenue. In

1970, Philadelphia police raided the Panther house. My father's neighborhood awoke to gunfire. By the late afternoon, the Philadelphia police chief strode down our avenue, declaring through a megaphone that all the dirty bastards living in this hellhole should be shot. Only a decade earlier, John Fitzgerald Kennedy had flashed by our sycamore-shaded house, smiling and waving in a motorcade on his way to the presidency of the United States, trailing hope.

In 1970, I was attending a Quaker boys' day school on an academic scholarship. There, I was isolated and admired in a world of affluent white boys. At home, I missed my father terribly, although I could not ever remember being close to him or hearing him tell me he loved me. I was lonely for my father. At the same time I hid from my father, I began to track him. I sneaked and went through his chest of drawers. I looked in his closets, his shoe boxes, fishing tackle boxes and toolboxes for the secrets of his heart. I went behind him, fingering the filters of the cigarettes he had smoked and left in ashtrays, hoping to finger some secret thought. Once I steamed open and read a letter he had written to the grandmother who raised him, hoping I would learn my father's true identity.

One day when I was eleven or twelve years old, and my father was out of the house on an errand, I made a fine, strange discovery. I found, hidden beneath a floorboard in our basement, his money box. The box was unlocked. There were several rolls of half dollars and dimes, and twenty dollars or so in old bills. Beneath the money box, however, there was a bundle of photographs wrapped in a brown silk scarf. The photographs were male physique photos—a series of white male nudes, well-made men standing in a sun-washed forest. I looked at each photograph of each man, carefully, as if each picture was a letter from some distant homeplace of the soul. My hands felt as if they were vibrating. When I was done looking at the photographs, I wrapped them as I had found them and replaced everything beneath the floorboard. I never mentioned the pictures to my father or anyone. Still, I always felt he knew I'd seen them after that day and that even before I'd seen them I'd felt them buried in his house. At times, I thought he left them there for me to find. Perhaps I am wrong, but I believe my father died waiting for me to unearth his softness. Somewhere inside the furnace of work he turned himself into, my father was a man crying for love between men, love that risked and healed the contradictions.

# LEV RAPHAEL

# TO BE A JEW

*To be a Jew in the twentieth century*
*Is to be offered a gift. If you refuse,*
*Wishing to be invisible, you choose*
*Death of the spirit, the stone insanity.*
*Accepting, take full life, full agonies . . .*
*Daring to live for the impossible.*

—Muriel Ruykyser

I was relieved in my late teens when our Washington
Heights synagogue, victim of a "changing neighborhood,"
became some sort of church. I'd only been inside once, for
a campaign speech of John Lindsay's, but my father's
small dry cleaning store was on the same block, and when
I worked there on Sunday mornings, I felt uncomfortable
and ashamed. I wished we were closed. Even though we
weren't remotely observant, it didn't seem right.

My father, whose childhood and adolescence resembled
the devout Eastern European life Elie Wiesel has described
in many of his books, had abandoned his religious belief
during the war—maybe in Bergen-Belsen, where his father
died three days before the Liberation, or earlier, as a slave la-
borer for the Hungarian army. Asking him to close the store
on *shabbos* would have been foolish.

21

As I watched from behind the scarred linoleum-covered counter, watched the men and boys in suits, the women lovely and correct, the girls trying to be, I felt alien. I had no idea what they *did* inside the high-fronted, vaguely Moorish-looking building, only that they did it without me. I had not been bar mitzvah'd, and neither had my brother. I suppose I didn't believe it mattered.

Though Yiddish newspapers and books filled our home, and my parents' only close friends were other ghetto and concentration camp survivors, I did not identify with them. I did not want to be a Jew.

I wanted to escape.

My first intense awareness of myself as a Jew had come in first grade, when an older child told me that "Germans threw Jewish babies in the air and caught them on bayonets." She acted it out while she spoke. This may have been around the time of the Eichmann trial.

I can't recall now if I mentioned that incident at home, but I know that afterwards, I began to learn at least partial answers to questions that must have been troubling me—how come I didn't have grandparents? Why did my father have terrible nightmares? Where was our family?

As with many children of Holocaust survivors, in my home there was a vast and deafening silence about the Holocaust. Details emerged piecemeal, unexpectedly, painfully. My mother told me only fragments of her ordeals, and my father said next to nothing. I don't think I ever completely understood a very simple truth: people had wanted to *kill* my mother, *kill* my father—and hadn't quite succeeded.

Until I was well into my twenties, I had no Jewish pride at all, I was *ashamed* of being Jewish. I was mortified by my parents' accents when they spoke English (even though they spoke a dozen languages between them), and by their use of

Yiddish in public because it seemed to stamp us as alien, different, inferior. When I was young I even imagined having a non-Jewish name. Like Tom Danbury, a name I had heard in an Abbott and Costello movie. Think of it: Tom Sawyer crossed with the name of a Connecticut city—what could be more American?

When friends or acquaintances in junior high or high school made anti-Semitic jokes or remarks, I never once challenged them. A fierce admirer of Martin Luther King from fourth grade on, I didn't have the courage to speak up for my own people in my own voice. I rarely identified with Jewish causes, except for a visceral support of Israel, and a terrible embarrassment when I read something disgraceful about a Jew in the newspapers. I had no close Jewish friends. Even as I read about Jewish history, I felt both attracted and ambivalent. Just as I wanted to love men but was afraid to speak my desire or touch another man. Silence reigned.

My parents themselves were deeply ambivalent about being Jewish. When I asked them why they'd come to America rather than Israel after the war, my mother was sharp: "Live with all those Jews? I had enough of them in the ghetto and the camps!" And when I was in first grade and a fire broke out one Friday night in the apartment of Orthodox neighbors, my parents both seemed to blame our neighbors' *shabbos* candles, nodding as if to say, "See, that's what happens. . . ."

They didn't know that the neighbor's son and I had once traded views of our nascent penises. One afternoon in my bedroom, we agreed to the exchange, and laughing with nervousness, I stripped completely. I waited for him to do the same, but he only pulled his pants and shorts away from his waist and and let me look briefly down. I felt humiliated. With my girlfriend Vicky, our genital displays and exploration were completely mutual, which might explain why I felt so cheated and ashamed.

Despite their contempt for the American-born teachers there, my parents made me go to a Workman's Circle Sunday school for too many years, where I was exposed to Yiddish-language lessons in Jewish history and literature. I was happy whenever I fell ill or overslept and didn't have to go to that school. Almost nothing made an impression on me there, except for one older boy—dark, sexy, slim—whom I sometimes annoyed because that was the only way to make him interested in me. What I remember best of all about my Workman's Circle classes happened one day in our excruciatingly dull Torah class, where the ratio of Hebrew to Yiddish on the page intrigued me. The thick square of Hebrew words, surrounded by the long Yiddish translation, seemed so dark and dense, impenetrable. We were studying *Koheleth,* Ecclesiastes, which is still vivid to me because of the vanity of vanities refrain—*"nishtikeit"* in Yiddish. It seemed powerful to consider this cynicism and despair in three languages.

My Jewishness in part consisted of a sensitivity to any threat to American Jews. I had more than a vague idea of the Jewish past, but Torah, prayer, and religious observance of the holidays were all another world, one I didn't even know enough about to truly ignore. It didn't exist.

I was culturally Jewish, or more accurately, the *son* of parents who were culturally Jewish. So I could feel superior, with my father, to the Reform rabbi of the synagogue down the street from his cleaning store, who drove to services in a Cadillac, and laugh with my mother at the women's "Easter" hats she found so appalling. I know I once wanted to go to *shabbos* services with a junior high school friend, was excited and nervous, wondering what to wear, how to act, but the plans fell through somehow and I never passed beyond contempt and distance, never prayed or even watched others pray in the synagogue two blocks from our apartment building. Perhaps not coincidentally, this same friend was one of the first teenage boys I showed my penis to, hoping he would reciprocate, but he didn't. This experience left me feeling stupid, weird, and worried that other kids would find out.

What *did* we observe in my family? We lit Chanukah candles (except on the days we forgot) and if my father did it, he said a prayer under his breath. My brother and I got the traditional Chanukah coins made out of chocolate. My parents each lit a *yorzeit licht,* a memorial candle, on Yom Kippur and on the anniversary of their parents' deaths. We ate "holiday dinners" somewhat fancier than the usual fare—to which my father was invariably late from the store. But we never had a Passover Seder. I resisted the huge Workman's Circle Seders because I knew I wouldn't feel at home there, and never went to a real one until I was twenty-six. Passover always embarrassed me, especially when non-Jewish friends asked what I did, where I'd gone.

I had no sense of Jewish holidays marking spiritual as well as historical time. I suppose I identified with other Jews but felt only nominally Jewish no matter how much history I read.

Partly because of my parents' very mixed feelings about being Jewish, and their professed superiority over observant Jews, I came to feel both estranged from more religious Jews and better than them—more rational and realistic, as if true observance were nonsense.

None of this seemed to matter until college when I met and fell in love with Beverly Sheila Douglas—a tall, blond, kind, lovely New Zealander. She was not Jewish.

We met in sophomore year at Fordham University's Lincoln Center campus, started dating, and fell in love our junior year. I had chosen a Catholic college because the campus was very small, my brother's Jewish girlfriend raved about her creative writing teacher there, and because it was Catholic. I'm sure of that now. I wasn't interested in converting, just hiding. Though as one of very few Jews there, I stood out; it was also the first place I'd ever heard the phrase "jew him down" as a habitual part of people's conversations.

Beverly intrigued me because she was so different from American girls, softer, quieter. It never felt to me that I was faking our relationship, that I was Odysseus bound to the mast of his ship to keep from answering the sirens' call. I had never had any kind of sex with a boy or man; it was all so out of the realm of possibility. Yet I was always aware of attractive men in the street, and my secret must have been visible in my eyes because men occasionally tried to pick me up.

The fact that Beverly wasn't Jewish didn't matter in the beginning. There was no conflict until we neared graduation and her visa was running out. It was time for couples to get married, or at least to become serious. Friends told us that Beverly and I were fun to watch and be with, and I suppose we did shine with the delicate snobbery of first love.

Friends told me what they thought about me and Beverly, what others thought, what I should think: a chorus, a babble deciding my life for me, or trying to help. Beverly, very British, could not talk about the future or her feelings; I, very scared and conflicted, could only stumble. I wanted to marry her, or maybe wanted not to lose her. Most of all, I wanted not to feel split and afraid of myself, afraid now of the feelings for men that lay coiled inside me like a snake ready to strike.

Several of our friends at Fordham were ostentatiously gay,

bragging about their wild nights in the Village, at the bars, the docks, the trucks. These men who camped and dished with us must have known about me, but they loved Beverly and insisted we get married. They *rooted* for us.

I began feeling that Beverly's being a Christian did make a difference, and I was drawn to the Judaica section at Brentano's on Fifth Avenue. I bought books about Judaism and read them with more hunger than understanding, searching, I now realize, to find what being Jewish meant for me. I didn't know enough to decide. Just as I hesitantly bought gay books, burying them in a stack of other paperbacks as if sheathing kryptonite with lead.

✇ Christmas 1974 brought deeper discomfort. At a friend's house with Beverly, the tree decorating was fun, but hearing the host read from the New Testament seemed unnatural to me, embarrassing. The carols at the piano drove me down the hallway to another room. I didn't belong there, I knew it, felt it, believed it. This was not my holiday or my place. I had always been somewhat uncomfortable during New York's Christmas madness, but never so intensely. I told Beverly that. The presents under the tree I'd helped string lights and popcorn on were gifts of love, but not appropriate to whoever I suspected I was. The hostess and I had once disagreed about the possibilities of Jews being conscientious objectors: "Look at the Bible," she'd said. "It's full of violence." And I had then only second-hand words for reply, none of my own.

Beverly and I did not get married. I knew more and more clearly that I could not marry a non-Jew, no matter how much I loved her. What pushed me over the edge? Imagining Christmas, so profoundly a part of Beverly's life, in "our" house. I couldn't do it or ask her to give it up. I couldn't confuse myself or any children we might have. I wanted a Jewish home. No—it wasn't that affirmative. I realized I couldn't have a *non*-Jewish home; that was as far as I got, and it meant much more to me than my subterranean attraction to men. When I told Beverly I couldn't marry a non-Jew, painfully, reluctant to hurt her, but forced to the truth by her coming departure, I closed that door forever. But I made a claim on part of my future.

When I returned from seeing Beverly off at Kennedy Airport, I found a package on my desk at home. My first selection from the Jewish Book Club had come: a heavy one-volume encyclopedia of Judaica. I was too bitter to laugh, too stunned to cry.


❧ My brother decided to marry the second-generation Polish Catholic he'd been dating for years, the woman he'd said he'd never marry, the woman my parents undoubtedly saw as "the enemy." Up at school in Massachusetts, I received a phone call from him asking for help. Mom was "getting hysterical," crying. Dad was upset for her, for himself. My brother was stubborn, angry, and his girlfriend understandably incensed. If she was good enough to come to dinner and to live with him, then why—?

I made phone calls, wrote a frantic letter, said anything to keep what little family we had from destroying itself in bitterness and violent regret. It sounded like a catastrophe. I could imagine them getting married, my parents not coming, and me in the middle. I'm not sure how much I helped, but my parents calmed down because they had to. My brother would marry whoever he wanted, we all knew that, but the shock and resentment on all sides were inevitable. Later, I felt strangely betrayed. I had not married Beverly; how could my brother marry the woman he'd said he never would? I wished my brother hadn't taken something away from the family by not marrying a Jew, but now I believe he had nothing to give. My brother was a Jewish Almanac Jew, the kind who likes knowing which movie stars changed their names.

I also felt bested by him, outmaneuvered in our unspoken rivalry. I was fairly sure I would never get married, and so even though my brother had dropped out of college, he was normal, and had just proven it.

He'd told me about his wedding plans before my parents, and the impending crisis sent me to Yom Kippur services in Amherst, Massachusetts, to a steepleless white clapboard ex-church, unused to being the scene of Jewish prayer, where I sat in a crowded balcony, hardly comprehending the English of the *Mahzor* (holiday prayerbook), but crying unexpectedly, moved by melodies I somehow knew, moved by the cantor's hall-filling eloquence, even by the children tramping on the stairs, moved by the fact that I was there, suffused by the beauty, the solemnity of group prayer for forgiveness, a publicly shared intimacy and hope.

I was roused and transfixed without understanding how or why, or what it all meant. I called home that night, to share my wonderment. My parents approved, just as they did next Passover when I didn't eat bread even though my matzo ran out. My parents approved, and might even have been proud, but like those who have stepped off a path, they could not fathom that I had felt the presence of a new possibility in my life.

My first synagogue service, my first Yom Kippur not listening to Kol Nidre on the radio or on a Jan Peerce album. I was twenty-three.

My brother's wedding, which took place in the United

Nations chapel, was performed by a half-Jewish priest and a rabbi who looked Episcopalian. I held one pole of the wedding canopy, the *chupa,* and was thrilled by the ceremony, by the Hebrew which I did not understand. But the experience was odd for me. I was too uncertain in my own Jewish identity to condemn what my brother was doing—or to feel comfortable with it.


🐚 That year was traumatic for other reasons besides my brother's wedding. When I published my first short story, the event was overshadowed by my parents' severe reaction to it. This story had burst from me in a day and a half the year before, nursed by Kris, my writing teacher in college, to whom I read the various sections over the phone as soon as they were finished, as if together we were tending a patient that might not recover. Her vigilance helped me begin to heal my own split from Judaism, because this story was about the child of Holocaust survivors who felt crushed by what he knew of his parents' terrible past. It won a prize awarded by a famous editor and was published in *Redbook.*

It scared me.

When my parents read it, they felt betrayed and outraged at the way I'd woven in autobiographical elements. Even worse, my mother had weeks of insomnia, as well as gruesome nightmares about the war, feeling, no doubt, violated by the son she had hoped to protect from the brutal realities of her past—a son who had unwittingly led her back. When I tried talking about the story—which I stupidly withheld from them until it was published—she berated me as though I were not just her son but her persecutor, and she sneeringly tore the story apart. My father had little to say.

But the story led me to begin confronting my legacy as a

child of survivors, and I started to read furiously about the Holocaust, steeping myself now in what had for years merely been bits of narrative gleaned from my parents, conquering my own nausea and fear of entering that Kingdom of Death. It was 1978, and Helen Epstein had made headlines with her book *Children of the Holocaust;* Holocaust curricula were being introduced all over the country; Gerald Green's "Holocaust" had filled America's TV screens.

I was experiencing profound chaos in other ways. While my brother announced his marriage, I was enmeshed in a murkier, less public drama. The night of my brother's bachelor party, I had left the Playboy Club assaulted by its almost surreal heterosexuality to find a bar and get picked up. That was one of the few contacts I had with another man.

At the University of Massachusetts, where I was doing an MFA in Creative Writing, I was in love—or something— with one of the roommates in the house I shared at the edge of Amherst. "Scorpio" was of Italian descent: short, dark, heavy-shouldered, heavy-cocked, cynical. I had cast him in a dual role: he was my beloved, he was my tormentor. Always there, always out of reach. It was the kind of obsessive, confused, and unreal relationship you have with another man when you don't respect or even understand your own homosexuality.

We never truly connected, we collided—with me usually feeling alternately bruised and elated, spending hours on the phone with friends trying to figure out what it all meant as if I was struggling to turn lugubrious Derrida into crystalline and witty Jane Austen. My parents and my brother knew none of this, and I felt stranded. Unable to ask for what I wanted, unable to comprehend just what that was, I stumbled through a year of living in the same house, my changing moods a puzzle to our other housemates. Scorpio didn't really desire me at all but wanted to put me in my place because I was a star writer in our creative writing graduate program. An occasional fuck could do just that. At one party, where my drunken dancing and enthusiasm galvanized the entire crowd, and attracted more than one woman, Scorpio got me away as soon as he could to prove in bed who was boss. These episodes sometimes seemed to occur in a parallel universe which we were only vaguely connected to, sealed off, remote.

When I wound up in bed with a feisty, sharp-tongued, and grandly multi-orgasmic woman who disliked Scorpio and had been actively pursuing me, promising me the love he could never offer, the situation became even more tortuous and melodramatic as I tried to keep our affair secret from him. She was only the third woman I'd slept with, but our lovemaking was incredible and liberating. For the first time in my life, I felt relaxed in bed, free of inhibitions, criticism, fear. Because she had also slept with women (and considered herself an "ex-lesbian"), I never felt judged.

But the lying, the frustration, the tension all burst after the semester was over and I was back in New York. I felt trapped in what was almost a ménage à trois. Every phone conversation with my best friend Kris was like watching a wounded animal trying to drag itself to its feet: it stumbles, falls, stumbles again.

Wisely, Kris said we had to cut through everything, that we couldn't spend the rest of the summer this way, but I had to pull myself out, to go as far away as possible. This was the same friend who advised me in college that, though I'd probably never meet a woman as kind as Beverly again (and she was right), marrying her when I wondered if I was gay, and felt uneasy about marrying a non-Jew, didn't make any sense.

Now, in the summer of 1978, Kris asked, "Don't you have relatives in Israel?"

Hysterically eager to drop everything and run from my confusion, I announced to my parents that I would spend the coming year on a kibbutz. Alarmed by my vociferousness, my parents suggested a few weeks just to see if I'd like it there, and I agreed. I called my uncle Wolf in Tel Aviv to let him know I was coming, and little more than a week later, I was gone—without telling Scorpio.

But the delight in not giving him any notion of where I was faded quickly. In my dark time, Israel was a bath of light, several rich, dense weeks of escape from a home that I hated to one I didn't know. Israel: stifling heat, long political discussions, bus rides, the unforgettable first vision of glowing Jerusalem, exploring Masada, surprising people with how much Hebrew I picked up, meeting my mother's brother Wolf for the first time, speaking Yiddish to his wife because her English was minimal. Israel: seeing a photo of *his* brother, the man whose name I bore as my middle name, Lev, the man lost in the Battle of Stalingrad. Israel: a dream more real than the dream of America, older in the mind of God.

Yet even there I ran right into what I had fled. On a bright, noisy, hot street, I'd pass a truck whose driver was more beautiful than any man I'd ever seen. And spending a few days on a heartbreakingly scenic kibbutz on the Mediterranean, I ended up having sex with a Brazilian Jew, who was even more withholding and uncommunicative than the man I'd left in Massachusetts. One night there, he fucked me, went off to shower, just assuming I'd come. Another night, after blowing and rimming him, I pushed up his heavy bronze-brown legs, but he shoved me away as soon as I entered him, claiming he was tired. Enraged, perplexed, I was unable to respond. In the morning, while he was gone, I contemplated ripping his clothes to shreds and destroying his few possessions.

Once more I was fleeing, this time back to Tel Aviv, where my puzzled uncle and aunt listened to my vague reasons for not staying at the kibbutz as long as I'd originally planned.

I returned to New York with a new name. Lev was now liberated from its Anglo-Saxon prison of "Lewis." Rocking one afternoon at my uncle's house, face-to-face with a picture of my mother, Wolf, and Lev, it had seemed dishonest to me to be named after Lev, yet not have his actual name. And the name "Lev" was a deepening of the link with my people and my history, because it had meanings in Yiddish (lion) and Hebrew (heart). Those languages even appear in the lives of Jews who don't speak or read them. Our religious and ritual terms are interchangeable, like *shabbos* (Yiddish) and *shabbat* (Hebrew).

I returned from Israel determined to speak Yiddish with my parents, to reclaim something of the past, and with a knowledge, undeveloped, unrefined, of the possibility of a deeper meaning of my life. Israel was another way, a different, difficult path, but far more rewarding, I thought, than graduate school. It was a life that could quench my thirst for meaning.

But I didn't take it. I had not even become a Jew—how could I become an Israeli?


❧ The feelings of the Yom Kippur service at Amherst lay dormant for another two years, what with finishing my degree, getting a part-time job in New York at my alma mater, writing and trying to get published, starting another degree, living at home again and reexperiencing why I'd wanted to leave: the coldness, the constriction. But I started subscribing to *Commentary,* which may seem laughable to some. For me, it was a big step to read *any* Jewish magazine. I chose it because it was the one I'd heard most about. I learned a lot in its pages, and felt, however tenuously, more Jewish. I also felt repudiated for wanting men, the day I read in its pages Midge Dector's notorious homo-bashing essay "The Boys on the Beach," a colorful diatribe about gay life on Fire Island and its threat to the American way of life.

I was so closeted at the time, and so devoid of actual homosexual experience outside of reading, that the essay fascinated and excited me. It was like reading a foolish book review in the *New York Times,* one that convinces you to rush out and buy the book it's condemning. Despite the invective, you're dead sure that the reviewer is short-sighted and wrong. Midge Dector made me *long* for the life on Fire Island she found so disgusting. I'd had a similar reaction to "The Boys in the Band" when I saw it at fifteen. While as an adult I'm most struck by the self-hatred in that play, as a teenager I was flabbergasted by seeing gay men together— and encouraged. The movie told me that gay men were out there, real, alive; I wasn't alone.

Teaching at Fordham from 1978–1980 as an adjunct instructor, I had the opportunity of giving a "January Project," a course different from regular semester offerings. One fall night in 1979, it hit me: I would teach Holocaust literature. All that I'd read before came back to me in a rush. I made a book list and syllabus, and plunged into three months of intensive research, reading even more than I had before, without stop: history, fiction, psychology, sociology, theology. I was certain that literature had to be grounded in the reality it attempted to deal with, and in interpretations of that reality.

Children of Holocaust survivors tend to feel they know a lot about those nightmare years in Europe, given the way the Holocaust has left its imprint on their parents. But like many others, I actually knew little in the way of facts before I began and came to see that I had wanted to know less because the Holocaust had stolen my parents' past not just from them but from me, had made reminiscing a dangerous and bleak prospect. This drive to learn and teach was intimately bound up with my search for Jewishness.

The course—a difficult and intense month of readings, films, reports—surpassed any I'd ever done. Two-thirds Jewish, the students ventured along with me bravely, confused, awed, horrified, searching too. What did it mean? we all wondered. How could we think of it?

If anything, we all learned the extremity of conditions in the ghettos and camps, learned that New York standards of behavior did not, could not, apply. And I emerged wondering if perhaps, as a son of Holocaust survivors, I hadn't found a *mission*. Traditional Jews observe 613 commandments; the philosopher Emil Fackenheim argues for the 614th after the Holocaust: to keep the memory alive. Perhaps that was what I could do. Teach others, give from my own special experience, transmit and interpret the past. In that spirit, I wrote the first draft of the somewhat autobiographical novel that would be published twelve years later as *Winter Eyes*. The intense privacy and immersion, the sense of deepening my craft, made me contemplate the role of my writing differently. It could serve a larger social purpose, as opposed to being my individual path to success. But neither writing nor teaching about the Holocaust would make me a Jew. One year later, I found out what could.

After seeing an advertisement in *Commentary,* I ordered a pamphlet from the American Jewish Community about "ethnotherapy" for Jews, group therapy to help those who had absorbed cultural stereotypes about themselves. This little pamphlet unexpectedly ripped me open. The ugliness inside finally came to light: I realized that I had not one Jewish friend, that I hadn't seriously dated one Jewish girl, that I didn't particularly *like* Jews.

It was a revolution. I tore unread books from my shelves and plunged into them that week, submerged in discovery: Irving Howe's *The World of Our Fathers,* Cynthia Ozick's *The Pagan Rabbi,* Adin Steinsaltz's *The Essential Talmud,* the *Penguin Book of Jewish Short Stories,* a book on ancient Israel, and Milton Steinberg's *Basic Judaism.* That last, the most important, was a relic of my days with Beverly. I'd read it back then, underlining everywhere, entering nowhere.

Now I read slowly, absorbed, released from the slavery of false pride and ignorance. I loved his clear, concise little book: it seemed so wise to me, and I knew then that Judaism, my religion of birth, could be my religion of choice. I loved the sensible way Steinberg discussed tradition and its modern application in every aspect of Jewish life.

It was a simple discovery to find that Judaism as a religion made sense, was even beautiful. Without having read about the death of European Jews, I don't think I could have understood or been able to appreciate their life, the tenets of a faith I'd known next to nothing about. And so, after feeling seared and overwhelmed by the horrors of 1933–1945, I found myself in surprising harmony with my people's religion.

I was primed for still more discovery and change when I arrived at Michigan State the semester after teaching the

Holocaust course. I gave a talk at Hillel about Holocaust literature and had chosen that field for my dissertation, but something very different compelled me. My neighbor at the graduate dorm was Jewish, and I accompanied him to what was only my second Yom Kippur service. I didn't fast, I wasn't ready to, but I achieved a nearness to prayer that now spurred a decision which rereading the pamphlet had made certain. Because I needed to be with Jews, I would move into MSU's Hillel co-op. I would live and eat and associate with Jews. What attracted me most about Hillel was not the well-stocked library but the small *shul* upstairs where an Orthodox congregation (*minyan*) met.

My *Commentary* subscription ran out and I ordered *Judaism* and *Midstream*.

᳔ Living with Jewish students was at first unsettling for me—did I fit in? Would I feel comfortable? As the routine took over, I realized we were as much students as Jews, maybe more so. This Jewish co-op turned out to be not very cooperative and not very Jewish. We did have one guy who was eternally vigilant and fanatical about kosher food, and some people attended Saturday morning services occasionally; still, the Jewishness was one of concern for Israel and worry about anti-Semitism, a Jewishness of discussion and jokes, of atmosphere and self-parody. But then none of the young men or women there was particularly in conflict about their Jewish identity or searching for ways to deepen it.

It was at services that I seemed to have found my pathway. The people there—Modern Orthodox—were relaxed and friendly, and one young couple began inviting me for *shabbat* lunch. Adina took me through the prayer book and explained what each prayer meant and what you did, and

both she and Josh shared their learning in an easy, nonjudg-
mental way. They were witty, well-read, helpful.

My transitions were smooth. One *shabbat* I donned a
*tallis* (prayer shawl), another I found myself swaying back
and forth during the Amidah: *shokeling*. The service began
feeling familiar and Hebrew stopped seeming completely
foreign and forbidding. After many weeks, I began joining
in some of the sun prayers. I began lighting candles on Friday night. I started wearing a *kipa* (yarmulkah) when I read
from a *siddur* (prayer book) or *chumash* (Pentateuch with
commentary) outside of services. I kissed the holy books
when I closed them (as Orthodox Jews do) not because I
thought I should but because I chose to acknowledge them
as sacred, and the act itself felt beautiful. The impulse came
from deep inside, where a sense of reverence grew in me.
Each service I attended gave me more understanding, beauty,
more belief, and connection. Prayer, once foreign and con-
temptible, enriched my life. Even when I was bored or tired,
being there was the Jewish immersion I had not known I
craved.

I had never bothered learning my full Hebrew name until that year in the co-op. I was a *Levi,* my father told me:
*Reuven Lev ben Shlomo ha-Levi.* Because *Levis* are supposedly
descended from Temple functionaries who sang the psalm
of the day, among other duties, this name connected me to
centuries of Jews. Up at the *bima* (lectern), saying the Torah
blessings, I felt the march of Jewish time, and felt myself a
part of it. Perhaps most profoundly, one Yom Kippur, the
first on which I fasted, I held the Torah while the plangent
Kol Nidre was chanted. It was ineffably moving to me, and
that evening I had a dream in which a warm voice sang the
words *Av Harachamim,* father of mercy. The dream told me
that I was welcomed and embraced.

Almost every week, I read the Torah portion in advance, or while it was being chanted, and plunged into the footnotes, feeling very much like a sort of feral child. Why had all this information about Jewish faith and observance been kept from me? And would I ever come to feel knowledgeable, truly at ease among worshipping Jews?

Mordechai Nisan, a visiting scholar from Israel, lodged in Hillel's guest room one weekend, and dined with the co-op members. He spoke movingly that *shabbat* afternoon about *shabbat* in Israel involving everyone and being a different kind of time. As he spoke, I thought of the *shabbat* prayer: "Be pleased with our rest." At lunch I'd told him about my background, or lack of it. Stumbling through *Birkat HaMazon* (the sung and chanted prayers after meals), I felt him considering me. When he left, he said, "I hope you find what you're looking for."


❧ But he didn't know that there was another hunger in me, as deep as my need to belong and fit in as a Jew. If I were a teenager in 1994, I doubt I would ever seriously date a woman, but given the times and my own conflicts, in the early '80s, I continued to date and enjoy my relationships with women (though the countervailing attraction never disappeared). Moving into Hillel's co-op, I was thrown together far more intimately with men than I was at the dorm. Rather than sharing a bathroom with one guy, I shared it with a handful. One of them had an enormous penis and joked about it as often as he could, eyeing me to see what my reaction was. Another became the model for "Eric" in my story "Shouts of Joy." And another whose intense camping trips with his "old buddy" and references to a bisexual woman friend were possibly unconscious signals. I felt somewhat besieged and afraid of exposure, both enjoying and fearing the random displays of nudity in the men's room, further heightened when someone's friend or boyfriend slept over.

After living at the co-op for a year, I moved out to my first apartment but still went to services and events at Hillel. The physical distance was matched by my burgeoning discomfort with the Orthodox restrictions on women and what I expected the response to my sexuality would be. Once I overcame the newness and excitement of being part of a prayer community, I felt increasingly uncomfortable with what I saw as the lesser role of women in an Orthodox service. And my own exclusion if I were openly gay.

Josh and Adina once mentioned a congregation they knew where a lesbian had been asked to leave when she came out. I found myself agreeing that it was "a shame" but tried to cover my disappointment when they went on to remark that the woman shouldn't have embarrassed her synagogue in that way. This anecdote, told to me in 1981, eventually inspired my story "Dancing on Tisha B'Av," but at the time it was more admonishing than inspiring. The lines were clearly drawn for me. I had to keep part of myself hidden.

Yet it was being grounded in a profoundly, unequivocally Jewish milieu that brought me real depth and success as a writer. After the shock of being published at twenty-four, and my parents' violent reaction to the story, I kept writing but somehow never wrote anything as good as that prize-winning story. It began to haunt me—what if I were like some character in a Hawthorne tale, doomed to be endlessly dissatisfied after the first taste of achievement? But in 1983, the drought was over. In Michigan, I'd begun reassessing my writing, wondering what I truly had to say and who my audience was. It was easier to disconnect from New York ideas of success and decide that being in *The New Yorker* or other national magazines wasn't the only way to find satisfaction as a writer.

I started sending my work to Jewish publications and the response was swift and amazing. Stories of mine, mostly about children of survivors, began appearing in Jewish magazines and newspapers. Editors loved my work, and so apparently did readers. Now I had an audience and a new sense of mission. For the first time in my writing career, I was thinking less of the glory of being published, and more about reaching people. But my success as a Jewish writer ironically drove me further into the closet. Having finally come to feel comfortable and accepted as a Jew, and established as a published writer, how could I risk either of those achievements by coming out? Especially in a city like East Lansing whose Jewish community was so small.

Still deeply uncertain about being gay, and at the point where I was finally comfortable in my new Jewish affiliation, I unexpectedly fell in love with a Jewish man I met at the university. He was, unfortunately, married with children. His research and writing about shame gave me a whole new set of insights about my past, my relationship to my parents, to Jewishness, my homosexuality. But it was more than a set of labels. It was freedom.

There were many similarities in our background—we went to the same high school back in New York, our fathers were in the same business—and it wasn't long before we acknowledged that we were soul mates. You could see it in the way we taught and wrote together. He and I would finish each other's sentences in class or as we worked on a piece of writing. Gersh is not a child of survivors, but he is the son of Eastern European immigrants, and we share a cultural landscape through which we move with ease and recognition together.

Our deepening bond transformed both our lives. Gersh was the first to know clearly what he wanted and that meant pain for himself and his family at the time. Gersh wanted a life together with me, and felt our meeting was *besherit* (fated)—but I couldn't imagine the possibility. I had never met a committed gay couple, let alone a Jewish one. It took several more years and great pain for us both until I could come to terms at last with what we meant to each other, to finally make a lifetime commitment.

Of course, as we worked all of this out, I withdrew even further from the Jewish community in East Lansing, after having a *bar mitzvah* at the age of thirty in Hillel's other, egalitarian *minyan*. My *bar mitzvah* marked my confidence and sense of belonging as much as it was a temporary farewell.

My Jewish journey was additionally complicated in the 1980s by Gersh's own problems with his Jewish background. His parents forced an unexplained and insensitive Orthodoxy on him from an early age, and our praying together only partially healed his pain and sense of separation from other Jews.

While I drew back from East Lansing's Jewish world, Gersh and I struggled with coming out, continuing to teach and write together. Our lives grew richer through the courses we codeveloped and cotaught at Michigan State University, the books and articles we wrote together, and separately with each other's guidance, and the many students we reached. The deepening of our love and commitment taught me the reality of that *shabbat* hymn, *kol ha-olam kulo*: "All of life is a narrow bridge, the important thing is not to be afraid." Just as my writing was beginning to include gay as well as Jewish themes, we bought a house and moved in together and that move gave me great courage. I was no longer afraid to publish fiction in my own name in a gay publication; I welcomed having my story "Dancing on Tisha B'Av" appear in George Stambolian's *Men on Men 2* in 1988. Meeting people in San Francisco or Provincetown who had read my work or recognized my name, I felt more settled and comfortable as a gay man, as a gay writer.

By 1990, I made a giant leap forward by proudly and unambivalently publishing *Dancing on Tisha B'Av,* a book of Jewish and gay short stories that was advertised as such—a book full of as many connections as contradictions. What is the role of gay and lesbian Jews in American Jewish life? How can their dual identities be reconciled? How do children of Holocaust survivors find meaning in their parents' lives? The questions this book raised had personal relevance for me, but also larger and current social implications.

Until that point, coming out as a gay man seemed to overshadow coming out as a Jew—but no longer. At the first national gay and lesbian writers' conference in San Francisco that year, I not only spoke to four hundred people about coming out in my writing as a Jew and a gay man, I had a pivotal encounter with the writer Jyl Lynn Felman, whom I hadn't seen in ten years. She had been in my MFA writing program, when neither one of us was out of the closet. When she shared her journey with me as a deeply committed Jewish lesbian (who also had a Jewish partner), I was electrified and stirred to action and commitment. That conference—which drew 1,200 people—opened me up for another one that was unexpectedly even more fulfilling.

Gersh and I attended the 1990 Midwest Regional Meeting of the World Congress of Gay and Lesbian Jewish Organizations, in Toronto. The experience was truly an answer to our prayers. There were *shabbat* services—led by a gay rabbi, in which the *siddur* recognized and included the experience of gay and lesbian Jews, most movingly, perhaps, before the Kaddish (the prayer for the dead), when we reflected on those who had never had *Kaddish* said for them, who had died with their true selves hidden. It was there, that *erev shabbat,* that Gersh and I felt completely ourselves, completely embraced by thousands of years of Jewish tradition and worship. That weekend there were seminars, meetings, shmoozing (and cruising), another powerful *shabbat* service, and an overwhelming tour of Toronto's Holocaust Museum. But the culmination for me was a final dinner, where our table of ten was laden with Yiddish speakers with whom I joyfully shared jokes and songs after we sang *Birkat HaMazon,* the grace after meals. My old world and my new world were united, joyously.

Since that time, we have attended World Congress meetings in London, San Francisco, Detroit, and Tel Aviv, appearing on the program in each city. Gersh is the country's foremost theorist and writer on the affect of shame, and his workshops have dealt with the intersections of shame and gay and Jewish identity. I have talked about coming out as a Jew and a gay man and combining the identities, and have read from my fiction. For both of us, these conferences have been an opportunity to give back to our community of lesbian and gay Jews, to offer what we know most deeply, by way of thanks, because we feel so nourished and connected.

Encouraged by the Reform movement's efforts to make a place for lesbian and gay Jews, Gersh and I joined our local Reform synagogue as an openly gay couple. Twice now, I've led the synagogue's Holocaust Remembrance Day service. The second time, it was a service I had written and compiled, which included homosexuals among the list of Nazi victims.

Gersh and I also belong to a Detroit-area gay and lesbian Jewish group called Simcha (joy), whose services we find far more meaningful than those at our Reform synagogue because they include lesbian and gay experience, and because the group is more intimate and friendly. Being there stills the longing for the closeness and warmth I first felt in the Orthodox *minyan* (even though I have never been by any stretch of the imagination "an Orthodox Jew"). Gersh and I are integral parts of Simcha, and our closest Jewish friends are there. It's in our involvement with this group and other gay Jewish groups around the country that I feel most committedly Jewish. My extensive reading tour after *Dancing on Tisha B'Av* was published concentrated as much on gay Jewish groups as bookstores, because I felt *this* was my primary audience.

I've seen that my work is helping encourage other Jewish gay writers to actively combine both sides of their life in their writing. There's a rich body of work by Jewish lesbians but far less writing by Jewish gay men, and hopefully my work can contribute to its growth. This sense of mission is somewhat like what I felt in the late '70s, when I contemplated teaching and writing about the Holocaust. But it's based on a deeper and calmer vision. It's truly social action in the Jewish sense of *tikkun olam,* repairing the world.

I'm not at all as observant as I was when I was still attending the Orthodox *minyan,* and I do sometimes miss the sense of excitement and immersion in ritual I had then. But I've also learned to accept the fluctuations in my own need to be involved in Jewish activities and rituals.

One of the most moving injunctions in the Torah is that "the stranger in your midst shall be as the native. For remember, once you were a stranger in the land of Egypt." This call is a central part of every Passover seder. Alienated for so long from other Jews, deeply divided about my own homosexuality, I have felt myself twice strange: Jewish in the gay community, gay in the Jewish community. In each, different, lesser, ashamed. But living with and loving a Jewish man, exploring our Jewishness and gayness together, have made it possible for me to do what Evelyn Beck has called exceeding "the limits of what was permitted to the marginal." Coming out as a Jew ultimately made it possible for me to come out as a gay man and then work at uniting the two identities. As Beck puts it so beautifully in *Nice Jewish Girls,* the "experience of being outside the bounds of society" as a Jew made me "more willing to acknowledge other ways in which [I stood] outside."

It was almost twenty years ago that I started exploring my Jewish past and wondering about a Jewish future. That search has been inevitably interwoven with coming out and finding love. In that dual journey, writing has been both a catalyst and a laboratory for change. Having just passed my fifteenth year as a published writer, and approaching my fortieth birthday, I feel the surprise and joy Lena does in *Light in August* when she says, "My, my. A body does get around."

● VESTAL MCINTYRE

# NAMING THE ADDICTION

The first time I saw my own semen, I had no idea what it was. I thought I was dying. I had been playing with myself, in the bathtub before school, which was my habit in the sixth grade, and all of a sudden my heart was beating in my ears and bits of white were flying out of me and I couldn't help but make splashing noises because my skinny, too-hairy-for-my-age body was writhing out of control, in a fit of what could only be thought of as possession, or death, or some sin that had no name. Afterwards, as I lay there panting, conscious of those bits of white sinking through the water to my skin, I wondered if my mom, who was making breakfast in the adjoining kitchen, had heard all. I stood up, pulled the plug, and quickly began to dry off. And I realized this white stuff was sticky and the more I tried to dry it off the stickier it got, and I suddenly understood sex. I understood how babies were made. (Sex was, of course, never mentioned in my house. Neither was *Three's Company* watched or the Lord's name used in vain.) So in those moments, dizzy with having just experienced some sort of insanity and with thinking rapidly, fearfully, I understood what it was that men and women did. There was some relief in this mystery being solved (before I had thought that maybe a man and woman sleeping in the same bed over a period of time caused the woman to become pregnant, or maybe some exchange of urine was involved), but there was also the terrible suspicion that I was the only person in the world who had done it with himself. As I pulled on my clothes and combed my hair, I muttered an apology to God.

"Hurry up, Vessy!" Breakfast was ready.

I went into the kitchen, kissed Mom good morning, and sat down to an egg sandwich, instant oatmeat, and hot chocolate while Dad, in his brown paisley bathrobe and drooping eyelids, began reading to me from a daily devotional. I was still spinning, and the new sin I had just invented was weighing heavily, and, cowering there over my breakfast, I vowed to myself and to God that I would never *ever* do that again.

I rode to school with my brother Evan, who was in eighth grade, and at that time Idaho law allowed fourteen-year-olds to drive during daylight. The ride to school took us between wide, flat fields of mint or wheat, past the sugar beet factory, billowing smoke, a series of trailer parks and subdivisions, into town. Nampa is small with streets named after other states or presidents. The buildings downtown are made of old brick; their cornerstones say "1910," "1895," and many have brightly colored aluminum facades. Southern Idaho being flat and dry, the sun shines on Nampa constantly, palely, with an almost artificial kind of light. The lawns are big and treeless. There are few buildings with more than two stories. There are no dark alleys.

The boulevard, lined with used-car lots and farm supply stores, led to our school—Nampa Christian, a Protestant, nondenominational school; a small, ultraconservative school in a small, ultraconservative town. (When I visit Nampa now, from Boston, I can't resist the temptation to drive by

Nampa Christian at least once. As I pass I don't turn my head, but glance only sideways at the those three yellow brick buildings that seem so much smaller now. It's silly, I know, but the fear of being seen, perhaps even recognized, haunts me still.)

It was here, at school, in a stall in the boys' bathroom, that I first broke my vow, less than two weeks after having made it. After battling the urge all through reading period, I surrendered, walked quickly to the bathroom (which was empty), and soon I was swooning, gasping, holding myself up against the wall with my free hand.

And as I wiped the evidence off the floor and toilet seat with a piece of toilet paper, I told God that this was *really* the last time. It was out of me. Never again. I flushed and returned to class.

On the bookshelf of my sixth-grade classroom there was a row of Christian comic books. Some were illustrations of Bible stories, some were the true-to-life adventures of missionaries, and some, the most popular, had "for ages thirteen and above" printed on the cover. In one of these comics two tall, muscular men with those comic book cheekbones and shadows beneath their pectorals were roving witnesses of the gospel. They came upon a town where devil worship was rampant. "What . . . what is that old man EATING!?! Oh my . . . it's HUMAN FINGERS!!!" There were detailed drawings of a young boy, possessed by Satan, writhing in a cloud of dust. Another comic book, about Catholics, had on the cover the silhouette of a bishop, his body dark except for glowing red eyes. On one of its pages was a single frame— a Protestant heretic bound to a stake in the center of some pavilion and, frozen ten feet before him, a bull mid-charge. The Protestant's head was bowed, accepting his martyrdom peacefully, reverently. And there was a comic on "the gays";

it began with the hulking, hairy men of Sodom gathered with torches at Lot's door, demanding the angels, and went on to men in grotesque makeup, and the lambda—a secret symbol used by members of the homosexual underworld.

These frightened and delighted me. I read every one and reread my favorites. They were Christian publications—guilt-free satisfaction for my taste for gore and the deliciously perverse. They told me "this is where your sin can take you," but also, "yes, you may sin but at least you're not screaming, clawing, possessed, or watching your skin melt as a result of an LSD flashback, or a man in women's clothing, or Catholic."

Friday afternoons at Nampa Christian, during the hour usually spent on math, the fifth graders would come into our classroom for singing and discussion. We were extra careful to behave because once there was too much whispering or if a note was caught being passed, the fifth graders would be sent back across the hall and the math would begin. So we sang loudly, attentively "Kumbaya," "Zacheus Was a Wee Little Man," or a song whose name I forget:

> I'm no kin to the monkey,
> And the monkey's no kin to me.
> I don't know much about his ancestors,
> But mine didn't swing from a tree.

And the discussion that followed often had the feeling of ghost stories told around a camp fire:

"My cousin got a Ouija board for her birthday, and she knew it was evil and so she threw it into the fire. She could hear the demons screaming as they burned."

"I read that astronomers found something way off in the

galaxy, heading toward earth. They say it might be Jesus, re-turning."

"My big brother played his Led Zeppelin record back-wards and it told him to worship the devil. So he broke it in two and threw it away."

"My mom told me, in the future, everyone will have to have a bar code tattooed on their arms and they'll have to scan it when you go to the store for you to be able to buy anything. That'll be the Antichrist; every number will end in 666."

And one Friday our teacher, Mrs. Stanley, who was tall and thin and had glasses with lenses that became dark when she went outside, but were never completely clear, told us about her recent visit to her son in San Francisco. "He asked me if I wanted to see the part of town where all the gays live, and I thought it would be interesting, so I said yes." Mrs. Stanley had a large key chain that fit around her wrist and she would finger the keys, twisting her wrist, jingling, as she spoke. "Well, driving there he told me to roll up the window and lock the door, and when we got there, there were all these men in women's clothing. My son told me that they all have to wear women's clothing. All except for one called the 'Queen Bee,' who's in charge. He wears men's clothes."

At night, after prayers and before sleep, these stories haunted me. I believed them all. They made the world col-orful and magical and terrifying. And yet I was still good, safe, God was still on my side. Up until that morning in the bathtub I had led a fairly sin-free life. I had cursed only three times in my life. I had never fist-fought with anyone outside my family (and with six older brothers and sisters, one must defend oneself). And I had always immediately turned away from those scenes of exposed bodies, sometimes shamelessly touching each other, which were always flashing before my mind's eye. I ignored the fact that these figures were nearly always male (sometimes Rick Springfield, or one of the Hardy Boys, or one of the members of my brother's basketball team). Naturally, there was no link between these flashes and the men pounding on Lot's door. Nothing in my mind had anything to do with dress-wearing San Franciscans. Certain sins are much less grave before they are named.

But it was during that sixth-grade year that things became more complicated. I lingered on sinful thoughts longer than I should. And that one sin—the one I had invented on that morning in the bathtub—was becoming a problem. I had started a cycle of promising God to abstain, resisting the urge for perhaps a week, then giving in. I told God I was sorry, but I really couldn't help it; I'd limit myself to once a week, and that I'd only think of girls while I did it. And only four days into the week I'd find myself in the bathroom of Dad's office, hunched in guilty pleasure, holding a tissue in my free hand so as not to make a mess, pretending that for this moment I was shaded from God's view. "I'm afraid I'm going to have to do it more often . . . Once every other day, but only thinking of girls . . . Three times thinking of girls for every once thinking of boys." I began to wonder how all this would affect my health. I wondered if I would run out of this white stuff. I considered keeping a record of how often I did it. And my negotiations with God continued. "Whenever I want, trying not to think of anything at all . . . Okay, never again . . . Thinking about boys, but only once a week . . . I'm sorry, God." But these agonized negotiations with him who was silent, whose position was unchangeable, could not succeed. I was addicted to my sin and to boys and was left to do nothing but apologize. "I'm sorry, God."

Within a year or two I would quit talking to God about it altogether. All Christians are instilled with the need to confess, but for us Protestants, of course, there is no confessional. The idea is to confess to God, who's seen it all already, or to let sin upon sin pile up on your soul until, later in life, you confess them to your friends as titillating anecdotes, or to someone on the other end of a phone sex line, or to a lover as the required information, or to a reader. For me, they piled so high that my soul finally collapsed and my sins lost their names again, and all of a sudden the spotlight that was God burned out, and my sweat dried, and I began to learn to see in the dark.

For my brother Roy, the world is still lit by God. Ten years older than I, a Southern Baptist minister, he and his wife recently went to Bangladesh to spend the rest of their lives as missionaries. (I, too, had once planned to be a missionary. It was in sixth grade, during those negotiations with God, that I abandoned that plan.) Roy and I have the same eyes, the same nose, our mannerisms are similar, and we're often mistaken for each other on the phone. (When he started losing his hair, I became nervous.) In the evening after his wedding two years ago, five of us seven kids—my two lesbian sisters, my gay brother, the straight one who doesn't care, and I—escaped the stiff atmosphere of a Baptist wedding reception to a bar by the water, just south of San Diego. The baby of the family, finally old enough to order a drink, I made the first toast: "To the *hope* that Roy is straight, because in this family he doesn't have much of a chance."

Roy and I never talk about religion. Needless to say, I wonder about him a lot. What did he do with his sins? Is he happy? How does someone as whiney and negative as one of us preach the gospel? And it makes me wonder where I'd be now if my soul hadn't collapsed.

❧ The sin that I invented was finally given a name, at a rollerskating party in the seventh grade. My best friend at the time was Suzanne, who lived in Boise and dressed cool and listened to Iggy Pop. Suzanne was an excellent source of information—it was she who explained menstruation to me and, in her description of a "daisy chain—something men in prison do"—gave me my first mental image of anal sex. (Soon after this I dreamt of having anal sex with a man in that same bathtub where my addiction started. I woke up angry. I was surprised at the things that were coming out of my mind. I hated them, hated loving them.)

"It's called masturbation," said Suzanne in her lisp, which would disappear a year later when her braces were removed. She was bent, lacing her rollerskates. "It's like having sex with yourself. Only gays do it." Again, that dim sense of relief in a mystery being solved, and in knowing masturbation was actually someone else's invention. But also the numbing horror of having, myself, been named. "Gay." The monsters that Nampa Christian had warned me about, in high heels and too much lipstick, crowded into my mind.

Over the next few years, I would be named again and again. When I dropped out of the football team, in eighth grade, my team mates named me "gay." It was whispered in the Nampa Christian halls. It was also in eighth grade when my friend Tom spent the night and, for the first time, I played those intoxicating games, and felt for the first time that amazing, hard-yet-soft feeling of someone else in my hand. Lying in the dark afterward, he on the bed and I in a sleeping bag on the floor, he started talking about unimportant things in a quick, cold voice. I didn't want to talk; I was thinking of too many things at once. For the first time, there was the hint of a realization that it wasn't just me pulling one over on God, that He had cheated me, too, forcing me to explore by myself in locked bathrooms what everyone else got to explore with others, behind the gym or in a dark corner at the roller rink. Then, out of nowhere, Tom asked in a bitter voice, "So when are you gonna tell your parents you're gay?" My thoughts froze. I had, once again, been named and Tom lay there, silent, comfortable in the bed, not naming himself. And suddenly it wasn't dark enough.

# Saved

"How intensely people used to feel!"

—James Merrill

I was fourteen and it was the middle of the nineteen seventies and I thought that everything I knew about religion could be easily contained, like a pair of quiescent worshippers in a big pew, in two sentences. *I believe in one God* was the first sentence, intoned weekly in my Profession of Faith in a booming voice that then trailed off into the assured murmur of the following sentences, only after all less condensed versions of the all-important one. The other sentence was the pale underside of the leafy, bright, manifest first, its hidden mate, seldom spoken, always assumed, the deep principle of everything: *I am a Catholic.*

Yet even though I took these simple declarations as a sort of irrefutable basis for my self, I was aware from an early age of something not quite right in the strain of my Catholicism. During mass I was subject to dual impulses. I wanted to give myself up, to surrender myself wholly to rapture, and I could not understand why, if we really believed what we said on Sunday mornings, we should go on with our lives in the ordinary way the rest of the week. But we did, so I wanted also to resist my passions. Yet how I loved the flamboyant artifice of the Mass, the resplendent escape, the exaggerated display! I could not help noticing, though, that I was not really supposed to love exactly these elements (yet, plainly, there they were!); or to love them in quite this way, or with quite this ardor. Something was obviously amiss, and religion came to signify for me a particular relationship to the ordinary. It was, itself, out of the ordinary: all that pageantry circulating, in a world of its own, with a kind of hysterical control, around the figure of a beautiful, doomed, naked man impaled on a cross. And, at the same time, my relation to it was not the ordinary one. Because I longed to be ordinary, I installed those two sentences as the cornerstone of my being, even as another, inverse sentence involuntarily formed itself within me, increasingly simplified, gradually stripped of equivocation, as the first two sentences grew ever more complex, sprouting modifying shoots. That sentence, the new one, I spoke finally when I was nineteen years old: *I am a homosexual.*

&#10087; I had recently moved with my family from one suburb to another farther away from Detroit, better insulated from the city by distance and cost, and one of the many distressing effects of the move, I soon discovered, was that it made necessary renewed avowals of identity. Nobody in our old neighborhood needed to be told who I was, or what. I was known. I was "Jimmy," good-natured loner, spelling-bee champion, Catholic, bad in sports but too amiable to be mocked, a bookworm, a tease who in turn could take his share of ribbing except in certain well-known and carefully avoided areas—bad eyesight, thick glasses, freckles, general scrawniness giving way to increasing huskiness. This identity had grown within me like the white sap coating the inner walls of a dandelion's hollow, mauve stalk—a charged image for my own mythologies of lost innocence, in memory of happy mid-spring hours spent decapitating yellow-headed weeds to suck their essence until the day Bobby Adams from down the block told me the white stuff was the flower's come.

Then I had not had to think about who I was. Now we were leaving my best friend, a house I loved, teachers who already knew in advance how smart I was, to whom I did not have to prove myself, in order to move into a new house, the lone structure in a still-unbuilt subdivision, surrounded by expanses of mud with here and there big rectangular holes, the basements of future houses, like craters in a lunar landscape. On top of that, I was expected to make myself known all over, or possibly to re-make myself, to endure yet again the humiliations of mutable but tenacious selfhood.

In our first week in the new house I was riding my bike along a street in an established neighborhood next to our undeveloped one when a girl called to me from one of the porches. It was a rainy afternoon, my slicker heavy on my shoulders, its yellow flaps concealing the shape of my body, my long hair falling in mid-seventies bangs across my forehead. The girl looked at me critically and tonelessly inquired, "Are you a boy or a girl?" I rode away without answering. This was not, I knew, going to be easy. I was going to have to start from scratch.

Is to speak one's identity necessarily to reinvent it? If so, that would serve to explain the existence of structures by which institutions keep even the most public facets of identity from being spoken. In elementary school, my identity as a Catholic was regularly made public through regulations seemingly designed precisely so that I would never be called upon to speak it, so that it could be made to go without saying.

On Wednesday afternoons, I and my fellow Catholics were excused from school early, whisked away without explanation, herded into buses and transported the half mile to St. Cletus for what must have seemed to our classmates, left behind, the inexplicable, exclusionary ritual of catechism. Election, communion—these are common terms in the public rhetoric of religious affiliation, but what is seldom noted is how the exclusionism the concepts engender threatens the quality of unspokeness they are meant to guarantee. The ritual itself, whatever it was we did during those Wednesday afternoon disappearances, may have remained undiscussable, mysteriously beyond the reach of those social categories given to white middle-class suburban late-baby-boom ten-year-olds.

But its trappings came in for thorough public scrutiny from the non-Catholics. For example, the bus that took us to catechism was the special-ed bus, squat, squarish, half the length of the normal bus with its sleek, rounded fenders. Our status as catechism-goers was therefore linked to the outward signs of abnormality, and Bobby Adams, irrepressible truth-teller, unleashed a gleeful weekly screed on the subject: "Retard bus, retard bus, you're going on the retard bus, they're getting it all ready for you, they're washing out the retard puke, hope you don't pick up too many retard germs!" It was also Bobby Adams who first articulated the disquieting properties of the very word—"catechism"—that named this unknowable act, this hebdomadal vanishing, with its remote but still distinct suggestions of kissing—evoking the kissing of cats, of others, of other boys.

What Bobby Adams could not have known, of course,

was that though we may have felt called on to defend it, the word was at least as disturbing to us as to them. For it could not be lost on us that, in spite of the appearance of institutional legitimization, a rhetoric of shame attended our Catholicism. It was, in fact, a socially authorized intrusion on normality, on normal desire. Though sanctioned by the school, it was understood as somehow ineffable, deeply private, a facet of personal identity, an ingrained attribute that, though chosen, was uncontrollable, seen as so profoundly rooted as to render choice nugatory; and was necessarily associated, despite its apparent social accommodation as a simple fact, with obsession, compulsive repetition, inner yearnings, ultimate dispositions. More than once was I enjoined to be proud of my Catholicism, and I saw only then that the injunction implied the previously unimagined possibility of pride's opposite.

It was weird, a weird thing that was somehow accepted. And my relation to it, to this weird thing, was not like other people's, compounding its weirdness. If society ever finds a way of acknowledging "alternative sexualities," that acknowledgment will probably resemble organized religion. What I knew then about inhabiting inverse identities I learned from being Catholic.

🐚 But I was fourteen, and had only those two sentences to go by, the creed of an accepted silence. All I knew is that we were changing churches just as we were changing houses and schools. Like the other houses in our neighborhood, our new church was still under construction, so mass took place with folding chairs and portable lecterns in the cafetorium of the junior high school I attended every day. The name of the parish was St. Rene, and the nuns wore ordinary dresses beneath a chaste wimple. The priests did not chant their prayers but spoke them in a normal voice, and they told jokes during their sermons. A man with hair as long as mine played guitar during the hymns. People wore blue jeans to mass. How different this was from St. Cletus, with its aura of permanence and its otherworldly ritual, its exacting separation from the habits of daily life. To get to mass at St. Rene, even though we went in by the back door of the school that was named for a failed astronaut, we still had to pass the gym and the music room where my French class met.

Gradually I came to see that my experience with church-going would exist in a new relation to the idea of the ordinary. Where formerly I had been susceptible to a kind of effortless transport from the modes of everyday life in church, now I was surrounded by them, and what church would have to be about was the nexus between the ordinary and the extraordinary. During mass I watched one of the altar boys light the candles and prepare the altar. His face was angular and sharp-boned with a prominent jaw and dark eyes that glowed with concentration as he moved slowly, ritually, extending a flame from elevated candle to candle. Then his air of caution disappeared and he drew back his staff, like a fisherman briskly drawing in his line, and blew out the flame at the end of it. He walked to his seat with an easy, loping gait. When he sat, easing his flattened hands palm down beneath his robed thighs, I saw that he was wearing corduroys and sneakers under his vestments.

All summer my mother said she was sick of seeing me mope around by myself. Mothers she met as the neighbor-hood grew had boys my age, and she kept threatening to get me in on their ball games. But I refused. Deprived of the friends who had surrounded me all my life, I decided it was

time that friendship, like other aspects of identity, became
for me a function not of proximity but of choice. By the end
of the first week of school, quirks of fate provided me with
three suitable but very different friends. Kevin was my table-
mate in algebra, a football player who looked like Robbie
in *My Three Sons*. Ronny, my locker-partner in gym, wore
leather jackets that smelled of cigarette smoke, and he had a
ready, trilling laugh that sounded like an imitation of Cousin
Itt. Craig was my chemistry lab-partner, and the difficulty I
had in placing him was explained for me in one of our first
conversations when he spoke with conviction a sentence
parallel to the one I recited by rote: "I am a Baptist," he said.
The compartmentalized, hierarchic nature of junior-high
culture made it possible to keep the three of them completely separate from each other. Faced with the challenge of
reinventing myself, I saw each of the three as a potentially
separate destiny, and I wanted the freedom to explore each
possibility in isolation, to see how it suited me. Kevin was a
Catholic like me, but the destiny he represented was the
least likely one, that of jockhood. Ronny held out the
promise of delinquency with tales of bad trips and sexual
indulgence that always sounded remarkably like the plots of
whatever movies were out that week. Craig was an intellectual companion, a fellow member of the chess club, from
whom I could learn, who might lead me toward asceticism.
No matter which of the three by turns equally appealing
fates I finally accepted, I knew I wanted to go *somewhere*,
and I knew I would have to be led there.


❧ At that age I could no more invent the man I have become than I can now fully imagine the boy I was. From time
to time I would try to do so, to foresee the cars I might

drive, the jobs I might hold, the women I might marry, the children I might have. But whatever pictures of this domesticated future my imagination supplied always lacked fullness and conviction. They were like images in a child's gray-plastic view-finder: dim, distant, static, reduced. Should I have been able to imagine in more ample detail my possible adult lives? Were others able to do so? It certainly seemed so: Kevin was already able in rhapsodic tones to describe his wife and kids. What was it that prevented me from similarly being able to enter the world of projected time? Would this lack recede as I grew, as the very time I felt I could not invent for myself transpired, unstoppable, with purposes of its own? Or would I be crippled by whatever it was that was missing, would I wear all my blighted life the outer marks of this lack, disproportionate limbs or the explosive scars of uncontrollable acne, unmistakable traces of a troubled transmutation into adulthood?

I can't say that these questions tormented me, if only because I wasn't then able to formulate them in exactly this way. But I began to glean that this growing sense of something missing derived from having taken too much about myself for granted. When someone in school asked me why I never said anything—for I spoke willingly only to Kevin, Ronny or Craig—I gave the stock answer that I remembered from my old neighborhood, what people used to say *about* me: "I'm quiet." This caused the asker to roll eyes upward and say something to the effect of, "You are just so *weird!*"—the final epithet tortured into multiple syllables. I knew from such encounters that the old answers were no longer going to work. But I was still able to cling to those two simple sentences: *I believe in one God. I am a Catholic.*

❧ Spirituality presents itself as a transcendent answer to human desire, but it is also necessarily an analogue to desire. Unamuno, in *The Tragic Sense of Life,* culminates a long tradition in describing faith as passion, as the only end of the unappeasable thirst of being, the hunger for immortality. The "vital longing for immortality" finds its closest fleshly incarnation in sexual desire: "Thanks to love, we feel all that spirit has of flesh in it." But that is not much. For Unamuno, love is as fully suffused with tragedy as any other earthly condition. In spite of the hopeful ardency of Unamuno's sermon on love—"Love is the sole medicine against death, for it is death's brother"—his bottom line is as starkly anatomic as Kant's description of marriage as a contract delimiting the use of a pair of genitals: "The species must renew the source of life from time to time by means of the union of two wasting individuals, by means of what is called, among protozoaria, conjugation." Sexual love, "the generative type of every other love," gives rise to suffering because it "seeks with fury, through the medium of the beloved, something beyond, and since it finds it not, it despairs."

In many spiritual traditions, it is recognized from the outset that what is sought, what is hungered for, cannot be found, and spiritual quest must be seen as an end in itself: Seek, but do not find. Or, in Bonaventure's variant: Desire faith; desire not understanding. Unamuno concludes, with his characteristic gentle severity, that sexual love is an imperfect analogy for faith because it is really a form of pity, born out of an intensity of identification with one's fellow-sufferers. Divine love eschews such identification: St. Teresa addresses God erotically not out of sexual hunger but out of an acceptance of her worldly state. Augustine imagines Adam's erections in the Garden of Eden with studious, not prurient, interest. I first read Unamuno at eighteen when my inner life was already very different from what it had been four years before. I recognized, without perhaps yet being able to articulate it, that the highest forms of desire were believed to surpass identification. We love God not because He is like ourselves, but because He is not, *because* he is unknowable. Yet the unmoored intensity of feeling, the fevered invocation of passion, the refusal to distinguish absolutely between sexual love and other kinds, the submission of suffering to an ecstatic lyricism, the intimate address, all that yearning talk of brothers!—surely some acknowledgment of my own relationship to Catholicism, fraught as it was with an ever more disturbing amplitude of the prohibited identification, was to be found there.

🍃 Craig was as different from Ronny and Kevin as I felt I was, in my yet-unformed state, from all three of them. Kevin and Ronny represented distinctive social types in junior-high culture, the jock and the burn-out. Most of the time, I had the long hair of the burn-out, but although this made me acceptable to Ronny, I let Kevin know it was more a sign of laziness than a gesture of solidarity. Nothing about me suggested even the raw materials of the jock, but Kevin thought I was funny, and my friendship with him allowed me marginally to penetrate that camp. I had not assented to social typology and was generally regarded as a little weird, but I was in a minor way able to traverse the classes.

My own position in junior-high culture may have been almost uniquely malleable, but what I admired about Craig was that he simply *had* no position there. He was not given to striking the same attitudes of superiority that certified outcasts fell back on, seeking lame revenge, as everyone instantly saw with the relentless gaze of the newly pubescent, for their own personal weirdness. Rather, Craig was above it all. The world of junior high, with its rigid structures and social jockeying, went on around him without attracting his notice. He was neither a player, like Kevin or Ronny, nor a vaguely tolerated reject, like me. I discovered with amazement early in our friendship that he didn't even know what a burn-out *was,* and that, unacquainted with the word's subjection to metonymy, he thought a jock was what you wear in gym, though he preferred the even more literal "supporter." One Saturday afternoon his mother dropped us off at a movie, *Young Frankenstein.* After laughing uproariously through the first half, I noticed that Craig was sitting in perfect silence, his arms folded, a distant smile on his face. He was not bored, clearly, and he was even giving off a kind of genuine pleasure, but a pleasure lodged deep within him, not given to laughter, resembling how a cat's pleasure might be expressed if purring were soundless. I felt chastened. I leaned back and folded my own arms, my laughter subsiding. On the way home he described the movie to his mother with invincible simplicity. "It was funny," he said.

A quality of purity was fully evident even in Craig's physical presence. The pressures of growth take their toll on most adolescents, and one reason that I was able to retain a certain hard-won equanimity amid the rank hysteria and casual cruelty of junior high was that I saw with clear eyes that, at least physically, no fourteen-year-old was much better than any other. For all practical purposes, my classmates constituted a richly varied gallery of physical freaks. Even Ronny with his stunted trunk and incongrously sinewy limbs, even Kevin with his rubbery grown-up lips pasted in the middle of a boy's face—a procession of misshapen, acne-splotched figures caught in the protracted act of growing up. But Craig was possessed of a grace that pervaded his frame even though it seemed otherwise untouched by the physical world. He didn't look like the strange hybrids surrounding him, part child, part adult, stranded painfully between irreconcilable conditions. Rather, he resembled the embodiment of the line drawings of nude males I watched him sketch in the margins of his chemistry notebook during class lectures. Like Craig, the figures in these drawings were fine-muscled and hairless. It did not seem unusual to me that Craig should be drawing such figures in his notebook. They were images of the saints, nothing but that, the saints in all their naked suffering. Yet I was conscious of the difference between his attitude as he drew and mine as I watched him draw. He drew with a kind of absent care, light-tipped pencil grazing the page, stopping after every few strokes to jot more harshly a note from the lecture. The inattentiveness of his drawing was at odds with the intensity of my gaze as he manipulated his pencil with blithe agility. In spite of its frozen passivity, my gaze was voracious, as if the strokes of his pencil traversed some furrow in space-time to caress unknowingly, causing it to pulsate irresistibly, whatever part of my body corresponded to the one he drew—supple legs, sloping shoulders, small but precisely detailed nipples.

Craig's otherworldliness was not lessened by those frequent moments when he resembled other boys our age. He was *in* the world, necessarily, but not *of* it. Once he remarked how funny it was that the word "embarrassed" contained the words "bare ass." Another time he suddenly asked, "Did you ever notice that asaparagus makes your pee stink?" I did not take these as lapses into standard adolescent crudity. I understood them as signs of a hallowed earthiness, like St. Teresa's, of a clear-eyed acceptance of the world from which he was inexorably turning away.

With this in mind, I was anxious about seeing Craig among his family. After all, my own impulses to asceticism were easy enough to sustain when I was by myself or at school, but they were routinely defeated the minute I returned to my family, with all their talk of farts and all their worldly acts. If I resolved in a solitary moment of spiritual intensity to subsist entirely on crackers and oranges, like St. Teresa, I could get through lunch but always fell victim at dinner to my reputation in my family as the Human Garbage Can, my plate a welcome receptacle for the leavings of my parents and my sisters, assorted items St. Teresa would no doubt have refused but which I could never resist. When Craig invited me to his house for the first time, I went in the hope that I would not be disillusioned, to find his home life too ordinary, too much like my own. The early signs were foreboding. The house was a ranch just like the one we lived in, the only variation being in the color of its brick and the austerity of its furnishings. The living room was uncarpeted and empty except for a single sofa. Craig's older brother Barry sat, bell-bottomed, against a wall strumming a guitar. His mother greeted me with the platitudes of a sit-com mother: "I always enjoy meeting Craig's friends" and "You boys just go on and make yourselves at home."

What I found out, though, was that Craig's way of relating to these ordinary circumstances was in keeping with what I knew of his inner life. For my part, I may have recognized keenly what I saw as the banality of my own circumstances and their distance from those of the saints on whom we were enjoined to model ourselves. But in spite of this recognition I could not detach myself from the world as I knew it but could only participate in it, helplessly, convulsively—bickering passionately with sisters, desiring ardently all advertised goods, robustly consuming the boxed

foods produced of a fallen age, the Sloppy Joes and Ham-
burger Helper. But Craig was no more a participant in the
structures of the larger world than he was a cog in the hierarchies of junior high. He took me to the basement to play
chess and discuss the implications of the gift of tongues. He
was heedless of the TV sets blaring from upstairs. He offered
me Fritos but referred to them as "corn chips."

Yet, although Craig rejected the things of this world, he
did so without ill spirit. Unlike me, he did not regard the
materials of his everyday life as inexpressibly banal. Instead,
he looked at them through eyes of cobalt blue that would
have pierced if he had let them, and he saw there evidence
of godliness. He did not regard the things of his daily life as
obstructions to his spiritual life but as the conditions that
made it possible. "Are you a Jesus freak like Craigy?" asked
Barry, interrupting our talk. He stood with his guitar tucked
under his arm, and when Craig looked from him to me with
his familiar remote half-smile, I saw that he was interested
in my answer. Before I could think of what to say, though,
Barry lifted his guitar and sang in broken tones, "Jesus
freaks, out in the streets . . ." Without transition he reverted
to speech: "What are you guys fagging around down here
for anyway? Why don't you come upstairs and muscle in on
the real world?"

"If you're lonely," said Craig, "you can stay here with us."

Barry laughed. "I'm not lonely," he said. Then in a slow,
deliberate gesture, he raised his guitar and lowered it gently
so that the bottom of the sound-box rested on Craig's head.
"Kabong!" said Barry, trilling his voice to imitate the sound
of reverberation. Craig only smiled. "What a nut case," said
Barry with a fond chuckle as he tucked the guitar under his
arm and shuffled away.

"It's your move," Craig reminded me.

The event was trivial, but to me it was revelatory. How adeptly—though without machination—Craig had resisted being drawn into his brother's wrangling! With what delicate perception he had seen past the contempt that would have infuriated me to the real need beneath it, refusing the imperatives of sibling rivalry without condescension. I knew that if I tried something like this on my sisters, they would tell me to knock off the holier-than-thou stuff, or would sniff the air in front of my face and ask whether the smell was that of my brain frying. But there in his identical house, Craig's was a completely different life, a completely different way of being. When his mother said good-bye, I noticed that her sit-com-speak had edged off into a kind of sour concern over the clear intensity of our engagement with each other. "What were you boys *doing* down there all that time?" she murmured. It was the kind of question that, when my mother asked, made me flush with anger and embarrassment, a reminder that I was after all only a boy in a fallen world. But Craig's tranquil smile persisted as I stepped out into the early dusk, going home.

On a muggy night in early fall Craig and I slept outside in a little red pup tent pitched in his backyard. The moon was full so the tent's sheer walls were palely aglow, crimson, holding in dense humidity. We lay side by side, inner arms touching, my left brushing softly against his right arm each time we breathed. "Do you think Christ knew he was God?" asked Craig. It was not a question I had considered before, and as always I was happy to listen to what he thought, hoping he would not notice the vacancy of my own response. He laid out the issues carefully, with passionate reason, showing me that it was an important question without seeming to instruct me, without patronizing me. The Son of God, Christ *was* God, yet he was expected to provide to men a model for faith, proving that faith can be found within the realm of the divine as well as in the world of the human. "It's not just that God *understands* faith," said Craig. "He made it, so of course He understands it, but even more than that, *He can share it.* He's what you're supposed to have faith in, but He has faith too, see? He wouldn't ask us to have what He couldn't share Himself. So He made Christ a creature of faith, who knew He was God only because He had faith, and who could even doubt so God could know doubt. Like when Christ asked on the cross, 'Why have you forsaken me?'"

I listened raptly. I could tell from the rhythmic pressure of his arm on mine, each of its hundred minute hairs making me tingle with its glancing contact, that his breathing was regular, as even as his reason. I tried to control my own breathing, measuring it against an expanding sensation in my chest that compressed and shortened each breath. "I'm hot," Craig said suddenly, and then he was leaning over me, bristly knees pressed against my arm where his arm had been. He drew his gray T-shirt over his head. He dropped the shirt in a bundle in the only available space, on the other side of my head. His chest floated above my face. I breathed in its heat. His torso blocked the light from me for a second so that his chest was the color of darkness. The crucifix suspended from his neck hung before my eyes, glinting when it caught the light. The base of his palm, where it curved into his wrist, pressed against the tent's floor next to my ear, supporting his weight as he leaned over me. It occurred to me that he remained there, his body suspended above mine, a moment longer than was necessary. Then he settled down again beside me, naked. "Now," he said. "Where were we?"

❧ I do not remember how the idea of conversion was introduced into our talks, but we began to discuss it soon after. Its appearance as a topic of our earnest conversations came by degrees, unnoticeable but somehow inevitable, like the appearance of the sun near the close of a cloud-choked day. Had he brought it up, motivated by the missionary zeal of the Baptist? If so, none of that zeal was evident as we talked about it. For him, the possibility of my conversion was simply an answer to a question, a step toward, not renewed, but *new* faith. I had recently had my Confirmation as a Catholic, but Craig explained that Confirmation implies a false equation between natural and spiritual birth in reaffirming in a state of knowledge the baptism that takes place in infancy. But regeneration is chosen freely by a self-conscious penitent, and salvation follows without reference to anterior spiritual states. For Craig, it was a simple matter. He wanted everyone to be saved; therefore, he wanted me to be saved. For me it was simple, too. I regarded conversion as a potential bond with Craig, a way of creating, by asserting, some elemental connection between us; or, to put it another way, of declaring that, through Craig, I had chosen asceticism as my destiny, so long as it meant I might spend occasional nights in tents with Craig's spectral body hovering, even for only a second at a time, above my face.

To convert is to speak a *new,* assumed identity while comprehending it as an authentic, originary one. "It may be a crisis experience," said one of the books I checked out of the library and hid under my bed. "But it will be definite." At night I lay in the bed under which these books were concealed and tried to make sense of my own fugitive impulse to conversion. Was it definite? Had I been mistakenly born a Catholic? Was I really a Baptist without knowing it? Did that explain whatever needed to be explained about my relationship to faith? Would conversion fill the lack I felt when I forced myself to look inward, so that I might no longer fear such contemplation? I wanted to save my soul, but a more immediate longing, to be close to Craig, compelled me. Would anyone find that out? Was it sinful? Was it sinful to conceal the compulsion, or to hide books under my bed? A new streetlamp had been put up outside my window and its dull-yellow ooze seeped through the drapes at night so that even when I closed my eyes the darkness was edged with light.

The third time I attended a service with Craig, converts were called forth. It was a week night, so only a few people were in attendance. Craig's mother dropped us off in their big blue van, Craig sitting in front next to her. The church was between the Farmer Jack's where my mother grocery-shopped and an apartment complex, where people I knew from school lived. It was brightly lit inside, and the pews and altars were made of plain, light-colored wood, in contrast to the dun-colored or saturated-auburn and densely ornamented wood of St. Cletus. Craig had explained to me that such services were intended to promote a greater sense of direct contact with God, unmediated by ceremony. Still, the rhythms of the service were so loose that I did not observe that converts were being appealed to until I noticed Craig looking at me with a beatific smile. Then I raised my hand.

I waited alone in a small back room. The room was in a style that I associated with schools, not churches. The linoleum floor was patterned in black spiraling curlicues meant to hide the dirt. There were three desks, chairs of white molded plastic with single chrome arms extending from under the seat in a metallic slope to support the attached congoleum marbleized desktops. Tubes of white glaring light hummed in the paneled ceiling. When the door opened, I was surprised to see that the man who entered was the same man who had been conducting the service. He wore a business suit and had thin, bright-silver hair that was so close-cropped it appeared to be inset into his scalp, resembling the rough-hewn coat of a mouse. In spite of the lustrous monochrome of his hair, his eyebrows were a deep, bushy black. He shook my hand briskly and said his name was Mr. Brill.

While Mr. Brill talked I tried to keep myself from tapping unconsciously on the floor with the toe of my shoe. Mr. Brill was saying the same things Craig said about atonement, conviction, repentance, perseverance. But these things did not seem compelling when Mr. Brill said them. He looked at the floor as he talked and both his hands were clasped together between clenched thighs. Even when he wasn't talking, he kept his mouth open so I could see his irregular gray teeth, and between each sentence that he spoke, he moved the tip of his tongue back and forth behind the bottom row of teeth. As he went on talking, it seemed to me that he mumbled the important words and then gave sudden, explosive emphasis to the unimportant ones. Suddenly he was leaning toward me, with his still-clasped hands now in front of his face, thumbs supporting chin, index fingers pressed together, their tips against the isthmus of skin between his nostrils. "When you pray," he asked me, "what do you pray for?"

I was startled to be spoken to. I removed my own hand from in front of my face, where I had been unconsciously biting into it. A fine strand of saliva connected my hand to my mouth, stretching and glimmering, and vanishing only when the hand came to rest on the desk. I was aware that some residual drool surrounded my mouth, but I did not wipe it away. For the poor, I answered. For the sick. For the starving. For the dead.

"For the dead?" One of Mr. Brill's husky eyebrows rose to a higher level than the other. "But surely the dead are past the need of human prayer."

"I pray that they'll be with God."

Mr. Brill nodded and leaned back. He placed his palms on the desktop, fingers curled. "Tell me how you under-stand the meaning of the Trinity."

I could tell him only what I had learned from catechism. I felt my face going red as I talked. I watched Mr. Brill's hands on the desktop. He spread his fingers methodically, flat now against the smooth, shellacked surface. He reached with one thumb across the desk so that its tip touched the tip of the opposite thumb. "Of course," he said, "you don't mean there are three gods."

"No. No, no, no. There is one." My incantation, my sim-ple sentence, was called for: *I believe in one God.* How is it that I did not speak it?

"There are three manifestations of God," said Mr. Brill.

"Yes," I agreed. "But there is only one God."

Mr. Brill looked both amused and contemptuous. "*Only* one?" he said. "When you think of God, what qualities come into your mind?"

"Goodness," I answered. "Love." I looked at the floor. The black curlicues were meant to hide the dirt, but I saw three footprints on the floor near my desk, the honeycombed shadows of big, cleated boots.

"Any others?"

"Goodness," I repeated.

"Self-existence?" said Mr. Brill. "Immortality? Omnipres-ence? Immensity? Eternity? Holiness? Righteousness? Truth?

Omnipotence?" He spoke each word with a measured tone. He closed his mouth, breathed deeply through his nose, then reopened his mouth, the tip of the tongue in the middle of one of its laggardly trips across the teeth. "Love," he said quietly. He stood up and held his hand out to me. My hand still retained the moist imprints of my teeth, but I extended it. My spit came into contact with the dry skin of Mr. Brill's hand as we shook. The expression on his face, superficially unchanged, was touched by disgust. At the door he turned back to me. "What sports do you like?" he asked.

I knew what the question meant. It was part of a code like the codes of devotion, but, I had thought, distinct from them. I liked no sports, but I could not say that. I thought of Kevin. "Football," I said. Mr. Brill nodded and went out, assured that I was lying, that my conviction was inadequate, that I would never be a Baptist, that—even if some of my prayers were for the poor and the sick and the dead—most of them were for the love of Kevin or Ronny or Craig.

On the way home, Craig clambered into the back seat beside me, leaving his mother alone in front. She regarded us nervously in the rearview mirror. "How was the service?" she asked. Craig placed his hand on my thigh and squeezed it tenderly. Then he rested his hand there. I was afraid that his mother could see this, but I also knew Craig would see no shame in the gesture. "Jim was saved," he told her.


🦋 Secretly relieved that I had not really been saved, that my life could go on as before, I avoided Craig for several days. I attended mass at St. Rene with my mother and sisters, and took Communion. If the masses lacked the inflamed theatricality that had previously so inspired me, I decided that, too, should be taken as a source of relief. The masses did not lack the spirit of God, after all, and their tractability was safer, more amenable to teaching myself, if I could not become a Baptist, how to be the right kind of Catholic. It had begun to seem to me that, in any case, the closer I came to exaltation, the further I was from God. Shooting the breeze with Kevin or Ronny, I felt I had come back to them after a long time away. There was something reassuring about their commitment to the known world, about the way they sought transport only in what was comprehensible—drugs, say, or football. Kevin told me he noticed I had been hanging around a lot with that Craig guy, whom Kevin had thought was pretty weird, and I agreed that he was. But then one afternoon Craig appeared at my door and suggested that we go swimming because he thought it would be among the last of the warm days. He had not brought his bathing suit with him, so I lent him a pair of my cut-offs.

It was already mid-fall, and cool, so the lake was deserted. After a quick swim we sat on the shore, arms hugging knees. Craig's chin rested on his knees, and he was shivering. He asked me how it felt, being saved.

"Okay," I said. Then I added sharply, "What's your deal anyway? It isn't *that* cold."

He looked at me. Seemingly by force of will, he immediately stopped shivering.

"I'm not like you," I went on. "I don't think it happens that way, being saved. Like, you walk into a church and then all of a sudden you're suddenly saved. I'm sure, man. I'm really just so sure. Going to heaven depends on what you do. It depends on how you act."

"It's not about going to heaven," said Craig.

"Then what's it about? I've listened to you talk and some of it makes sense, like that stuff about a personal God and all. But not everybody believes all that stuff, you know? Not everybody even thinks that way. I mean, there's Baptists, yes, but there's Catholics, too. And that's not all there is. What about Jewish people? I mean, all I'm saying is not everybody believes the same way and you shouldn't act like your way is best all the time."

"I didn't know I did," said Craig. "I didn't know you thought I did."

I remembered the night we slept in the tent. I had listened to him speak of God that night. I had been in a state of sustained rapture. It had been his words that had brought about that state, his words that had sustained it, but it had also been, I realized, his voice, his body. And later, after his voice subsided, he asked me in a low whisper if I, too, were not hot. Had he wanted me to take off my shirt as he had his? Would it have produced in him something of the inarticulate bliss his nakedness caused in me? Was it possible to reconcile that unspoken ecstasy with the spiritual transport he was able to describe so fully? "No," I had told him. "I'm not hot." I had refused; I had not wanted to get too close to the source of my feeling, because I feared it. But now on the cold shore of this empty lake, I was telling him that I was not like him, because I wanted him to consider forms of our kinship other than the spiritual.

"That's not what I mean, either," I said. "This isn't coming out right." In frustration I lay back, facing the sky, stretched out on the rocky shore.

Suddenly he clambered on top of me, straddling me. He was holding a ridged, variegated rock, the size of a hockey puck. "This all comes down to something basic," he said urgently, his weight on my thighs. "Do you see this rock? Do you believe God made it?" With his free hand he gently clasped my wrist. Gently he lifted my hand to the rock he held, and I closed my fingers around it. He held one side of the rock and I the other. "Do you believe that God made this rock with His own hands?"

I did not answer. Then the rock was pulled away and the pressure lifted from my thighs. I looked at my hand, at the traces of dust there from the rock. When I sat up, I saw the rock hurtling through the air. I saw Craig standing on the shore, his back to me, his arms at his sides. The posture of his body suggested repose. I had not seen him throw the rock, yet I did not doubt that it was he who had done so. Why, then, merely because I had not seen God fashion the rock, should I doubt that He had done so? I watched the rock soar through the sky. I looked, nearer me, at Craig's back, its clear proportion, the precise column of his spine, at the cleft in the seat of the shorts I had lent him. In a second the rock would hit the surface of the lake. It would make a splash that would perhaps be lost amid the rising din of the wind. It would create outward-moving circles as in liquid glass that has not yet found its final, solid form, and these would, before disappearing, interlock mercurially with the many other ripples on the top of the already quivering lake. But for another second the rock was still in midair, and it was *that* second when I knew that, whatever else, I thought Craig's *body* was beautiful; that I would have to find a place for such knowledge among whatever other knowledge I could forge; that my future life, which I could not before imagine, would depend on it; that in this way the lack I had perceived within me might yet be overcome. The rock reached the crest of its arc, buoyed up and suspended aloft but falling still, as if from an immeasurable height.

## ❧ A N D R E W   H O L L E R A N

# THE SENSE OF SIN

The attempt of gay men to merge their Catholicism with homosexuality has always seemed to me touching but doomed. I used to walk past the church on Sixteenth Street in New York where I knew Dignity—an organization for gay Catholics—was meeting, but I never went in. I felt sorry for the men inside, sympathetic to their attempt, and superior to what seemed to me their naivete. Don't even try, I thought, as I walked past, on the way from the gym to the baths (my new church), you're just kidding yourselves. There can be no commerce between, no conflation of, these two things. Fellatio has nothing to do with Holy Communion. Better to frankly admit that you have changed gods, and are now worshipping Priapus, not Christ.

There was a certain bitterness in these thoughts as I passed St. Francis Xavier—no one can jettison his childhood beliefs without a sense of dislocation; especially a set of beliefs in which sex had no place whatsoever. On the other hand, I suspected even then that it would be too simple to ascribe this disjunction to my Catholic upbringing. The sense that sex was incompatible with one's ideals of social and spiritual life seems endemic to much of human culture. "There is a prejudice against you here among the 'fine'

ladies and gentlemen of the Transcendental School," a friend
wrote Walt Whitman from Boston more than a hundred
years ago. "It is believed you are not ashamed of your repro-
ductive organs." I was; even as a child. Presexual innocence
ended the day I began spouting on our patio one morning
the "dirty" words I'd just learned—ignorant of their meaning, not their power to shock—and my mother washed my
mouth out with soap. By the time I saw, while visiting family friends, the large crucifix that hung on the wall above a
marriage bed that had produced seven children, I was already disturbed by the apparent contradiction: How could
people make babies while Jesus on the Cross was watching,
I wondered. Jesus and the saints were sexless, and, so far as
I knew, so was family life. Whatever the reason, a disgust
with our private parts, an embarrassment about the way we
are manufactured, was certainly in me by the time I had to
confess my first "obscene acts, alone or with others" in the
hush of the confessional.

As Anthony Burgess wrote: "It is never the object of Confession, at least in the Catholic tradition, to present oneself
as a likeable character." No, the object of a Catholic Confession, and education, was something else entirely: growing
up Catholic meant refining what may have been an already
intrinsic sense of sin. (Though one could say the same for
Calvinism, too.) Faced with the list of sins in my missal, as I
examined my conscience before Confession, I became a
connoisseur of the evil that lurks behind our every act, of
the duplicity, the obfuscation with which we hide our true
natures. "Obscene acts, alone or with others" was only one
item on a list: False humility, joy at the misfortune of others,
envy, covetousness—the phrases still come forward, intact,
from the almost transparent pages of the missalette. Growing up Catholic meant being intoxicated with the sense of

one's own evil. (Though surely this varied according to the Catholic; the sense of Sin is distributed unevenly among people, I think, like hair color or temperament. I know Catholics serenely unperturbed by all of this.) Each Sunday in church one was given what seemed to be a clear message: Jesus was a solitary, celibate, lonely man whose death had freed us; and if you couldn't become a priest or saint yourself, you would have to settle for merely marrying a woman, and forming, as a kind of second-class citizen, a part of the community which crucified Him.

This sense of betrayal, of Sin, meant that when puberty arrived in the life of a Catholic idealist and the body asserted itself in a way that nothing in Catholicism had prepared you for, that single phrase on the pages of the missalette—"obscene acts, alone or with others"—was literally breath-taking, heart-constricting, to the child who heard the screen slide open and knew he was about to say these words to the priest. "Alone" meant you had jerked off in the bathroom. "With others" meant you'd compared penises with the boy next door (the son of a Protestant minister, in my case). Either one was terrifying; a new order of guilt—so great one started to postpone, and fear, a sacrament which till then had been eagerly sought.

When Confession was good, it was great, on a Saturday afternoon, when my friends were all at the beach, the very emptiness of the huge church confirmed my specialness, my devotion to Christ. Christ, who hung on the large Cross above the altar, His beautiful face bleeding from the Crown of Thorns, ignored by the world rushing past this shadowy church on their motorbikes and cars as I examined my conscience with the thin, thin pages of the missal beneath my fingers. The soft thudding sound of the confessional screen being closed and opened in the rear of the church as the

priest moved from one penitent to the other only empha-
sized the amplitude of Time in which I could kneel near the
magical warmth of the banks of burning votive candles in
their blood-red cups, and peel away the layers of my soul;
even while my mother sat outside in a baking car in the hot
sun, waiting. This, after all, was for Eternity: the more time I
spent, the better, as I tried to work up a contrition that
would be real, unmistakable, beyond doubt. (*Jealous of
Suzanne because she got a 98 on her math test . . .*) Afterwards I
said my penance, mercifully small, it seemed, the holy water
drying on my forehead, reborn, renewed, remade, almost
afraid to return to the world that would send me back here
laden with new, inevitable sins; unsure what to do with my
newborn cleanliness—just as years later I would pause on
the steps of the VD clinic in New York after the doctor had
told me the Diotoquin had cleared up my intestinal para-
sites. What to do with health, with life, with one's body,
would always be the problem, in a world of good and evil.

At that point I need not have worried; both the pleasure
and dread of Confession seemed to vanish when puberty,
and its obscene acts, coincided with a dissipation of religious fervor. By the time I got to college, I was already skeptical; reading Nietzsche in the basement of the Catholic
Club deepened that; and by the time I went to bed with another man, at the ripe age of twenty-six (surely a conse-
quence of my Catholic upbringing), it was no longer an
issue of Sin and perdition.

Or so I thought; till I found myself the next morning in a
shower washing my mouth out with soap—not my mother,
me—to clean the orifice which till then had been used for
the "innocent" purposes of speech and nourishment: my
first glimpse of the fact that we never really leave Catholicism behind. On the other hand, after this mouth-washing,

this soapy purification of the Temple of the Holy Ghost, I was off and running. A sense of sin never held me back thereafter. The mouth-washing was momentary remorse. I was no exception to the fact that as we grow older, we redefine Sin, all of us; and this redefinition of Sin is precisely one way we change into the persons we become.

Jesus said: No man can serve two masters; either he will love the one and hate the other, or hate the one and love the other. (Or *perhaps* Jesus said this, according to the new book that claims only about twenty percent of what's in the New Testament can be attributed with any certainty to Christ; there may be little left of Christ after science and scholarship are finished.) Well, when you're a gay man having sex, and a Catholic, you have a problem. The Church says sex between people of the same gender is a sin; homosexual desire, according to a Vatican document of the late eighties, is "tendency ordered toward an intrinsic moral evil." In other words, don't do it. If, as Socrates said, happiness is virtue, and, as the Church says, the virtuous homosexual is celibate, then Happiness=Celibacy for the gay Catholic.

I guess it was here I made my choice, in my late twenties; after returning to celibacy for almost a year after the mouth-washing, an awful loneliness forced me out of the closet once again. Celibacy did not seem a realistic option; the Church itself called celibacy a vocation, a gift; it made sense only with a call to the priesthood or to the monastic life, it seemed. I went on with my homosexual life, and stopped going to Mass and Communion, except when home visiting my parents. Like Jack in *The Importance of Being Earnest*, I was one thing in the city, and another in the country; that somewhat pathetic figure: the lapsed Catholic—a strange mer-man, half-in, half-out of the Catholic sea, believing with the heart, but not the head, no longer a Catholic in the eyes of some, yet still unwilling to cease the internal dialogue between my Catholic self and daily life. But one thing seemed clear: Celibacy, sans faith—celibacy, in 1970— seemed pointless. The life of Gerard Manley Hopkins—the most brilliant example, perhaps, of a man who extinguished his sexual self on the altar of Catholic idealism—seemed to me a tragedy. Christ, so far as I knew, said nothing at all about homosexuality; He said to love one another. The rest was commentary—the work of human priests, the ones Nietzsche accused of resentment. I said to myself as I walked past the church in which Dignity was meeting: If God is Love, and sex is love, then sex between two people of the same gender can only be looked upon benignly by God. The real sin would be to live, like Hopkins, like the protagonists in Henry James, without ever having this contact with another human being, and the relief from isolation it provides. I took my mantra from St. Augustine—"Love, and do as you will"—and distinguished between a human and a divine church; made my own list of sins; and became in the process what is known as a cafeteria Catholic.

The cafeteria Catholic—I'll believe this, and that, and leave the rest, thank you—is no doubt emblematic of the late twentieth century, a time Santayana compared to the Alexandrian age, when many faiths, many religions, flourished in cities. The more I read, after college, the more eclectic I became—till concluding I belonged more to Greece than Israel, to Athens, not Jerusalem. I'd been the hapless inheritor, through Rome, of a Semitic civilization more parochial and puritanical than that of the Greeks. I agreed with Santayana, sadly, that religion is probably no more than a marvelous imaginative construct of man. I was happy to learn the Sufis believed God was found in the arms of a beautiful youth. I began spending more time lifting weights than praying, looked for ecstasy in the discotheque, not mass; found myself kneeling everywhere but pews. Homosexuality at times seemed to me as passionate as Catholicism but without belief—a sort of peripatetic, all-male brotherhood outside of marriage, and town; the habits of adoration transferred from the invisible world of Christ to the Puerto Rican messenger on his bicycle waiting to cross the street beside you. In other words, life became aesthetic.

And Christian imagery and homosexual life mingled; it was all a celebration of the male form. The lean man lying in his room at the baths, feet-first toward the hallway, resembled exactly Mantegna's painting of Christ descended from the Cross. The magic of his embrace was the same ecstasy Teresa of Avila and John of the Cross described in their meditations on Christ the Bridegroom. The similarities between the Catholic and the pagan worlds—which had, historically, been as much a continuum as a change—seemed so abundant that it startled me on my way from the gym to the baths to walk past the church in which Dignity was meeting (a meeting the Pope has since banished from his churches) and feel the sudden stab of anger and certainty that they were, because of homosexuality, irreconcilable. But they were. Dignity: The very name was poignant—testimony to the pariah status of Catholic homosexuals; it seemed incredible to me that one needed to meet in a group to acquire a sense of worth! I could not imagine the homily a priest or lay person would give to such an audience; the mind boggled. Treating one's trick with Christian lovingkindness? Please. Getting him to call back was the object; the cardinal virtues were irrelevant to that. What mattered in real life, it seemed, was the body, not the soul; and not even that so much as body parts.

Of course I was aware of a system of ethics in homosexual life; and Sin was still, despite Whitman, a useful concept. It was Tennessee Williams, however, who now supplied the definition: deliberate cruelty to another human being. Under this rubric, one still had to examine aspects of gay life: promiscuity; hiding one's sexual orientation from one's family (the real Sin, unless you thought it crueller to reveal it); withdrawing from one's full potential because of the shame, or the difficulties, of having a secret vice. (At least that's what Proust called it.) At times it seemed to me I was involved in a life which didn't seem terribly kind to its participants, which valued Beauty more than character, and subjected us to diseases that, with the onslaught of AIDS, climaxed in scenarios of sadistic cruelty—which, to the fundamentalists, looked like nothing more than a good, old-fashioned Old Testament come-uppance; the first in years, if not decades, of moral relativism. AIDS shook everyone's "faith" in homosexuality; seemed to prove that, if not a sin, same-sex eros should be at least included among those things the Old Testament forbade the Israelites out of concern for their hygiene, health, and safety. As Irish American Catholic conservatives like Pat Buchanan—and even Protestant conservatives—pointed out on the talk shows, whatever you thought of homosexuality, it seemed to cut short the life span of young men.

Indeed, it did—the toll AIDS was taking deepened the line people of all faiths, cultures, races wanted to draw in the shifting sands of moral values that Pat Buchanan called not merely a cultural, but a religious, war. Blacks and whites, Catholics and Protestants, fundamentalists and sophisticates could agree on this: the idea that homosexuality and heterosexuality were on a moral par was nonsense. To the fundamentalist, homosexuality was *the* Sin: and gay men a horde of hedonists defying Scripture so flagrantly that

AIDS only restored the natural order of things. To Jerry Falwell, the man who came out was selfish. (To the gay person, it was an act of courageous authenticity.) To a sophisticate, it was at best a dangerous, lonely, and tragic lifestyle. To the Pope, moral disorder. To the average gay man trying to keep his sense of—yes, dignity—against what seemed to be the slings and arrows of outrageous fortune, not to mention Cardinal O'Connor, Pat Buchanan, Jerry Falwell, William Dannemeyer, the Pope, and the beds on which one's friends lay dying, it was hard enough to think, much less think clearly, about whether one was living in Sin.

It is terribly important, of course, to be clear in your mind about what constitutes, and does not constitute, a sin. One had to decide, first off, whether believing in Sin was itself a sin. Over a century ago, Walt Whitman had written:

> I think I could turn and live with animals, they are so placid and self-contained . . .
> They do not sweat and whine about their condition;
> They do not lie awake in the dark and weep for their sins;
> They do not make me sick discussing their duty to God.

In other words, one could legitimately decide, with Santayana, that religion was a human construction, and that it was nonsense to even worry whether homosexuality was a sin. One could say, reasonably, that religion was only mankind's superstitious response to the terrible problem of Death, that Montaigne was right when he said "Nothing human offends me," that the poetry of the ancient Greeks was full of pederastic sentiment, that one should no more feel guilty about homosexual desire than a pear should feel guilty for not being a pomegrante. Or—if you believed in God—that the Church is both human and divine, subject to the temporal prejudices of its time, and that eventually its judgment of homosexuals would change. That it was possible to live one's whole life worried about one set of (sexual) sins while committing meanwhile another set much worse. (As Proust said, our venial sins may cause those who love us much more unhappiness than our mortal ones.)

You could believe all this, however, and still have to ask if any of it was entirely rational or subject to mental scrutiny. It was one thing to say, reasonably, that religion was only superstition: it was another to extinguish the self that had spent so many warm, happy hours in church preparing for Confession. As William James said: "The test of a belief is whether we act on it." I suspected the fact that I kept my sexual identity secret was not so much an exercise in diplomacy, for instance, as it was my own feeling it was a shameful thing; despite my mind's conviction that there was nothing wrong with sex with another man. When my mother asked one evening if I was gay, I replied, "Of course not!" and stalked out of the room, thinking, as I left, that I'd denied this more quickly than Peter denied knowing Christ.

Of course Walt Whitman—when asked by John Addington Symonds in a letter if he was homosexual—wrote back indignantly denying such a suggestion and claiming to be the father of six illegitimate children. The reflection, which followed my lie, however, convinced me I was nevertheless a sort of mess; a living contradiction between two selves; not only a cafeteria Catholic, but a cafeteria human being— a little of this, a little of that. I hadn't the courage of my convictions—if they were convictions, which I'm not sure they were.

In fact, my chief argument against the Church on this matter was not that homosexuality involved affection, but that it did not involve, so far as I could tell, free choice; it was simply part of God's handiwork, the vast variegation of Nature Hopkins had celebrated in poems like "Pied Beauty." Clearly, I would have argued with the Pope, that the homosexual was part of God's creation, not a threat to the family, but a supplement to, a part of it. Clearly we were—in every generation, for whatever mysterious reason—part of His design (in Hopkins's poem, "All things counter, original, spare, strange"). I thought I understood the Church's venomous opposition—only sex that created Life could be approved; religion, like philosophy, is a reaction to Death—I even found myself prudishly disapproving when I met a Jesuit who ran a college and took boyfriends on vacation. (The perfect living example of my intellectual theory.) But mostly I agreed with Freud, when he wrote the American mother, worried about her son, that homosexuality was "no vice, though assuredly no advantage." (It was, of course, institutions like the Church that made sure it was the latter; and worse.) I thought it simply one's lot in life—the way one had turned out, for reasons no one comprehended; a condition that might even, in some people's view, be that most Catholic of things—a cross one had to bear.

That one kept thinking in Catholic phrases was, of course, part of the legacy of a Catholic childhood. The gay Catholic operates on two levels, I suspect; on the one hand, he believes it is quite moral to act on his sexual orientation, to form a sexual bond, of whatever duration, with another man; that the antihomosexual tenets of Christianity are parochial, culture-bound, and heterosexual; that the active gay man has acquired, and provided others, a human dimension available uniquely in erotic intimacy; that kindness, beauty, tenderness, love can be experienced only through the medium of another person. On the other, he suspects that he has turned sex into a form of fast-food junk; that he is trapped in a way of life from which there is no escape and no real chance of finding any lasting peace of mind. In other words, this was cognitive dissonance as a way of life.

Dignity, of course, was an attempt to counter that—I was simply too puritancial, too pessimistic, too Catholic, perhaps, to think it could be done. I even took the next logical step and asked: Is my Catholicism perverting my homosexuality? Is my guilt over homosexuality so great that I keep it secret, furtive, detached, compartmentalized? Is it still so ineradicable, this Catholic world view, that I have programmed homosexuality to fail? (Or have I just not met the right man?) Who knows? There may be no way of knowing the answers to these questions, but ask them I had to; as we all have to ask, sooner or later, if we're pleased with the way we have spent our life. In other words, we are always going to Confession.

The sense of Sin is, of course, missing in some people, keen, more keen, keenest in others. When I drew up a list of my own one evening, I was surprised to see that all of mine amounted to sins that did not include homosexual acts themselves but the consequences of hiding them from people who loved and expected more out of me, perhaps, than I'd given the world. In other words, I suspected myself of shame, withdrawal, and finally that most classic of Catholic sins, despair. Still, none of them seemed correctable; I hadn't any more faith in homosexuality's virtues, really, than I did in the existence of God—though the latter was not something I could bring myself to entirely disbelieve, either. It startled me, for instance, in the eighties when a Catholic friend told me as we were leaving church that it was rude to go to mass and not take Holy Communion—like going to someone's house for dinner and refusing to eat; and that if, as I said, I was troubled by the necessity of going to Confession first, then I should just go into the woods and confess my sins to a tree. (So *that's* how things have evolved, I thought. Well, not for me.) I still took it seriously enough to believe that if I received the Holy Wafer on my tongue in a state of unconfessed, accumulated sin—countless obscene acts, alone and with many, many others—I'd be doing something profane. In other words, I agreed with Flannery O'Connor who said about the Eucharist: "If it was a symbol, I'd say to hell with it!"

This is a confession of indecision, of course—not the serene reasonableness of a Santayana. (Santayana spent his last years in the care of Blue Nuns but left strict instructions that even if Extreme Unction were brought and he seemed to nod, it must not be construed as a conversion.) How can the person who believes there is no evidence for the existence of God—and nothing wrong with homosexual acts— be afraid to take Holy Communion? Simple. I *am* afraid. I am not merely rational, but irrational, too. It would be nice to say there is a clear, precise, logical "solution" to this dilemma—this conflict between the Church and the gay Catholic—but in reality most of us are a motley mix of child and adult, logician and frightened animal. The central question of Christianity is still very simple: What think ye of Christ? If you think He was not divine, then all this is merely a discussion of human ethics. If you think He was, then this has to do with the future of one's soul in all eternity. It becomes a question of authority. Years after entering the confessional with my heart in my throat, I was listening to an evangelical preacher on the radio while driving through the Florida backwoods one evening. He warned against doubting the Bible and acquiring the detachment and cynicism that characterize "the hardened heart." And I had to ask myself: Is my eclectic potpourri of beliefs, my cafeteria Catholicism, merely the work of a selfish, rationalizing sensualist who doubts God's Scripture?

I think not. The sexual instinct waxes and wanes, of course; St. Augustine wrote his confessions after a life of debauchery. And I'm sure one can lose one's "faith" in homosexuality as well as in God; ending up, perhaps, with a double loneliness. I cannot predict the eventual overview of my life, if one is allowed me; and I know homosexuality at fifty is not what it is at twenty-five. But looking back now on the sins I suspect have characterized my life, homosexual acts are not among them.

The way I've treated others because of the conflict between my religion, society, culture and those acts may well be, however. This conflict is not merely external, but internal as well. Imagine, if you will, the Catholic who retains the sense of Sin without availing himself of the sacrament, which relieves it and absolves him. What worries me most, perhaps, is the sad fact that even if others may be willing to "forgive" gay Catholics their sexual orientation—family, friends, doctors, even priests—too often we refuse to forgive ourselves.

# THE WAY OF
# SOME FLESH

A week before Christmas 1993 I found myself with my friend Sean, at a restaurant in Washington, D.C. Sean spent his early twenties in a monastery before turning secular and hitting the noisy, bumptious, ultra-ego world of Washington broadcast news. Despite his steady professional success in the news trade, he had begun to contemplate returning to the monastery.

"I have no time for solitude in my daily life," he told me, no time for the vital moments of clarity that had ordered his earlier monastic life. Because of the timing of broadcast deadlines and the antic nature of the daily news spin, he found himself progressively divorced from more primal daily rhythms, from witnessing and acknowledging what a day really is. Before, in the monastery, the celebration of each day had been codified in the vespers service. Unlike the fixed daily deadlines of news, vespers is the fluid marker of the day's completion, driven not by a clock but by the trajectory of the sun, the length of the shadows, the imminence of night. The implications of the word—vespers, taken from the Latin word for evening star—were joyous, reflective of a fragmentary, early Christian hymn that told of the happiness that came in seeing the light of God reflected in the vesper star.

Sean and I continued to talk about the tension between monastic rhythms and news rhythms in the back of a taxi that was delivering us to Washington's tawdriest sex bar, a place called La Cage à Folles. La Cage, which is noted for providing happy evening moments to congressional staff, military men, and lobbyists, features buff boys naked down to their boots, undulating their limbs atop the club's two long bars. A certain discontinuity struck me about our conversation and our location.

At first flush I supposed this sex temple—really a sex fantasy temple—to be one of the polarities Sean was examining for himself, inasmuch as he takes the vow of monastic celibacy seriously. Fleshpots and news deadlines on one side. Silence and prayer on the other. But that was only the most superficial way of reading the evening.

Later, as I would replay in my mind the tableau of Sean and the other customers sitting on the bar stools and the young, beautiful men dancing on top of the bar, I began to contemplate the qualities of happiness that the vesper star brought to the faithful. As much as the star shifted in the heavens, it was a continuous companion in the Mediterranean night, a beacon from God that night was not death, and a reminder that the physical world and the celestial world were connected. The rhythm of darkness and light was integral and rooted in physical experience, the act of seeing. Not to be forgotten, either, is the fact that the name of the star, like the iconography of the stars in the heavens, derives from the pagan religions of Greece and Rome. Though the early Christians may have claimed vespers as their own, they took it from the rituals of pagan belief, which never separated the physical from the celestial or the human from the spiritual.

And what of these young men, hustling their buns for a few dollars, and the middle-aged men, their eyes uplifted just at knee level? All too many of the men on the stools dwell in the arid, officially desexualized domain of bureaucratic Washington politics, a world where they dare not even wander into the section of the chain bookstores where gay material is displayed. Like the late congressional power broker Wilbur Mills, who splashed about the Tidal Basin with his "Argentine Firecracker" Fanny Fox, many of these men only find it possible to explore the unity of the flesh and the spirit in the shrouds of night. They sit, gazing on the star-boys. They reach up to touch forbidden flesh, and they gratefully deposit their offering—a single, a five, a ten, occasionally a twenty—into the gym sox that ride above the boys' leather boots. In that moment—sad surely, undeniably objectified, and utterly ritualized—there is often, if not always or even usually, a sublime unity of spirit and flesh, a touch of continuity in a cold, greedy, brutal, and discontinuous city, where news passes for reality, and deadlines substitute for a day's end.

As for the boys atop the bar, some characterize their work as "just a job" in which their young flesh is their most valuable tool. Some say, too, that they experience the sublime, that they take delight in the grace of their own beauty, that they derive sustenance from a quality of comradeship unthinkable, unimaginable, in their classes at Georgetown or on their rounds in the Senate office buildings. Maybe they are simply narcissists. Certainly, as critics gay and straight will rush to note, the bawdy overlay of teasing sexuality at La Cage has nothing to do with conventional love or intimacy that most Americans assert is the only proper venue for erotic contact. And yet, as readers of Boccaccio and Chaucer will recall, bawdy escapades are not entirely absent from the monastic orders. For as much as the monastic impulse is to withdraw from the transactions and relationships of the secular world, the monastery often insists that its brothers immerse themselves in the physical experience of being on the earth, of touching the soil, crushing the grapes, wrapping the cheese, cleaning the dirty. As much as any human institution, the monastery requires ritual immersion in the physical simultaneously with personal removal from the world. To be in a state of contemplative solitude is not to withdraw and sever the spiritual from the physical, but to order and contain the physical in sublime celebration of the continuity between spirit and flesh.

I don't know that Sean, who continues to opt for deadlines over vespers, finds anything at all monastic in the experience of visually fondling go-go boys. I do not know how many of the men sitting around that bar stuffing bills in boots over Christmas week would talk of any spiritual or crypto-religious intimations at La Cage à Folles. I do know that for Sean the periodic taxi ride to La Cage takes him into the territory of the sublime. And while I seldom allow myself to escape my own role as witness-reporter, I do find myself increasingly drawn into those meditations precisely because the physical contact humans make with one another at sex temples like La Cage is so strictly ritualized, so repetitive, and so protected from the confusions and obligations of conventional emotional intimacy. The provocative power of these moments is possible specifically because, in almost all cases, fully intimate exchange is impossible, reducing contact to a momentary arc of synaptic connection. Though we are surrounded by the most crass, market-driven of surroundings, where even now the police might raid at any moment, exposing all present to ridicule and ruin, we are offered the possibility of losing ourselves in raptured contemplation of the sublime.

By the sublime I don't mean the merely beautiful, although, of course, only the most conventionally beautiful men are chosen to dance atop the bar. Unlike the figures on a Grecian urn, these men are not preserved in timeless eternity. They are momentary. They will be replaced. The hardness of their bodies and of their market strength will soften and sag. They may, in only a few years, compete with their current customers for space on the bar stools. That is the key to the rapture.

None of this, of course, is or should pass for the more conventional raptures of religion, with which I have had modest contact. I was not raised with benefit of any religious instruction. My early spiritual sensibilities were at best a fuzzy-focused pantheism expressed in the color, taste, texture, and grandeur of the oak trees, tobacco plants, and autumn apples we harvested each year for our living. My father shielded us from the local organized churchery and itinerant preachers, who peddled Bibles up and down the highway. He was not antireligious, but he found more hate and condemnation than love and forgiveness in their fire and brimstone oratory. And so, aside from a few months when I accompanied neighbors to their church, and learned the tune and lyrics to the basic gospel hymns, I was, and would still be considered, a heathen.

Yet despite the obvious evil that has been committed in the name of religion, especially of the Judeo-Christian-Islamic variety, I have never felt hostile to the religious impulse. Much as the organized churches of my own state, Kentucky, have felt constrained to view queer people with revulsion, I have never seen them as necessarily committed to my repression. Perhaps perversely, I have even felt sympathetic toward them, for I suspect that their obsession with the uses of the flesh constitutes a tacit admission of the fundamental connectedness of flesh to spirit—just as I suspect that many of my secular, straight liberal colleagues would neutralize all mystery about sex and spirit by relegating it to the realm of passionless hormonal chemistry. The first step to spirituality, it seems to me, comes in contemplating the mystery, not in resolving it.

The matter of mystery in ordinary life recurs frequently in talks with Gene, the man I live with in Brooklyn. Some summers ago Gene began putting out a garden in his long, narrow backyard. He starts, as many city people do, in February. He pores over seed catalogues, looking for exotic flowers and gorgeous vegetables.

Unlike many Park Slope yuppies, Gene doesn't grow his garden in order to have his own fresh, organic vegetables. For the table he's generally quite happy with the Pathmark produce section. Gene's garden is sacramental. It is, to him, a mystery that the packets full of rattling grit that arrive in early March should be transformed, by his hand, into vining clematis, curly lettuce leaves, and goofy Cosmos by August. When, during the first winter I lived with him, his first seedbeds failed to germinate, his faith in the process seemed genuinely shaken, as though his own life and health were somehow put in jeopardy by his failure to germinate new plants.

"There's nothing very mysterious about it," I would say. "You overwatered the seedbeds, just like I told you you were. Seeds probably rotted."

I had been planting or helping plant gardens in our heavy, yellow Kentucky clay since I was seven years old. You wait until warm weather, till the ground, cut a row, drop the seeds, cover them up, and hope for rain. Usually by July or August there would be plenty of squash and limas and pole beans, tomatoes and corn, cabbage and cucumbers. We never had great gardens, but generally there were plenty of fresh things to eat. The notion of starting in February with tiny seeds carefully sown in high-priced potting soil would have struck us as so much silliness. Gardens were work, not mystery.

Of course, the most compelling mysteries are the most quotidian, the ones we accept sunrise to sunset as articles of faith. If we continue our ordinary work successfully all day long, we call it technique. And technique can be learned. But to those who look on the tawny, crinkled lettuce leaf as evidence of grace and coherence in this world, then the technique is itself infused with grace. The beauty is not merely the leaf but the orchestration of acts and observations and new acts that have caused the leaf to rise there, covered with the sweat of morning dew, safe from the decaying slug that was salted to death the night before.

Sean's and Gene's reflections on the power of Nature's rhythms have provoked me to reflect on the actual "religion" of my early life, where acres of barren, winter orchard turned out thousands of tons of apples. The apples themselves were not altogether free of religious taint. Not only were they the Christians' forbidden fruit, but we also sold them in violation of Christian law. As with most orchards, our biggest sale day was Sunday. We earned most of our year's income on a dozen Sunday afternoons of autumn as people drove up onto the mountaintop from miles around to buy them—except for the preachers, who would choose them on Sunday and pay for them on Monday.

At the time I took their actions as simple evidence of religious hypocrisy. In retrospect—now that all the blue laws have disappeared and even the supermarkets are open on Sunday—I suppose they were preserving the ritual rest of the Sabbath. If they could persuade themselves that they were not transacting business on Sunday, then most likely they could experience it as the easy, relaxing autumn outing it also was. To come to the orchard along with hundreds of friends and neighbors was to enjoy a picnic of the senses and appreciate God's or Nature's multiple bounties and beauties. To a degree, and though it provided our family livelihood, the collection and presentation of the harvest was a seasonal vespers, a marking of the inevitable closing of the growing season and preparation for the dark months. Unlike all the other fruits, the apples these country people bought would last them through the winter until the sun returned.

That sense of persistent continuity, linked to the marriage of sun and earth, expressed in the fecund, drenching beauty of spring bloom and the terrible wrath of hail storms and earth-cracking drought, remains my fundamental liturgy. It is not Nature as a placid, benevolent, or curative force. The ecology of creatures that live in the fields and the orchard is brutal and rapacious, a predatory dance of fruit and leaf and insect and fungus. There are no pacifists in the natural liturgy. Nor is there denial of concupiscent appetite. To enter it fully is to enter the territory of the sublime.

The sublime is not peaceful any more than a real engagement with the force of Nature is restfully pastoral. The sublime moment, as the Romantic poets recorded it, is the moment in which we see ourselves at one with the awesome, majestic, and ultimately unknowable power that drives the exquisite beauty of Nature. Unlike prayer to the personified Christian deity, it blinds us with our humble inseparability from that force, reminding us that we are neither more nor less than any other organisms in an infinite food chain that is busily eating itself to death—descendants of amoebas, waste of viruses. Yet paradox of paradoxes, the same sublime comprehension that so reduces us also can release us into an ecstatic joy for our inclusion in the infinite. In the territory of the sublime, terror guards beauty, just as it did for the poet Shelley, who when gazing in awe at the face of Mont Blanc wrote that he was consumed with "an undisciplined overflowing of the soul," and dwarfed by "untamable wildness and inaccessible solemnity."

The experience of the sublime, Kant wrote, is "brought about by the feeling of a momentary check to the vital forces followed at once by a discharge all the more powerful, and so it is an emotion that seems to be no sport, but a dead earnest affair of the imagination." We are hit, as we experience the sublime, by a shattering recognition of a presence vastly greater and more powerful than ourselves, a presence that takes all that we have conceived in our minds, that consumes our minds and presses us beyond what our minds can contain. We are left in the infinite, which our finite faculties cannot order.

Kant considers how we experience the churning sea in a storm: "The broad ocean agitated by storms cannot be called sublime. Its aspect is horrible, and one must have stored one's mind in advance with a rich stock of ideas, if such an intuition is to raise it to the pitch of a feeling which is itself sublime—sublime because the mind has been incited *to go beyond the senses* [emphasis added], and employ itself upon ideas involving higher ends." The horror of the tempest is not itself sublime: first comes the jolt of terror at our incapacity to order the boundless beauty and savagery displayed in Nature; but we can only touch it and render ourselves sublime when we return to the security of intellect witnessing the tempest, erecting in our minds a method of comprehending a sensual experience that overcomes our senses, generating the metaphors that transport us beyond the finite limits of the fragile flesh. We are like the anxious airline passenger at takeoff who stares down the terror of his own imminent destruction and instantly senses the lift of the air rushing over the plane's wings as though he were himself in flight. We comprehend ourselves as being simultaneously out of and at one with time.

To feel the force of the sublime—perhaps Christians would say to feel the force of God or the Holy Spirit—in observed Nature is a commonplace experience. Our poets and painters have left us a clear and easily read legacy. When that is not enough, there are always earthquakes, monumental floods, and volcanic eruptions, chromatically packaged and pumped onto our videoscreens. We feel dwarfed, or at least we witness those who were dwarfed by it. But to experience the grammer of the sublime within ourselves, within our own bodies, is another matter.

When finally as a young man I began to figure out what sort of sex my body wanted, I was fortunately free of the usual internal taboos that the Church and Synagogue system had stamped into most people I knew. I had no trace of moral abhorrence at the prospect of men mating with one another. But I could not, until much later, integrate the morally neutral fact of same-sex desire with the apparent biological imperative of complementarity between the sexes. Whether expressed in the Eastern terms of yin and yang or the hormonal distributions of estrogen and testosterone, the natural world seemed to revolve around the interrelation of sexual opposites. The same-sex erotic option seemed to represent a refusal to engage in the most integral dance of life, the will to regenerate, nurture, and continue the species. Fundamentalist Protestants and Jews, as well as doctrinaire Catholics, of course, make a similar argument, employing a form of faux modernism to argue that Old Testament prohibitions are a reflection of Nature's (and thereby God's) laws. The mystery that eluded me—and which the Christians refused to acknowledge at all—was how our animal natures consistently produced homosexual eroticism, generation after generation, millennium after millennium, throughout the range of species. Not that I saw abstinence as an answer; I actively pursued erotic, homosexual adventures. It was the realization of unity between my flesh and spirit that eluded me.

Two events in the summer of 1988 brought me closer toward resolving the impasse.

I had begun work on *The Culture of Desire* and was living in Oakland, California. Gay San Francisco was just beginning to emerge from the darkest terror of AIDS—a generally unstated fear that everyone would be wiped out. The passionate, sexy resurgence of "queer" activism hadn't yet arrived, but the rebellious militance around AIDS had displaced the defensive despair of the mid-'80s. There was an air in the streets redolent of late-sixties exuberance, but better than the sixties, when my own sense of sexual displacement had seemed inadmissibly frivolous, we as queer people were at the center of a national cultural battle with life and death consequences. AIDS had moved the gay discourse from the sentimental to the sublime. For the first time (and arguably very belatedly), I had begun to figure out how to apply twenty years of professional technique to the examination of my own existential condition. And I was in my tenth month of chronic, painful muscle spasm in the lower back.

The original pain and muscle seizure had happened one afternoon the previous November as I sat down at my desk inside the Washington NPR office. Moments earlier I'd been in a yelling match with a colleague I liked and respected. It was one of a seemingly endless series of pointless, bureaucratic battles and power struggles that had become commonplace and that led many fine staff members to quit, or at least to depart the home office for foreign assignments on the opposite side of the globe. I had come to the Bay Area on leave the following summer both to exit the company's stifling atmosphere and to confront the gay story I had so long avoided. But the pain persisted. Chiropractic, acupuncture, diet modification, Alexander technique, better posture, and regular exercise had not released the clenched muscles that lashed the lower vertebrates in place.

Then one evening the pain dissolved and disappeared as though by magic. The curative technique was absurdly simple: I allowed myself to be penetrated by a young man who, for a variety of reasons (including the fact that he wore multiple layers of condoms), I judged to be safe. The act took place at seven in the evening. My nearly year-long muscle spasm was gone by midnight.

A few weeks after my "eroto-chiropractic" breakthrough, I had a long conversation with a gay, former Catholic novice; afterwards, I began to think about what had happened in radically new ways. Bruce Boone no longer considered himself Catholic, but he was a profoundly spiritual man. He spoke, using the language of the French writer and philosopher Georges Bataille, of the sacred interrelationship of sex, ecstasy, and death. Particularly, he recounted how his first experience sucking another man's cock had been "like Holy Communion." Knowing how easy it would be to slip into cheap sacrilege, he reminded me that for genuine Catholic believers, to take the Holy Wafer and the wine is to bite into and become one with the body of Christ, and therefore one with the unity of God. Thus his first time at fellatio was like Holy Communion, not because there is anything "holy" about phallic, homosexual sex, but because until that point he had not experienced the sublime "oneness" of his own physical and spiritual selves. Just as the Communion Wafer delivers, through transubstantiation, a oneness with the true presence of Christ, so the touch of Boone's mouth to the sex organ of a man released him from the psycho-spiritual barrier that had kept him a divided being. Like Shelley gazing upon the face of Mont Blanc, the act had propelled him into a sublime and timeless moment "where silence and solitude were vacancy."

Though Boone's story was profoundly Catholic and though I had had minimal experience with Catholic cosmology, it haunted me. Had I had an equivalent moment when, after years of AIDS anxiety, I took this young man into my own body and my body responded of its own accord by letting loose the compacted tensions of my own flesh? I wouldn't have said so then. I had no such sense of sublime spiritual unity. I was not conscious of that transcendent quality of one-ness through which we enter the inseparable continuity of time and space and body and spirit. So surely it was not the same experience as Boone or Shelley had had. My secular, materialist friends would say simply, "What a marvelous technique! I'll ask my chiropractor about it." (I've no doubt that all network news would be vastly improved if "the technique" were applied to all employees on an annual basis.) Few, however, bought much of the spiritual explanation. They preferred a straightforward neuro-kinesiological explanation: the sex felt good, the other man's hips and penis probably stimulated new muscle groups, and therefore I had been able to relax my back more effectively.

What is missing in the neuro-physiological explanation is something we all know about back pain: In many if not most cases, it is symptomatic of profound stress. In my case, much of that stress reflected standard mid-life aspirations and obligations. However, to an equal if not greater degree, the power of the AIDS epidemic had been pressing steadily closer. During the previous October, shortly before the muscle seizure, the AIDS quilt had come to Washington and filled the Ellipse behind the White House. At the network, none of the editors considered it worthy of a story until some of the gay staff convinced a weekend show host to do her own essay. Nor did I feel capable of producing my own story: My own losses, though they were still few, felt too personal, too precious, to be converted into journalism. And yet by failing to merge my personal concerns into my craft, I felt even more surrounded by the bleak horror of the epidemic, more guilty for not bringing this collective gay story forward in my own gay voice.

The relentlessness of the epidemic had equally powerful effects on sex itself. Sex had become wrapped in disease. Penetrative sex had become both metaphor and method for death's invasion of our lives. Many men I met that summer told me that since the advent of AIDS they had narrowed down all their sexual contact. No matter how much they had loved to be fucked, they could no longer imagine such sensual release of their bodies. Actual intercourse had disappeared from the screen of conscious consideration.

I go back to the moment of my own penetration.

For seven years I had not had receptive intercourse. As I lay there, looking upward at the man who was about to enter me, examining all the calculations I had made of who he might be, of who I thought I was, at the weight the act would carry for both of us, I felt the unbearable jolt of our presence.

For any male to be penetrated by another in the Judeo-Christian tradition is a profoundly disordering experience. It is a challenge to one of the most fundamental principles by which we have been taught to know ourselves. But then to dress the experience with the terrifying imagery of the body's own rot and decay precipitated by the penetration of an unseeable virus opens us to the possibility of touching all the unknowable terrors and beauties of Nature.

Unlike the work of any other microbes we know, HIV's attack on our immune systems reveals, in reverse, the technique by which we remain alive. Its genius is that *it* does not kill us; instead it builds a theater of our own flesh, from which we watch as participant-observers the spectacle of dying—the chemical, electrical, and physical disconnections that offer us up to our countless predators in the food chain. In AIDS we experience ourselves being eaten by the force of nature. As the ordering of cells that give us life degenerates into the disordered material of our prey, we find ourselves revealed as merely exquisite pigments in a palette whose shape we cannot see. At best we are witnesses to our own oxidation, neither good nor bad, moral nor immoral. Denied the capacity to order our experience or know our fate, we have only one choice: To witness or not, to be penetrated by the experiential wave washing over us, or to stand aside, blind, dumb, and untouched.

As surely as this epidemic has brought us to the eye of Nature's god, it has also surrounded us with a public spirituality that contains the sublime. I cannot think of that act of physical penetration in the summer of 1988 independent of that broader collective experience, which resulted in what I now see as a second "coming out." Let me explain what I mean by the notion of a second coming out.

I had been open about my sexuality for many years, with friends, with family, and with colleagues. I had occasionally reported for NPR about gay matters. In several investigative reports on the Iran-Contra scandal, I had broadcast the bizarre homosexual twist of how Col. Ollie North had relied on gay men to raise money secretly, and illegally, for the Nicaraguan Contras. But my "sexual identity" had remained incidental to my work and to most of my social life—as it was for most journalists and political people I knew in Washington.

Once I began to integrate those identities and began to participate in what has come to be described as the second gay liberation movement, or queer liberation, of the late '80s and '90s, I entered into a bargain of faith. As a journalist I have not been alone. Since 1988 there has been a massive, nationwide coming out of journalists in newsrooms and broadcast studios. For a multitude of reasons, not least the magnitude of AIDS deaths in our lives, we have all taken that act of faith: We have said that our presence as professional observers cannot be separated from our duties as human beings. We are human observers. But by observing (and coming out is a public self-observance) the queerness of ourselves, we inevitably change how and what we observe in the world as well. Those things we cause ourselves to see—love, bigotry, deceit, courage, chicanery—change because the way we see and hear has changed. The distanced language of heterosexual normalcy that we once employed to separate our observer selves from everything queer becomes unusable, and is replaced by unselfconscious terms of ordinary intimacies. Adjectives of the exotic become nouns of a new normalcy. Finally the spirit with which we observe ourselves alters the spirit with which others observe us. The moment at which we recognize that we cannot remain outside ourselves, the moment at which we acknowledge ourselves *in* the force of a wave that we cannot hold back, is surely as powerfully sublime as Kant's tempest or Shelley's Mont Blanc: We can no longer retreat into the alienated, internally divided selves of our pasts.

The act of observing ourselves *in* the world we are observing constitutes more than psychological self-consciousness. It is a dialectical process with ontological implications. I am not only talking about writers and journalists. The experience of collectively witnessing that which before had been unspoken, that is, telling the stories of lives free of demonization and disguise, alters both our lives and our subjects' lives. It is not only, as Foucault has written, that "homosexuals" did not exist as a distinct human category before the rise of nineteenth-century Victorian science. More importantly, the incipiently queer individuals coming of age today are qualitatively, developmentally, and existentially different from those who were coming of age twenty-five years ago. The coming out experiences of today's adolescents, a year or two past puberty, with a rich literature of queerness available to them, is not comparable to the experiences of my generation coming out at age thirty after years of denial when most available "homosexual" literature was either pornography or abnormal psychology. In the act of crafting a collective story, we have brought into being a collective spirit, which, willy-nilly, has irrevocably reshaped who we are and how we comprehend Nature.

We have shattered the *frisson* of our own exoticism. Through creating a literature whose very meaning is the ordinariness of our sexual difference, we reconfigure and destabilize the conventional polarities of what is queer and what is natural, throwing into question our entire society's acceptance of "the laws of Nature" and, therefore, the accepted hierarchies of the spirit's relation to the flesh. That destabilization of traditional hierarchy governing spirit and flesh is at the very heart of today's so-called "culture wars" because it threatens the terms of traditional religionists' faith. If I can enter into and be "at one" with the mysterious rhythms of "boundless nature" through the "perverse," revelatory penetrations of my own flesh, then I, like St. Gregory in the desert, have access to the sublime moment in which all being is unitary.

❧ Evangelical Christians speak about "receiving Christ" and undergoing the rapture of the Holy Spirit, through which they, too, say they are born again. If the still new language of American gay liberation sounds remarkably like the Protestant language of reawakening and being born again, it is hardly accidental. For more than three hundred years American culture has been shaped by the paradigm of rebirth in the promised land. Queer activists' embrace of terms like "safe space" and "liberated zones" falls easily into that tradition, just as nineteenth-century utopian socialist communities did and as twentieth-century spiritual cultists do. As radically different as their particular faiths and ideologies may be, the underlying spirit is a profoundly American faith in rebirth, both individual and collective, in a place where we will come to a revolutionary comprehension of our place in relation to God or Nature.

While I have grown up and lived uncommonly outside of conventional religion, I have been, like most native-born Americans, profoundly shaped by the spiritual paradigms through which the country has constructed itself. Our national heritage of periodic ritual "rebirthing," from Jonathan Edwards's Great Awakening in the eighteenth century to Gay Liberation today, has shaped my own sense of "sublime spirituality" just as surely as it has the messianic Christians.

I would not equate gay coming-out experiences with the Christian rapture of being born again, nor would I equate either with my own contemplations on the sublime. But equivalence is an irrelevance. What seems to me vital is the sublime pursuit into the mystery of our place in Nature, and that may just as likely take place between a bureaucrat and a go-go boy in a sex palace as between a child and her savior in a backwoods chapel. These are questions of technique and tradition; neither offers any guarantees.

As for my friend Sean, the once and possibly future monk, he continues his contemplations of the sublime in distinctly secular venues, joyous temples of the night that seem to offer respite from the rigid deadlines of the day.

KEVIN KILLIAN

# CHAIN OF FOOLS

Again I approach the church, St. Joseph's at Howard and
Tenth, south of Market in San Francisco. It's a disconcerting
structure, in late Mission style, but capped with two gold-
domed towers out of some Russian Orthodox dream. I'm
following two uniformed cops. In the late afternoon this
October, we're followed by the sun as we mount the steps to
the big brass doors and enter into the darkness of the nave. I
see the pastor, Filipino, short and shambling, approach us
from the altar, where two nuns remain, arranging fall flowers around the vestibule. I fall back while the cops detain
the priest. They're passing him a sheaf of legal papers re-
garding the closing of the church, which has been damaged
beyond repair by the earthquake of '89. Anger crosses the
priest's handsome face, then he shakes the hands of the two
policemen; all shrug as if to say, *shit happens*. I glance up at
the enormous crucifix where the image of Christ is sprawled
from the ugly nails. His slender body, a rag floating over his
dick. His face, white in the darkened upper reaches of the
church. His eyes closed, yet bulging with pain. Again I bend
my knee and bow, the body's habitual response. Across my
face and upper torso I trace the sign of the cross, the marks

of this disputed passage. I'm dreaming again—again the dreaming self asserts its mastery of all of time, all of space.

🐚 Late in the '60s, Mom and Dad enrolled me in a high school for boys, staffed by Franciscans. I was a scrawny, petulant kid with an exhibitionist streak that must have screamed trouble in every decibel known to God or man. My parents had tried to bring me up Catholic, but as I see myself today, I was really a pagan, with no God but experience, and no altar but my own confusing body. In a shadowy antebellum building high on a hill above us, the friars rang bells, said the Office, ate meals in the refectory, drank cases of beer. In the halls of St. A—, bustling with boys, I felt like the narrator in Edmund White's *Forgetting Elena,* marooned in a society I could hardly understand except by dumb imitation. In every room a crucifix transfixed me with shame: I felt deeply compromised by my own falsity. My self was a lie, a sham, next to the essentialism of Christ, He who managed to maintain not only a human life but a divine one, too. He *was* God, the Second Person of the Trinity.

But I talked a good game, as any bright student can, and did my best to get out of my schoolwork, so I'd have more time to develop my homosexuality. I spent a year in French class doing independent study, reading *Gone with the Wind* in French, while the other students around me mumbled "*Je ne parle pas*" to an implacable friar. Presently I was able to convince the history teacher that reading *Gone with the Wind* in French should satisfy his requirements, too. Then I would go home and confront my appalled parents by saying, "This is something I have to read for school."

Later on, when I was a senior and drunk all the time, a friend and I invented an opera, a collaboration between

Flaubert and Debussy, set in outer space and ancient Rome, that we called *Fenestella*. George Grey and I flogged this opera through French class, music class, World Literature, etc. We recounted its storyline, acted out its parts, noted the influence of *Fenestella* on Stravinsky, Gide, etc., you name it. Our teachers slowly tired of *Fenestella,* but we never did. The heroine was an immortal bird—a kind of pigeon—sent by St. Valentine out into Jupiter to conquer space in the name of love. On the way to Jupiter, she sings the immortal "Clair de Lune." I must have thought I, too, was some kind of immortal bird, like Fenestella, like Shelley's skylark. None of our teachers pointed out the unlikelihood of Flaubert (d. 1880) and Debussy (b. 1862) collaborating on anything elaborate. We had them quarrelling, reuniting, duelling, taking bows at La Scala, arguing about everything from *le mot juste* to the *Cathedrale Engloutée*. Nobody said a word, just gave us A's and praised us to the skies.

I had no respect for most of these dopes. In later life I was to pay the piper by dallying with several teens who had no respect for me. Nothing's worse than that upturned, scornful face that throws off youth's arrogance like laser rays. When I was sixteen, I had the world by the tail. But in another light the world had already made me what I was, a blind, struggling creature like a mole, nosing through dirt to find its light and food.

In religion class Brother Padraic had us bring in pop records which we would play, then analyze like poetry. It was a conceit of the era, that rock was a kind of poetry and a way to reach kids. Other boys, I remember, brought in "poetic" records like "All Along the Watchtower," "At the Zoo," "Chimes of Freedom." The more daring played drug songs—"Sister Ray," "Eight Miles High," "Sunshine Superman," or the vaguely scandalous—"Let's Spend the Night Together." When it was my turn, I brandished my favorite original cast album—*My Fair Lady*—and played "Wouldn't It Be Loverly." Now, that's poetry, I would say expansively, mincing from one black tile to a red tile, then sideways to a white tile, arms stretched out appealingly. After the bell rang, a tall man dressed in black stepped out of the shadows between lockers and said, "Have you considered psychological counseling?" I should have been mortified, but I shook my head like a friendly pup and, with purposeful tread, followed him to his office. When the office got too small for his needs, he drove me to what I soon came to think of as *our place,* down by the river, the weeds and waterbirds.

Getting in and out of a VW bug in those long black robes must have been a bitch. Funny I didn't think of that til later. It happened in front of my eyes, but I didn't really notice. I was too—oh, what's the word—ensorcelled. He—Brother Jim—wasn't exactly good-looking, but he had something that made up for any defect: he'd taken that precious vow of celibacy, though not, he confided, with his dick. First I felt for it through the robes, then found a deep slit pocket I was afraid to slip my hand into. Then he laughed and lifted the robe over his legs and over most of the steering wheel. And down by the gas pedal and the clutch he deposited these awful Bermuda shorts and evocative sandals. And his underwear. His black robe made a vast tent, then, dark in the day, a tent I wanted to wrap myself up in and hide in forever, with only his two bent legs and his shadowy sex for company. So I sucked him and sucked him, Brother Jim.

"Why don't you turn around?" he asked. "Pull those pants all the way down, I like to see beautiful bodies." He made my knees wobble as he licked behind them. Wobble, like I couldn't stand up. On the wind, the scents of sand cherry and silverweed, the brackish river. The squawk of a gull. Scents that burned as they moved across my face, like incense. After a while he told me how lonely his life was, that only a few of the other friars were queers, there was no one to talk to. "You can talk to me," I told him, moved. Every semester he and the few other queer monks judged the new students like Paris awarding the golden apple. Some of us had the staggering big-lipped beauty that April's made from; some of us were rejected out-of-hand, and some of us, like me, seemed available. Then they waited till they felt like it, till they felt like trying one of us out.

He made me feel his . . . dilemma, would you call it? Boys, after all, are tricky because they change from week to week. You might fancy a fresh complexion: act right away, for in a month that spotless face will have grown spotted, or bearded, or dull. You might reject me because I have no basket, well, too bad, because by Christmas I'll be sporting these new genitals Santa brought me, big, bad, and boisterous. This was Jim's dilemma—when you're waiting for a perfect boy, life's tough. So they traded us, more or less. Always hoping to trade up, I guess. "Don't trade me," I pleaded with him. "Oh never," he said, tracing the nape of my neck absently, while on the other side of the windshield darkness fell on a grove filled with oaks and wild hawthorn. "Never, never, never."

I wanted to know their names—who was queer, which of them—I *had* to know. He wouldn't say. *I* named names. How about the flamboyant arts teacher, who insisted on us wearing tights, even when playing Arthur Miller? No. None of the effeminate friars, he told me, was gay. "They just play at it," he sneered. How about the gruff math teacher, who had been the protégé of Alan Turing and Jon van Neumann? If you answered wrong in class, he'd summon you to his desk, bend you over his knee, and spank you. If you were especially dense, you'd have to go to his disordered room in the evening and he'd penetrate you with an oily finger, sometimes two. "No," said Brother Jim, my new boyfriend. "Don't be absurd. None of those fellows are fags. You'd never guess unless I tell you." I told him I didn't really want to know, a lie, I told him I'd never done this with a man, a lie, I told him I would never tell another about the love that passed between us, a lie. And all these lies I paid for when June began and Jim got himself transferred to Virginia. But then another teacher stopped me in the hall. "Jim told me about your problem," he said, his glasses frosty, opaque. This was Brother Anselm. "He says you feel itchy round the groin area."

He's the one who took me to see *The Fantasticks* in Greenwich Village and bought me the record "Try to Remember." If you're reading this, Anselm, try to remember that time in September when life was long and days were fucking mellow. As for you, Brother Jim, whatever happened to "never"? You said you'd "never" trade me, but when I turned seventeen I was yesterday's papers. Thus I came to hate aging, to the point that even today I still pride myself on my "young attitude." Pathetic. I remember that our most famous alumnus was Billy Hayes, whose story was later made into a sensational film called *Midnight Express*. At that time he was mired in a Turkish prison for drug smuggling. We students had to raise funds for his legal defense, or for extra-legal terrorist acts designed to break him out. Students from *other* schools went door-to-door in elegant neighborhoods, selling chocolate bars to send their track teams to big meets, but we had to go around with jingling cans, asking for money for

"The Billy Hayes Fund," and you know something, people gave! They didn't even want to know what it was, good thing, too. Later when the film came out its vampy homo-erotics gave me a chill. Later still, its leading man, Brad Davis, played *Querelle* in Fassbinder's film of the Genet novel. And even later still Davis died of AIDS and I con-flated all these men into one unruly figure with a queer complaint against God.

Standing on the desert's edge, a man at the horizon, shaking a fist against an implacable empty sky.

❧ At first I resented Jim and Anselm and the rest, their careless handling of this precious package, me. But after a while I grew fond of them, even as they passed me around like a plate of canapés at a cocktail party. Anybody would have, especially a young person like myself who thought he was "different." I watch the E Channel and see all these parents of boys, parents who are suing Michael Jackson, and I want to tell them, your boys are saying two things, one out of each side of their mouth, or maybe three things, one of them being, "Let me go back to Neverland Ranch where at least I was *appreciated.*"

Unlike Michael Jackson, the religious staff of St. A— wore ropes around their waists to remind themselves, and us, of the constant poverty of St. Francis of Assisi. One of them quoted St. Therese to me, to illustrate his humility: "I am the zero which, by itself, is of no value, but put after a unit becomes useful." I pulled the rope from around his waist, teasing him. I took one home as a souvenir. These fat long ropes, wheaten color, thick as my penis and almost as sinuous. I believed in those ropes. I said to myself, why don't *you* become a friar, think of all the side benefits? I walked down to the grove of trees by the river's edge one April afternoon, thinking these grand thoughts of joining the seminary. Beneath my feet small pink flowers, a carpet of wood sorrel or wild hepatica, leading down to a marshy space tall with field horsetail, up to my waist. "God," I called out, "give me a sign I'm doing the right thing." I felt guilty that I had sinned in a car, guilty and stained, like a slide in a crime lab. I waited for His sign, but zilch. Above me a pair of laughing gulls, orange beaks, black heads, disappeared into the sun. *Is that my sign?* thought I, crestfallen. *How oblique.* But right around that time I began to realize that there was something stronger than a Franciscan brother.

Marijuana leads to heroin, they used to say. I don't know about that, but after a while friars just don't cut it, you want something stronger, something that'll really *take you there.* You want a priest. Ever see *The Thorn Birds,* the way Rachel Ward longs for Richard Chamberlain? Or Preminger's *The Cardinal,* with Romy Schneider yearning for some gay guy, it's a thrill to think, y'know, with a little luck, this man licking my cock could turn out to be the Prince of the Whole Church, the Supreme Pontiff, in ten or fifteen years and right now, you can almost see his soul shining right through his thinning blond hair, already he's godly. Again the dreaming self rises above the squalid air of the black back room, the hush of the confessional, breaking free into a world of pleasure and Eros and hope, all I continue to pray for and more. Out in the snowy East of Long Island I bent over Frank O'Hara's grave and traced his words with my tongue, the words carved into his stone there: "Grace to be born and to live as variously as possible." Another lapsed Catholic trying to align the divine with the human.

And because I was so willful, I made spoiling priests a kind of game, like Sadie Thompson does in *Rain.* Under those robes of black, I would think, are the white limbs of strong men. I trailed one priest, Fr. Carney, from assignment to assignment. I was his youth liaison—encouraged to inform on my peers' drug habits, I had first to increase my own. You have to be a little hard, a little speedy, to become what we then called a "narc." He also got me to bring along other youths to retreats staged on isolated Long Island mother houses. When I graduated from St. A— I continued to traipse after Fr. Carney, like Marlene Dietrich slinging her heels over her shoulder to brave the desert at the end of *Morocco*, all for Gary Cooper's ass. "You don't have to call me Father Carney," he would say to me. "Call me Paul." I felt like king of the hill, top of the heap. Oh, Paul, I would say, why am I being treated so well? "Because you are who you are," he told me. "You are someone special. You are Kevin Killian."

I grew more and more spoiled, and he must have enjoyed my ripeness, up to a point; and then he left me, in this valley of tears. I remember standing in his room, watching the cold, green spectacle of Long Island Sound, leaves of yellow acacia tapping into the window, with this pair of black gym shorts pulled down just under my buttocks, and thinking to myself, I'll bring him back to me with my hot skin and my healthy boy type sweat. And he, Paul, slouched on his king-size bed, turned away from me, bored, extinguished, his breviary pulled next to him like a teddy bear. "There's a list on my desk," he said. "Some of them may be calling you." So when I pulled up my pants I'd have this list to turn to, the names of other priests, *next!* Like one of those chain letters, filled with the names of strangers, to whom you have to send five dollars each or Mother will go blind. "You're trading me, too," I said, before the door hit me on the ass. Thump.

So the next guy called me, Father some Polish name, and he turned out to be—*really into the Rosary.* Around this time I got to thinking that despite what they told me, I was not someone special after all.

These men were connoisseurs all right. They pulled out my cork and took turns sniffing it. Meanwhile the *sommelier* stood by, a smile in his eyes, attentive, alert. Disillusioned, dejected, I began to read the whims of these men not as isolated quirks, but as signs of a larger system, one in which pleasure, desire endlessly fulfilled, is given more value. Within the Church's apparently ascetic structure, the pursuit of pleasure has been more or less internalized. By and large, the pursuit (of violence, danger, beauty) *is* the structure. I had to hand it to them! Under their black robes, those long legs were born to *can-can.* Pleasure, in a suburbia that understood only growth and money. Aretha Franklin said it best, singing on the radio while I moped from man to man. "*Chain-chain-chain,*" she chanted. "*Chain of fools.*"

❧ I met Dorothy Day in a private home in Brooklyn, when Fr. Paul took me to meet her. She was seventy then, and had been a legend for forty years, both in and out of the Church, for her activism, her sanctity, her saltiness. I had read all about her in *Time* magazine. She sat on a huge sofa almost dwarfed by these big Mario Buatta-style throw pillows, gold and pink and red. Her hands were folded neatly in her lap, as though she were groggy. The way to get closer to Christ, she asserted, is through work. Fr. Paul argued mildly, what about the Golden Rule? Isn't love the answer? No, she responded sharply—work, not love. Last night on TV I watched *The Trouble with Angels,* in which mischievous Hayley Mills raises holy hell at a Long Island girls' school, till she meets her match in imperious, suave Mother Superior Rosalind Russell. At the denouement, she tells her plain girl-friend that she won't be going to Bryn Mawr or even back to England. She's decided to "stay on," become a nun, clip her own wings. I remember again wavering, on the brink of be-coming a priest, saying to myself, why don't you do the *Hayley Mills thing?* Saying it to myself from the back row of this cobwebbed movie house in a poky town on the North Shore of Long Island, fingering the beer between my legs, all alone in the dark.

Now I'm all grown, Dorothy Day is dead, and when I open *Time* magazine I read about altar boys and seminarians suing priests. One quarter of all pedophile priests, they say, live in New Mexico. I have no interest in pursuing my "case" in a tribunal, but I'd like to view such a trial—maybe on Court TV? Or sit in the public gallery, next to John Waters, while my teachers take the stand and confess under pres-sure or Prozac. I'd get out a little sketchpad and charcoal and draw their faces, older now, confused and guilty and perhaps a little crazy. Then their accusers would come to the stand, confused, guilty, crazy, and I could draw in my own eyes into their various faces, into the faces of my pals and brothers.

Oh how I envied them their privilege, their unflappable ease, the queers of the Church. If they were as lonely as they claimed, weren't there enough of them? If their love lives were dangerous, surely they would always be protected by the hierarchy that enfolded them. I remember one monk who had been sent away years before to a special retreat in Taos and he said, *I didn't want to have to come back and see any boys. But then I wanted to come back, it must have been to meet you, Kevin.* And I pictured this empty desert sky with nothing in it but one of Georgia O'Keeffe's cow skulls staring at me through time. My face broke into a smile and I said, "That is so sweet."

❧ I broke with the Church over its policies on abortion, women's rights, gay rights, just like you did. Perhaps its hypocrisy angered you, but that's just human nature, no? What scared me was its monolithic structure. It's too big either to fight or hide within, like the disconcerting house of the Addams Family. I tried to talk to It, but It just sat there, a big unresponsive sack of white sugar. So good-bye. And yet I suppose I'm a far better Catholic now than then. I dream of this God who took on the clothes of man and then stepped forward to strip them off at the moment of humiliation. This renunciation for a greater good remains with me an ideal of society and heaven. I try to get closer to Christ through work. I tried love for a long time, but it only lengthened the distance between Him and me.

So I try to call the number of St. A— to see where the twentieth high-school reunion will be. So that's when I find out the school's now defunct, for the usual reasons: indifference, inflation, acedia. I continue to see the Church as the house of Eros, a place of pleasure and fun, and I continue to regard men in religious costume as possible sex partners, yearning to break free. Such was my training, my ritual life. I can't shake it off, I'm not a snake who can shed its skin. Every time I pass a crucifix I wonder, what if it had been me up there instead, could I have said, *Father, forgive them, for they know not what they do?* I don't think I'm so special, not any more. At the church here in San Francisco, I bow down and make the sign of the cross, the logo of the Church, an imprint deep within forces me to replicate this logo. Up, down, left, right, the hand that seeks, then pulls away frustrated. The hand tightens, becomes a fist, the fist is raised to the sky, on the desert's edge, angry and queer. Inside the church burns incense, tricky and deep penetrating, strong, and perdurable, like the smells of sand cherry, silverweed, trillium.

# Trying Grace

The church in which I grew up was the first church organized east of the Mississippi and west of the Alleghenies; behind it flows the muddy and mostly shallow tributary of the river in which my grandfather, father, and uncles fished when I was a boy and in which my father was baptized. To get to the good fishing, you have to walk past the church cemetery's new graves, through the old stones flat and gray and leaning or fallen and broken, make your way past some stones thrown back in the bushes with leftover plastic flowers and pots in a dirty garish reticulation of the memorial. Downstream a bit, limestone has flaked to leave an ear in the cliff, a cave out of which a cold, clear stream (and in the summer, steam) flows.

Since old Mr. Hix (who owned the farm through which some of the creek runs) has been dead for decades now and the sharecroppers who once lived there have moved, I can't go back to that cave anymore without trespassing. There are signs now—in addition to the occasional copperhead, water moccasin, or innocuous black snake sunning on rocks as you make your way down the steep bank—to keep you off the land and away from the water. The last time that my father, sister, brother and I went down to the creek to fish, we walked by some high-school boys skinny-dipping in a pool, where the sun made its way through the water maples and beneath the waist-deep water. They stopped their ballyhooing and swinging from a grapevine to stare at us strangers as we walked past with our poles and rattling boxes of lures. My beautiful, athletic sister must have been part of what made them uneasy, but my own momentary gaze, I felt, gave me away, as did my dogged looking askance as if intent on not sliding in as we balanced on the thin trail of muck mixed with wet sand.

I am no longer a Baptist, though baptized when I was nine in the baptismal tank of the church sanctuary. The minister's large hands held me under for the full three beats of the Trinity as intoned by his bass voice, and I felt I was drowning. As I coughed and gasped for air, climbing the slippery steps from the tank, I looked down to notice my nose bleeding on my robe. My mother, who was there to greet me after the service, frowned.

🕸 My father is a Baptist deacon, though now inactive. When I was a child, my mother read to me from a book of Bible stories presented to my parents by the hospital when I was born, and she told me once that this is why, she believes, I write. (I think she's right.) I remember at the age of five or so being horrified and confused by the story of Job, at the picture of him squatting in the dust with those broken pots, picking his sores—horrified even more, of course, as a child, by the thought of God giving to Satan, as a kind of test that Job had to pass, the bodies of Job's wife and children. I also remember the long sermons on those summer mornings before the advent of air-conditioning in the Ohio River Valley; the pains of hell felt literal in my bow tie and jacket. (The paper fans in the pews had advertisements for undertaking establishments on the backs of images of solemn, praying children.) One Sunday I ran to the kitchen, jumped on the kitchen counter, and began stuffing my face with Wonder bread—the bread of eternal life without which one would suffer an eternity of heat and torture. I remember thinking of hell as a literal place beneath my feet that might open at any time to engulf me. I had to tread lightly.

❧ My paternal grandfather, crippled by polio, struggled with my grandmother to raise my father and his four siblings. The house we often visited when I was a boy was spare, the one exception to the lack of art or ornament an enormous triangular portrait of Christ. My grandfather's faith was deep—and distinct in feeling and tone from doctrinal piety, perhaps in part because of the difficulties of his life. His Bible was marked with his pencillings—underlinings and marginalia. When I came back from college one summer, we had a conversation about two lesbians and the town's disapproving rumors that they had driven to another state for the expressed purpose of marrying one another, which one apparently could do in some such other place. His anger at people's gossiping surprised me, when I think back on it. He chuckled to himself as he wondered aloud—innocently, naively—"which one played the man."

❧ My parents, with an urbane wisdom I later came to understand, were skeptical of the value of revival enthusiasm; it was "country," yet dangerously powerful and intoxicating. My father, I believe, thought tent meetings and such the provenance of suspect feminine passions. I remember him sheltering me with his arm when I was very small as some older women of the church asked to take me to a tent meeting; it was hot and summer, and we stood outside in the gravel under the maple trees as the breeze moved the leaves and gave us some small relief, all the more welcome for its intermittence.

In junior high, I took part in a revival sponsored by a coalition of churches, primarily Methodist and Baptist. A few itinerant preachers came in, all of them, as I remember, fairly young, in their twenties. They played the guitar, sang socially relevant songs, and sought to lead us to enthusiasm and spiritual revival. The open microphone was there for the confession of sins and for testimonials as to the power of the Spirit.

I remember that after a couple of the revival services, I followed one of the revival leaders like a lovesick puppy. One night outside the sanctuary, his itinerant colleague turned to him: "There he is again." A surge of anger and disgust focused on me for one hot instant, and though, at the time, I was baffled, in retrospect I think I know what made me "unworthy" in the eyes of the young preacher I had so inappropriately and mostly unconsciously adored. I learned again the feel of being moved between the cold dark of separateness and the hot eye of anger.

My sense of human evil arrests me, but in ways my revivalist beginnings would never countenance—the suicides contemplated, attempted, or committed by gays, lesbians, and bisexuals raised in churches that ask them to see themselves as misshapen pots on God's wheel, made by their maker to be made over in another image or utterly discarded. The moral conundrums one faces in writing about people one knows tempt one to remain absolutely silent. Instead, I'll talk only as specifically as feels safe. A teenager tells his father he is gay; he is sent out of the house, excluded from the family. A young woman with anxieties about her sexual identity is directed to counseling with her preacher; she tries to take her own life. A gay man is bashed by a group of boys with two-by-fours and left unconscious on a sidewalk, his jaw broken and his teeth knocked out. I write about these events in the literary present, because, like plots in some horrific book, they are always happening.

I understand why in the eyes of some a gay man belonging to a church is analogous to a Jew belonging to the Nazi party: the collaborator.

"Get over it," I've been told: I must invent myself, make myself up out of nothing and cast away the sentimental or Gothic underpinnings of my history which is so tied up with puritanical particulars and masked unkindnesses. I have learned through experience that the same man who gives up several weeks' wages to help the victims of natural disasters and feed and clothe the hungry can be the same man who believes that all homosexuals—as well as unclean unbelievers of all kinds—will roast in an eternal hell. A volunteer who works for hours a week with disabled children can be the same adult who hates African-Americans or Jews and wonders why God in his infinite wisdom allowed for their existence. What I'm looking for is a grace unannealed by the false fires of hypocrisy, self-hatred, or self-sanctification.


❧ In my early twenties, I was confirmed within the Episcopal church, and I still attend services. I work and pray for the "dignity of all people"; my intercessions are for the "victims of hunger, fear, injustice, and oppression." Driving by the shot-gun shacks of the small city where I live, I pass people, particularly older people, who walk as if under some enormous weight. Communal action in organizations like Habitat for Humanity can make small lifts from what seems a hopelessly onerous mass of past and present racial and economic injustice.

Yet like some of the literary figures I love—Milton, Dickinson—I often have to make do with the little claustrophobic room of the heart. That room is nothing more than a necessary way station, a place to stay before being found by God in the face of friends and strangers. To reveal such a need to others directly, however, in many contexts only intensifies the isolation. Sounding such a bell of announcement so somberly can serve only to scare away light-footed grace.


The institutional Church, which as a mystical Protestant I distinguish from the "invisible Church" of the saints of all creeds and states of creedlessness, has for much of its history responded to the message of the Cross by raising the Cross. A Jewish lesbian friend told me that she can't fathom how anyone of conscience would live in the South. Along the backroads of the state in which I live, one finds enormous crosses erected in threes. She told me, half-jokingly, that she's afraid that if her car breaks down while she's driving through the South, she'll be nailed to one of those crosses.

A former student of mine from Hong Kong, an adolescent of fourteen, once stumbled into the Castro in San Francisco. He told me he was disgusted; as he spoke to me, the memory left his face screwed up and contorted. Neither Christianity nor the South has a monopoly on bigotry. He told me that he did not understand how we Americans let such people be. In China, he said, such people were forced into bamboo cages and thrown into the ocean.

I came to the Episcopal church circuitously. First, I took instructions in the Roman Catholic church. In high school, my girlfriend's brother converted to Catholicism a few months before he died of cancer; thinking of him, my girlfriend and I went to mass at the Abbey of Gethsemani in the neighboring Catholic county. On Christmas Eve, the monks processed into the nave of the abbey beneath us, at midnight the light of their candles unfolding like a white flower fragrant with incense. She died a few months after that when she was struck and thrown into the air by a car driven by a drunk.

Just after her death at the end of my senior year of high school, I left the Church. I no longer believed in a just and loving God; his existence was not compatible with my experience. My father frequently exhorted me to come to church with him, demanded it, threatening penalties only to stop threatening after he realized their uselessness. I said I would not go, and I did not go.

Yet at some deeper level, the image of a retributive God governed my ensuing depression. I was being punished through her death. God was punishing me for being attracted to a man, another student whose feelings were not like mine. Desire of any kind—for a man or a woman— became excruciatingly painful. I must have been in love with my tormenter, have afforded myself some self-worth through these economies of pain.

Four years later, near the end of my undergraduate career and in the midst of an emotional crisis, I felt Catholicism would offer me freedom. Catholicism's ritual seemed to offer some protection from the unrelenting manipulativeness of the Baptist minister, whose rhetoric, I felt, was always itching to hold me over the pit, that "Pit—with Heaven over it" that Dickinson describes and which I felt. The elderly priest who gave me instruction was a bitter man dying of cancer, and he insisted on my unconditional submission to Catholic doctrine, which, I came to discover, was in many respects very close in its rigidity to Calvinist doctrines. My roommate, whom I had found through an ad in the paper, was a lapsed Catholic and went with me to my sessions. One day, I stumbled on a pile of his paramilitary magazines in the kitchen; the ads were for weapons and mercenaries.

🐚 My first relationship with a man was with an Episcopalian. We danced around one another, just outside one another's orbits, when we worked together on productions or performances of music and theater. Some church friends knew of our developing relationship, a few guessed, and many (I guess) thought of us as close friends working toward a common end out of common interests.

My partner and I maintained a long-distance relationship for some seven years. He spoke several times about meeting his risen Lord *within,* an experience of spiritual resurrection like that of the early Gnostics, perhaps—those who saw the primary Christian message as spiritual rebirth out of death, triumphing over pain and meaninglessness. For a while, he lived in an apartment whose bathroom and kitchen shared the same space, separated from the bedroom by strings of beads. He lived in the mountains, a day's drive from where I lived and worked: intimacy without the difficulties of visibility or the daily sustenance of companionship.

The high school where I taught had recently fired two teachers—a gay man and a lesbian. The man had been accused by a student of unwanted sexual advances. The woman, I was told, had not "fit in." She didn't shave her legs or underarms and was not a "team player." My partner felt vulnerable at his jobs as well; one of his hats was as a church musician.

Once, in the middle of a blizzard, he explained to me the power of Bach's Christmas *Oratorio,* particularly the final movement during which one can hear the Good Friday hymn "O sacred head sore wounded" beneath the triumphant trumpet—a meaning within, and despite it all. Joy is, perhaps, something distinct from happiness, an emotion which does not detach itself from pain and morality but gleams instead like light on discarded engine oil.

His gift is that of a *magister ludi,* teaching people to play in community, to break the shell of the isolated individual. He once dressed as Father Christmas, leading a congregation with his commanding tenor voice through a series of songs and strange processions that mixed everything and everyone up. A matronly boules player sat at the head of the table in a wimple beside her husband in leotards. I felt then that one of the most lithe incarnations of the sacred is laughter.

When I was a graduate student, the choir at Saint John's sang Bach's "Wachet Auf" ("Wake up" or "Arise"), a piece written by Bach not long after a significant portion of his congregation had died of the bubonic plague. I had sung the piece with my friend Jonathan who had died of AIDS—as had my first choir director at Saint John's.

American churches have fueled the growing social intolerance of people with AIDS—despite the ministries of many churches. Yet I feel that only as part of the Church can I ever hope to change the Church. When bigots interact with those whom they hate, their hatred sometimes transmogrifies through a series of painful lurches into something else, sometimes even collaborative friendship. This seems one of the lessons of the Civil Rights Movement, which Americans in general and Southerners in particular have imperfectly learned. Separatism in many ways risks capitulating to inertia and reaction.

But in saying this I must say that most people who see me in the church where I now worship do not know my sexual identity. My risks have been piecemeal and relatively minuscule—in my poetry, scholarship, and my developing friendships. I have chosen a relative silence in order to be able to profess some truths and work in some ways for change. Unlike Martin Luther King, Jr., and his models Jesus and Saint Paul, I have not been an "extremist for love."

In my more paranoid moments, I worry about my physical safety. The rabbi of the local synagogue, when he dared to respond to our governor's claim that we should be mindful that we are "a Christian nation," found himself threatened by a chorus of voices, some of them avowedly Christian, threatening his life, along with those of his wife and young children. The priest of my parish, whose church stands across the road from the synagogue, was one of the few Christian ministers who, in print, defended the rabbi's response. As Frederick Douglass wrote more than a century ago, "between the Christianity of this land, and the Christianity of Christ, I recognize the widest possible difference . . ."*

---

*Frederick Douglass, *Narrative of the Life of Frederick Douglas, An American Slave Written by Himself* (New York: Signet, 1968), p. 120.

Abolitionists had to fly in the face of Paul's injunction that slaves obey their masters, as women who have sought the right not only to speak in church but also to take on holy orders have also defied Paul's exhortations. The larger biblical truths of justice, compassion, and salvation have forced believers to use Scripture and tradition against themselves to overturn centuries of what we have come to see as inhumanity and wickedness.

In my early twenties, I had a drink with an older gay man, a friend of a friend. Monogamy was incompatible with homosexuality, he said; it was a kind of crazed drag, an inappropriate miming of heterosexual marriage. (Since the AIDS epidemic, he has begun singing a new song, the joys of monogamy.) Sex, he argued, is overvalued because it is denied; it is as unimportant and essential as water. At the time (though he may now find my account uncharitable or inaccurate), I couldn't help wondering whether he was particularly thirsty.

Some younger gays I met in California talk about those who are "more committed than thou" and disdainful of "predatory sex." There is sometimes a divide between those who see sex as a kind of communal celebration of identity, a lubricious mixing of members in Dionysian selflessness, and those who affirm an approach to sexuality closer to the heterosexual paradigm of marriage, a holy echoing of desires like Christ's love for the soul or the Church's desire for God. Others see monogamy as a necessary stopping place, a kind of unpleasant escape from the even worse evils of disease and loneliness.

When priests and parishes within the Episcopal church sanction gay relationships, as they sometimes do informally or tacitly, they insist that they be like heterosexual marriages are supposed to be: monogamous and loving. Yet the realities of the world are such that the Church itself makes the maintenance of monogamous, committed gay and lesbian relationships extremely difficult. Often, couples are asked, directly or indirectly, to keep their relationships private; few churches bless or sanctify unions. A commitment celebrated and yet confined within the cloisters of the couple itself becomes a hothouse capable of sustaining gorgeous and outlandish flowers, flowers that are frequently short-lived.

In a recent conversation, a stranger commented on the number of gay men he knew who were going to church. He'd left the Church, he said, when he discovered he was gay. He wondered, perhaps cynically, whether those who went back to the Church were trying to get right with God before they died.

I have witnessed what feels like an unusual number of deaths, some of them by AIDS. Jonathan is one of those. We sang together in our church choir. He was a tall man; I remember him as 6'5" at least, with a voice as powerful as the entire bass section. There was no blending with Jonathan. His voice rocked the church. When I first met him he had a girlfriend. A year later, he had given up his attempt, he said, at going straight. Jonathan found a partner and married shortly after that. His gay wedding, I heard, was a high Latin mass celebrated with great solemnity over a period of several hours by members of our choir and other singers whom Jonathan had enlisted. Jonathan lived out a rambunctious mix of the radical and the conservative, a not uncommon blend for the gay Episcopalians I've known.

He married a man whom I was not to meet until

Jonathan's funeral. I spoke with Jonathan when he was ill, and his lover closely monitored the length of the conversation so as not to weaken him. Within weeks after he was diagnosed, he died of a parasitic infection. The service, which he had choreographed, was conducted in a Lutheran church by friends of his who were gay ordained ministers. A table with pictures of Jonathan as a child, adolescent, and young adult stood near the front of the church. A procession of ministers sprinkling the congregation with juniper branches wet with holy water began the service, and a version of Job's "I know that my redeemer liveth" was performed by a mostly nude man, his body painted green, around the altar.

❧ The liturgy for me can be a window into timelessness. I recognize the dangers of idolatry, of making the window into the place for which you long, the ineffable realm that makes speech possible and toward which all speech tends. The liturgy, the liturgical year, give form to my spiritual yearnings. I can remember, when I take Communion, the hands of Ben giving me Communion. Or I can imagine beside me at the rail those whom I love and who have since died.

Ben, an engineer who had lived with his family in an oil-rich Islamic state, died of cancer. Ben—straight, comfortable with himself and others—had been particularly good for Jonathan, helping Jonathan to affirm his own identity as a gay man, to have the courage to believe in himself as he was. Jonathan spoke of Ben's prayers and healing meditations, models that Jonathan was to follow as Jonathan himself became ill. Ben's wife, Laura, remained close to Jonathan until his death.

The liturgy can help me to cry, to break through the defense mechanisms that let me get through from day to day but keep me from breaking through to any kind of healing. Though I don't believe, like Luther, that pain is a sign of election, an evidence of God's grace, I know that what heals often hurts.


※ Last summer, I visited my ex, who was then directing a church camp. Streams tumbled down over rounded boulders from the surrounding mountains. We went rowing, and I nearly knocked us into the river through my clumsiness. Lunch was punctuated by prayers, songs, and story-telling. After lunch, his charges were painting the exteriors of their cabins with angels and scenes from the gospels. The cabins were small, more like booths than living quarters, so I thought of the Transfiguration. One of the younger campers, a kid of about seven named Enoch, asked to ride me piggy-back. We trotted around the camp for a while, and he asked me to find John. He gestured toward John and asked him to come closer, to hear a secret. Enoch brought our heads together, John's and mine, and said, "Here. Like this. You two should kiss."


※ What is love? "Agape"—the word used by Saint Paul—is translated, I have been told by a classicist friend irked by the low style of biblical Greek, as "something like kindness that is unmotivated by self-interest." "Charity" and "love"—the two most common translations in English—don't quite capture the idea. Yet the sexual and emotional love that can exist between two people is one of the most powerful enablers of such "kindness"—toward others, oneself, and the larger world. But the Church has set up stumbling blocks.

If I speak in the tongues of men and of angels, but have not love, I am a noisy gong or a clanging cymbal. And if I have prophetic powers, and understand all mysteries and all knowledge, and if I have all faith, so as to remove mountains, but have not love, I am nothing.

1 Corinthians 14

🍥 P E T E R   M .   K R A S K

# THE WAY THE STARS COME HOME

*The Lord was passing by: a great and strong wind came rending*
*mountains and shattering rocks before him, but the Lord was not in*
*the wind; and after the wind there was an earthquake, but the Lord*
*was not in the earthquake; and after the earthquake fire, but the Lord*
*was not in the fire; and after the fire, a low murmuring sound. When*
*Elijah heard it, he muffled his face in his cloak and stood at the*
*entrance of the cave.*

*Then there came a voice.*

—I Kings 19: 11–12.

It was when he kissed me—lightly, on the tip of my ear—
that I knew. Of course, he had kissed me on the lips as well.
But there was something about that sensation, that tremor,
released by his mouth on the outside of my ear that let the
truth out. I thought of this later, watching him sleep, his
body broken up by shadows cast from the window.

*You have changed your life.*

I had never watched another person, another man, sleep
before, so I sat there on his bed, looking at this stranger I
had met in a park a few hours earlier, looking through the
dark at his stocky white body. Before I fell asleep, before the
sun rose, I pulled his body over mine like some cool, damp
blanket and shut my eyes. There was no going back.

Six weeks later I entered a monastery.

Jim told me his name as we left the park and headed some-where to find something to eat. As we walked, afraid to look at each other, I answered his questions. I was in summer school, my final class before graduation from the University of Maryland. After that, I was going to live with my parents in Frederick to save up money for graduate school. Over dinner, I told Jim of my monastic plan. He was baffled. Some people backpacked across Europe. I was going to live in a monastery for three months. Was it that unusual? I smiled, knowing full well that it was. Pass me the salt, please. His hand touched mine and we stopped talking. Nervous, sick with fear that dinner would end soon, I withdrew my hand.

"Your hands are beautiful," he said.

Those words lingered, weighted with the implications of what we knew was next. Inevitable. Jim paid the check, ending the silence with a question: "Are you sure you're not running away from something?"

The Order of Cistercians of the Strict Observance was founded in 1098 at the Abbey of Cîteaux in Burgundy, France, by Robert of Molesme. Known as the Trappists, after the seventeenth-century reformer of La Trappe, Abbé Armand Jean de Rancé, the Cistercians live under the old and compassionate Rule of St. Benedict. "Do not rub the rust too hard lest the vessel shatter" wrote Benedict in his effort to balance a life of work, study, and contemplation. As recently as thirty years ago, the Trappists practiced a rule of silence, slept on straw pallets, and lived on a diet of bread and water and boiled potatoes. Today there are twelve Trappist monas-teries in the United States, many filled with the aging men who entered during the monastic boom after World War II.

My first contact with the Trappists came in a college honors seminar, "Alternatives to Violence," taught by *Washington Post* columnist and former Trappist, Colman McCarthy. After we read works by Gandhi and Tolstoy, Colman gave us passages by Thomas Merton, the Trappist poet, essayist, and political figure. Merton's advice to seek happiness over success connected with my recent and painful decision to pursue a music degree; these were potent words for a twenty-year-old boy, from a family of scientists and lawyers, who was eager to embrace the arts.

I read as much Merton as I could, probably understanding little but knowing that his words were beautiful: "God utters us as a word that contains a partial thought of himself. A word can never understand the mouth that spoke it." I was entranced. However, all of the stuff about monasticism, which was substantial, left me stumped. There was only one way to know. McCarthy suggested a retreat. Stay in a monastery. Find out. Go.

In November 1987, I spent the weekend at the Abbey of Our Lady of the Holy Cross, in Berryville, Virginia. The weather was cold. If you make a retreat at Holy Cross, you do not stay in the monastery proper. The guesthouse, with room for fifteen retreatants, is about a mile down the road. To enter the monastery—its chapel actually, the only room open to the public—you have to walk past farmland, away from the Blue Ridge Mountains and Shenandoah River which shelter it. Past the monastery cemetery and a sign on a gate that says "Private. Monastic Enclosure. Do Not Enter." You are told to bring a flashlight, because at night, aside from the stars, there is no other light.

The monastic day is divided into a series of hours called the Divine Office, in which the monks gather to chant from the Book of Psalms. The first Office, Vigils, begins at three-thirty in the morning. If you are coming from the guest-house, you must rise at three in order to attend. In November, the wind blows hard from the mountains. Even if you have a flashlight, the air remains black.

Inside the chapel, the air feels warm, almost hot. A lone monk or two sit opposite each other on benches near the altar. Their bodies are hard to see because the cowls over their white robes are black. They seem to be only heads, floating in the darkness. The chapel, a long rectangular box, all white walls and plain wood, is bare except for a cross suspended over the altar. A single candle burns, in the back, by the tabernacle. Although the flame sputters, it lights the entire room, giving that hanging cross a strange glow.

All of the monks enter, some with their robes snapping behind them likes waves; others slow, nearly late. And the stage is set, for that's what it looks like, only there is no curtain to be raised. The retreatants who have managed to wake themselves sit and watch: the darkness, the disembodied heads, the cross with its yellow aura, and the varnished floor shining like ice. Someone rings a bell, which seems loud because it has been so quiet. Another monk raps his fingers on the cover of a psalter. A voice starts to sing: "O God, come to my assistance. O Lord, make haste to help me." An hour later, when you leave the chapel, remember to turn on your flashlight, if you've brought one, so you don't fall down the stairs.

When my retreat was over, I understood those bitter-cold November days as my first real experience with God. On Sunday, before I left, I spoke with one of the monks who was available for "Conversation." A brochure about the abbey was lying on his desk. It mentioned the possibility of extended retreats within the monastery for interested men. I read it and knew that if he asked me, I would go. Father

George looked at me and took my hand in his to say farewell. Then he asked. I said yes.

Nine months later, during a hot, hot August, I entered the monastery, ready to stay for three months.

*Why are you going?*

That was the first difficulty, answering that question. A few stumbling explanations later, I managed to formulate some vague reply. People assumed it was about finding myself, if they would call it that. I suppose they were right, but I did not know it. I didn't know why I was going or what I hoped to accomplish there. To say I must go but don't know why was the truth, but the truth did not help much. In the meanwhile, I enjoyed fostering a sense of mystery, a kind of ascetic glamour.

"The Trappists? They're the ones who don't talk, right?"

"Well, not quite. They have a rule of silence but . . ."

Had I known what would happen while I was there, I would never have gone or been quite so coy about going.

The cliché is more than true: my parents were the last to know. Friends at school found out first and they were amused, encouraging, and not surprised. Brothers and sisters were next and they were puzzled, encouraging, and not surprised. Then my parents. I was surprised. Delighted. They responded in the way I had hoped but surely did not expect: We love you. We do not understand this choice, but if that is what you want. We just want you to be happy.

And I was happy. Relieved even. The truth was out. The next step could be taken. One week after I returned home, a family friend, the woman they thought was my girlfriend, told me about a discussion my parents had had. My father was furious. "Betrayed," he said. Frighten his mother this way. How could Peter do this to us? Live in some monastery. When will he learn?

I told Jim all of this, my head resting on his chest, the breath of my words stirring the hair around his nipples. As usual, I lied to my parents—sort of—to be with him. Told them I was spending the evening in College Park, visiting some friends from school. Saying good-bye before leaving for the abbey. Don't wait up for me. On the way to Jim's apartment, two men exposed themselves to me: one on the subway from Frederick to Washington; the other, an old man, in the bathroom of a pizza parlor, where I had stopped to wash my face and comb my hair, near Jim's home. He turned to me, with his pants down and expectant eyes, his hands filled with the wares he was offering. I fled.

Jim laughed when I told him this story, although I didn't think it was funny.

"You ran from him?"

Breathless, I said yes. Still laughing, he brushed my sweaty hair away from my face and kissed me. I dropped my bag and kissed him back, hard.

Sex first. We could talk later.

Which we did as he walked me back to the Metro station. We looked straight ahead, not at each other.

"Is there anything left you wanted to say?" Jim asked.

There was one question in my mind: What do I mean to you? I couldn't ask him, though, and said something vague.

"There is too much to say," I told him, "only there are no words."

"What words?"

Silence.

"I've told no one about you," I said.

"Don't let any of the monks hit on you."

More silence and the subway station fast approaching.

"It's been real fun," Jim said. "A party."

Good-bye? As I descended the escalator into the station, tears streaked my glasses. When I turned back to look for him, he was gone.

❧ Every afternoon, I sat in the monastery library, the scriptorium, and wrote in my journal, a bundle of loose-leaf paper in a binder. The windows that flanked the long tables were always open. Because of the cross breeze, it was usually one of the cooler rooms. If I looked up from my writing, after the wind riffled my papers, and looked out the window, I could see Brother Michael shoot past the trees on his motor scooter and disappear in a blur. Or Brother Thomas would be mowing the lawn, high on his tractor, and the scent of cut grass would hiss into the room.

I have kept this journal for four and a half years. From time to time I pull it out from underneath a pile of books on the bottom of a shelf and flip through those pages. I am alternately saddened, amazed, and embarrassed by what it contains. When I sat down with it, to begin this essay, I was astonished by a sense of clarity in the words and the thoughts they encompassed; a clarity I cannot recognize today. It seems alien, written in code. There are pages filled with quotes, difficult thoughts from the serious books I was reading—Simone Weil, Carl Jung, Meister Eckhart, Buddha—and I barely understand them. Did I understand them when they seemed important enough to be written down? Did I understand any of what I was trying to say?

Those thoughts seem private, like a letter to a lover, not meant to be shared, not in their raw state. Let me rewrite them now and change the names that should be changed; let me protect the innocent.

## AUGUST 1, 1988

It begins and, strangely, I am not afraid, even if I didn't sleep last night. I am glad Charis brought me. She has been such a source of comfort and information since I decided to come here. I'm still stunned by her graduation present—a plane ticket to visit her this Thanksgiving in Utah. How long has she been saving up for this? She is right: Her name does mean "grace." She tried to help me carry in my boxes filled with books, tapes, and papers, the suitcases packed for three months. One of the monks stopped her at the door to the cloister. When she went to the car to bring the rest, he politely said, "You mean there is more?"

Neither of us wept when we parted on the gravel path outside the abbey. I waited for her to leave my sight before I mounted the steps and shut the door. A letter from Jim—a note, really—was waiting for me on my bed. Just a few words to say welcome and that he missed me. I am elated. Another monk, whose name I don't know, told me, "Time stops when you enter here."

## AUGUST 2

My room—or cell, as they call it—is very small. I barely have enough room to walk around, even since I stacked up all of my boxes. I live downstairs in the Old Dormitory which is attached by a long porch to the Mansion, an old stone farmhouse. The rest of the monastery radiates from the Mansion and forms an upside-down J. I think there are about twenty-five or thirty monks that live here. They've been friendly, but I haven't actually spoken to any of them. Only hellos.

Another person is making a retreat, a retired surgeon

from the Navy. He stays in the room next to mine. Our beds
are attached to the same wall, and I can hear him snore at
night. The walls must be made of cardboard or the thinnest
Sheetrock. None of the joints are sealed. Narrow cracks separate the walls and the ceiling and floor. When I was awak-
ened by this mysterious snoring noise, I realized all of the
angles of the room were glowing from the nightlights left on
in the hallway. I look from my window and can almost see
the mountains covered with the fog that rises from the river
at dawn. Waking up at 3:15 wasn't as bad as I thought it
would be.

## AUGUST 3

I cannot stop crying. Another letter from Jim. Weeping into
my pillow. He wants to stay for a weekend in the guesthouse
so he can see me. All I can do is cry. In ninth grade, when I
switched to a public school, someone wrote "The Faggot"
on my locker with black markers. The janitor never got
around to cleaning it off until the end of the school year. I
hug my pillow and sob. I cannot stop crying. I cannot ever
have children. No one knows. No one must ever know. Jim
wraps his letter in a thick sheet of blank paper so his secre-
tary, or anyone in his office, cannot read it. No one can
know. Who can I tell? My body is shaking. My throat is
hoarse. I've told no one. My parents. *My parents.*

Snot covers my face. I cannot stop weeping. I weep—*no
children ever*—into the blanket, hoping that—*in college, the
football player who lived*—the man next door will not hear
me—*next door used to tape fliers for the Gay and Lesbian Student Union to my door.*

I had never slept with anyone until Jim. The sheets stick

to my face. Someone drew a life-size picture of two men having anal sex on my dorm-room door with purple markers. I
cannot make any more sound and still cannot stop shaking.
My family. *My God.* I fall asleep heaving, twisted in the bed
sheets. Later, sometime in the night, I wake up startled. The
room does not glow. I get out of bed and open my door as
quietly as possible. The hallway is black. No one turned on
the night lights. I grope my way to the bathroom. If I turn on
the light, I will wake everyone. In my underwear, in the
dark, I wash the dried salt and mucus from my face. I cry
some more, when I return to bed, but not as hard. Silently.

## AUGUST 4

The schedule has absorbed me into itself with ease. I'm surprised, in fact. You just have to show up in the right place—
chapel, work, the dining room—when the bell rings. I don't
wear my watch anymore. I work in the bakery every morning and two afternoons a week. The rest of the time is my
own. I like to sit and write in the library on my afternoons
off, or sit under the trees and watch the mountains. After
Vigils, we're supposed to meditate or read, but I've been going back to sleep until Lauds at 6:30. Thank God we get a
nap in the afternoon after lunch.

About half of the monks work in the bakery. Usually, we
bake twelve hundred loaves of bread a day in addition to a
couple of hundred Monastery fruitcakes. They're gearing up
already for the Christmas fruitcake rush. I help punch down
the vats of risen dough. The gas from the yeast is so strong
that, with the heat from the ovens, it makes me weak—not
to mention the fermenting fruit for the cakes. At the end of
the shift, we eat the rejected loaves, right out of the oven,
with butter and honey and cold lemonade.

A young monk dropped a sixty-pound sack of flour on the floor and it burst with a spectacular cloud. "Fuck!" was all we heard through the whiteness. Brother Jorgé, a novice from Chile who speaks little English, turned to me and asked, "What is this *fuck?*"

## AUGUST 5

During lunch, a monk reads aloud while we eat. It is a luxury not to have to talk during a meal. The only sounds are the forks and knives, and a voice over a weak loudspeaker with spiritually edifying words. This week we listen to a biography of Mother Teresa. Today's chapter told the story of a noted British doctor who made a pilgrimage to meet her. Apparently, the physician got rabies while she was in India and didn't know it. When she finally met the famous nun, she started to foam at the mouth and fell down to the ground, barking like a dog. She died six hours later. I choke on my food, trying not to laugh. No one else looks amused. While we wash the dishes, an older monk pulls my sleeve and says, "Father John always picks the most dreadful books."

## AUGUST 6

I don't know why or how I can sit in the chapel and chant with these men. I watch them united in the mystery of their prayer and know that I believe so little of what they sing.

Wrote postcards to my friends saying I am well and that they should go to Giant or Safeway and buy Monastery bread because I put secret notes in the bags that say "Help Me."

### AUGUST 7

Brother Andrew, I discovered, plays the piano. I heard him as I walked back to my cell last night. I thought I was hallucinating. I looked through the window, through the lace curtain, and there he was, playing Haydn as elegantly as he could. When we talked about music this morning, he never mentioned that he played. His fingers are thick and the curl of his beard, beneath his lower lip, waves as he speaks. Another letter from Jim.

### AUGUST 8

It is time to tell someone. After lunch, I asked Father David if I can talk to him. The first thing the Retreat Master suggests is a spiritual director. Watch the monks. You'll see one to ask. David agreed to meet me that night in his study. When the time came, I walked to his office, to a part of the monastery I had never been in, wanting to throw up. He asked me all sorts of polite questions: Where was I from? Was I comfortable? What did I study? *Why was I here?*

The words came out of my mouth as if I were vomiting a two-by-four: *I am a homosexual.*

"Wait!" David said. He got up from his chair and bent down on the floor. "Look." A baby frog had gotten into the room and rested on a book. "I know what to do," he said. David found a box and gently tapped the book, and the frog jumped right in. He took the box outside, while I sat there, and set the frog free.

"Go find your home," he said and then returned. David smiled and scratched his beard, which was the color of strong tea.

"Yes. So you're gay. What brings you to Holy Cross?"

AUGUST 9

I've been rereading Jim's letter. Now I sit under a tree, having dropped his words onto the dirt because they made me weep. He writes that he has been thinking about me:

> Where do you fit into my life? Our age difference. Twelve
> years seems so great. Contemplating us . . .

As if a few nights spent together and some letters and phone calls had produced an actual *us* to contemplate.

> . . . something about the way you looked at me when we
> met on the sidewalk. Something in a smile. You seem like a
> strange old man to me. Or a flower. Delicate. Rare. So young
> and so old. Where do you belong? Have any of the priests
> hit on you yet?

Two weeks before entering the monastery, I stayed with Jim. We sat on his porch high above the city, shirtless and spent. It was late, and police sirens kept going off. I sat across from him. My feet rested on his thighs. He laughed and said I was much too serious for my age. "I still don't think you're twenty-one," he said. I got up and went to the bedroom. My wallet had fallen out of my pants, which were lying on the floor. I marched back out and gave him my driver's license.

The next morning Jim dressed for work, in a summer suit, as I watched him. When he came home, I sat there waiting on his bed, ready for him. That was the most time we had ever spent together.

AUGUST 10

I write long letters to everyone.

AUGUST 11

I check the loaves of bread as they come off the line before they go into the oven. The seams in the dough must face down or the loaves will split as they bake. I drown in the tears in my body. My other job is sorting raisins. I hate this. We talk while we work of nothing in particular. I feel the weight of gravity crushing my body and wait to collapse in the piles of shrivelled fruit. Songs run through my brain as we talk, endlessly: "What a guy/What a fool am I/To think my breaking heart/Could kid the moon." My head will explode soon.

AUGUST 12

Charis writes. She can tell the monastery is doing me good. Something in my letter said so. She spoke with my parents. My father hopes that I won't stay all three months. "There's no shame in leaving," he said. She's sorry she won't see me before school starts and can hardly wait for Thanksgiving. I speak with David tonight.

AUGUST 13

On Sunday, the local families come to church here. Father Pius gave the sermon. He is a big, round man. If there were a hoop in the bottom of his robes, he would look like a walking bell, clanging through the hallway. His word accents are all wrong. "THE Vatican says we must TOE THE line. Look AT the world. PregNANT teenAGERS. HomOsexuals ramPANT."

None of the monks seem to listen to him preach. David tells me that it is not uncommon for retreatants to think they are losing their minds. A kind of madness sets in.

AUGUST 14

Most of the monastery buildings are painted gray. I cannot see them when I walk to the bakery in the morning because of the fog. I walk down the dirt road. Only the trees are visible. The cold wet air rests on the hair of my arms. I wade through it, as in a sea that offers no resistance. Only later does the air heat up and stick to me.

My favorite service is Compline, which takes place at dusk. Brother Lawrence plays the guitar, and it is the only time the chant is accompanied. Often I lose focus of the words. "From fears and terrors of the night." I am too busy watching the chapel dim. "So when we close our eyes in sleep."

We sit there in the quiet when the song is over. Darkness burns around us like blown glass. The bell rings. The Great Silence begins and we retire. As we leave the chapel, in rows, the abbot blesses us. He dips a stick in a bucket of holy water and sprinkles us. We kneel before him. The water splashes across our chests, then we leave through the night to sleep.

AUGUST 15

St. Paul writes that we must create our own salvation. I have a crush on a monk. I work beside him in the bakery and can see the hair on his chest creep up from his open collar. His curly hair grows from his skull like the rings in a tree. He always looks either bored or deep in thought. I cannot tell which. I sit across from him during dinner trying to figure out what he wears under his robes, hoping he doesn't notice my stare.

My parents called last night. I'm starting to receive many letters. Two from Jim. I've never written so much before. Am seeing David tonight.


AUGUST 17

Only one room in the abbey is air-conditioned. David thought it would be good to talk in there. We went into the basement, into the computer room where they process the orders for fruitcakes. David pulled out folding chairs for us to sit on. The room is small and we were almost on top of each other. I began my litany of complaints: *Being gay is this sick cosmic joke. How could God be so cruel? That's what makes me the angriest. How unbelievably cruel. Bolt a starving person in a chair and place a plate in front of him. Just out of reach.*

David became a monk when he was nineteen. He still looks like a boy.

*All of these things you are supposed to have to be decent and you can't have them. Grasping through windows, through glass.*

It's his posture more than anything: slightly bent, like most boys who never quite mastered their height.

*Leave the food beyond reach, but not beyond smell, and ask if they'd like some.*

He couldn't get comfortable on the little chair and kept folding and unfolding his long legs. He stopped.

"Peter, who told you this?"

I thought he was joking.

"No. I'm serious. Where did you get this idea?"

"My family. My school. The Church. The world," I told

him. "I know you're a monk, but just think about it. Didn't you hear the sermon this week? It doesn't take Einstein to figure it out."

"And you've figured it out correctly? You're sure."

Breathless, I said yes.

"Peter, what if you're wrong?"

What did he mean?

"Are you so sure the world is right?"

*My logic is flawless.*

"Are you so willing to lie to yourself?"

I began twenty sentences at once and said nothing. Oxygen vanished from the air. I felt the hardness of my chair and stared. All David said was, "Oh, Peter," and then he embraced me. We were both quiet. My head rested on his chest, a little below his heart.


AUGUST 19

It rained today. I spent most of the day sitting on the porch writing letters. In the rain, it's hard to tell what's mountain and what's cloud.


AUGUST 20

This is what happened. It started this afternoon, this feeling of weight. Imagine the air is a vise that imperceptibly twists around you. It squeezes you slowly. Maybe you feel the pinch or a twinge; but it's not enough to hurt, not at first. Silently, it tightens, pressing your arms against your ribs until your elbows cut into your lungs. You can still walk this way, but where can you go to make it stop? When granite is crushed, it turns to dust.

After dinner I kept looking for someone to talk to. Anyone to get in conversation. I brushed my teeth twice. I walked everywhere except the chapel. I couldn't go in there. No. I was too afraid. I couldn't breathe. And always this weight bearing down on me. I washed my face, looking in the mirror to see if anyone was behind me. No one. I don't remember how, but I wound up in the chapel. It was empty. I sat there feeling the weight of the sun as it set. Felt it sink into the earth. Felt it scorch the ground. And then the word came from my mouth. Alone, on my knees and terrified, I said yes. Yes to everything. To all of it. I ran out of the room, suddenly weightless, and hurtled into David and the monk I have a crush on.

## AUGUST 21

What metaphors can strain after the mystic? Nothing happened last night, I tell myself. Nothing. I am a gifted liar.

## AUGUST 22

A monastic joke: Once a year Brother Guerric was allowed to break his rule of silence and speak two words to his abbot. At the end of his first year, he said, "Bed hard." At the end of his second hear, he told the abbot, "Work long." When the third year was over, he said, "Food lousy." And when the fourth year was up, he shouted, "I quit." The abbot looked at Brother Guerric and said, "Frankly, I'm not surprised. You've done nothing but complain since you arrived."

## AUGUST 23

We sat under the tree for hours. When Charis first arrived, and met me on the path, she embraced me.

"I have been waiting for you to tell me for so long," she said.

My letter, the one that said I am gay, came earlier that week. I cried when I wrote it and I wept when she greeted me.

The bugs were thick in the air. They kept biting and biting.

"I couldn't figure out why you would never kiss me," she said.

We sat there and began to unravel what seemed to be a blanket of little betrayals. Later that evening, one of the monks asked me if I had been sick. I had missed all of the services that day. Charis had embraced me when she left. Before she got in her car and drove down the gravel driveway, she looked at me and said, "I think what you are is immoral."

AUGUST 25

Spent the day taking photographs of Father Adric. Yesterday he wrecked an old truck, although no one knows how. Adric is sixty-seven. He became a monk when he was seventeen. He lives in a different monastery and spends his summers at Holy Cross. They think he was speeding as he drove to the barn, on the rough road. He must have hit a pothole and lost control before crashing into a pole that anchors the gate to the cowpen. Adric was thrown from the cab but wasn't hurt.

"You should have seen it," he told me. "What a great crash!"

We walked down to the site together.

"This is where I began to swerve."

The truck was wedged into the gate, the driver's-side

door open, the axle bent. The shattered windshield was blinding in the sunlight. Adric lay down on the ground, not far from the hanging door.

"Take a picture," he said. "Wait until they see this at home."

That afternoon we went to see the basketball court he built. I took pictures as he sank every shot. He wore a white sweatsuit and a floppy tennis hat. He is very small. "You'll be sure to send these to me, won't you?" he asked. *Bounce. Bounce. Whoosh.*

Must talk to David.

## AUGUST 25

Brother Mark talks with a terrible stutter. Every conversation with him is an effort. We have worked together, and the wait for him to get directions out can be excruciating. Once, when we were clearing debris from a renovation project in the Old Dormitory, he carried an entire wall by himself to the Dumpster. Yesterday, he gave me his grandmother's recipe for raisin pie. I watched him during Vespers. He came in early and loomed above the benches as he prayed. He never moved, just stood there, except for the slightest shake in his fingers on the wooden pew.

Wrote Jim that I will be home in one week: When can we see each other? The things we must discuss, the things we've been writing each other can no longer be confined to paper.

## AUGUST 27

Today I walked the grounds with the other retreatant. We haven't spoken much to each other since our arrival. I didn't realize how much land the abbey owns. We explored the river, and an island in the middle of it, where he told me that his marriage was unhappy and his children were angry. "You don't know how lucky you are," he said.

In the afternoon, we picked blackberries and raspberries. The berries were ripe and delicate, and I crushed quite a few. Juice was everywhere. I kept having to wipe the sweat from my eyes. We gave the bucket of berries to the cook, who told us we looked as if we were bleeding.

AUGUST 28

Caught a glimpse of Father Pius this morning. He sits in an alcove ironing little white squares of cloth used during mass. Sweat ran down his bald head and the folds of fat in his neck, and made his T-shirt transparent. He sat across from me in the library today. All I had to do was unclench my fist and stretch out my fingers to touch his hand. He looked up and smiled. "It's going well for you, isn't it?" he asked.

AUGUST 29

Said good-bye to David this evening. It was my turn to ask questions.

"What do you miss the most?"

He didn't have to think about it. "The ocean."

David told me a story about the last time he saw the sea, three years ago. "I was in Oregon at a conference about Trappist Spirituality. We had one free afternoon, and even though it was autumn and much too cold to go to the beach, a few of us got in a car and went. I took off my sandals. The sand was cool. I watched the waves for a while and then decided to go in. The water was cold, but I could stand it. I stood there at the edge of the land with my robe hiked up around my waist, and the foam sticking to my calves. A mist fell, and I knew it was time to go home."

I heard him walk down the hall, with his curious loping gait, and the loose sandal strap that slapped against his heel. I'd know his walk anywhere.

## AUGUST 31

It seemed strange not to work this morning. I stayed in my cell to pack. I carried my suitcases and all of those un-opened boxes to the front porch. Took a walk through the entire monastery and then sat in the chapel. My brother-in-law will be here soon. My father was supposed to come get me. I went to the bakery to say good-bye. Everyone was working, and most of the men could only wave. They gave me a few loaves to take with me. Walked back up the hill to the abbey. My hands are too full to wipe my tears. The fog should have burnt off by now. The sun is out and the air is luminous, but it is difficult to see.

When I first learned how to draw, I would make quick, short strokes, stabbing at the paper. The lines were so deep I could never erase them without tearing the page. An artist makes a line with one long steady stroke. If he erases it, the line disappears. But sometimes a faint grayness remains—a blurred shape, no longer tentative. That's what all of the trees look like now. I come home to a funeral. My grandmother has died the night before.

❦ One page—the page that begins this story—cannot be found in this journal. It is in a different book, a different bundle of papers. A binder that was filled six weeks before I entered the monastery. Let me include it now.

## JUNE 23, 1988

This is what happened. I sat there, waiting and hoping, and watching him. We sat in the circle with five men between us. That morning I felt that the air would crush me unless I finally went. I took the subway to DuPont Circle, the "Fruit Loop" as my gay friends call it. Benches encircle a large fountain and men are everywhere. It was hot, and most of them were shirtless.

He walked by me, as I sat there waiting. All I did was smile. As he left the park, he turned toward me and smiled back. I knew that if he returned, if he asked me, I would go. My stomach in knots of desire. I could not breathe. I didn't know how much longer I could sit there. He sat down and began talking to the group of men beside me. We looked at each other, silently, and he kept talking. The men left. I sat alone, waiting. I knew that he would ask me. The word was forming in my mouth.

"Can I see your newspaper?" he asked.

Breathless, I said, "Yes. My name is Peter."

Later, back in his apartment, I felt the weight of his body press against mine, his breath on my neck. Neither my shirt or shorts had buttons, only little squares of Velcro. With one quick tear, everything was open and I stood naked.

❧ I have not spoken to Jim in one year. The last words we had were heated, ugly. He loves another man. I knew this from the first day we met. Jim's lover is HIV+, and Jim is bound to him, bound to wait for the sickness that will kill him. The last time I saw Jim, I borrowed money from him which I cannot pay back. Not now anyway.

When I saw him, I had just come out to my parents. My father had written me a letter that said, "Those boys in college were right. You are a fruit, a fairy, a faggot, a queer."

He didn't speak to me for three months.

## AUGUST 30

I didn't write this before, but when you arrive they have a place with your name on everything: a towel hook, a place mat, a mailbox, a cup, a door. My name is typed on faded paper. I can tell the typewriter is old by the shape of the letters. Received another letter from Jim today. I stood there at my mailbox, opening an envelope, sent by a man whose tongue had caressed my ear, and looked at the name tag on the outside of the box. It looked as if it had been there forever.

**DAVID PLANTE**

# IMAGES OF THE BODY FROM MY RELIGION

Recently, at a party where I was speaking to a young man about trouble he was having with his job, I all at once became aware of his face, which before this moment hadn't appeared to me in any definite way, but which suddenly appeared to me very beautiful.

The attraction roused in me more than the desire to kiss him, but to make love with him, as if his naked body would be his face more revealed. It occurred to me that I have always been attracted, first, to a person's face, and that for me sexual attraction to a face is sexual attraction to an entire body. Then it occurred to me, surprising me because the simple thought had never presented itself so immediately before, that when I am drawn to make love I am most drawn to a body made whole and exposed in the bed of an individual personality. I am not excited by the anonymous body in parts, and the very idea of making love with someone whose face I couldn't kiss, much less see, rouses nothing in me but the incomprehension of how it can for others.

I accept that, though sexual desire for me has to be made whole within an individual personality, others would find their sexual desire roused by *depersonalizing* the body, roused, even, by fixing on parts of the body as if they did not belong to a whole. I think my desire comes entirely from my having been brought up a Catholic, taught, from the very beginning, that as long as we are on this earth our souls are indivisible from our bodies, and that we are in the wholeness of our personalities what we are because we are both body and soul.

Though I say I can't understand someone wanting to see the body devoid of the personality, devoid, in effect, of the soul, I can, really, when I consider the responsibilities imposed on a Catholic to save his soul by denying himself his body. I can understand a Catholic who is brought up to believe he will most likely condemn his soul by giving in to sins of the flesh rather than save his soul by remaining pure, throwing off all the imposed beliefs to live entirely within the freedom of the soul-less body, a body freed even from sexual responsibilities toward other people. Catholic gays have done this with a vengeance, and they have been right to do it, for, according to the Church, they are condemning their souls utterly by any expression of their sexual attraction to their own sex.

I, as a Catholic, threw off, with a kiss, any sense that I was condemning myself by kissing someone of my own sex, but—and I have no idea how, except that it might have had something to do with the kind of Catholic I was, a Franco-American Catholic from a small Franco-American parish in New England—I retained, as if with the sense that it gave me more than it took from me, what I see as the basic Catholic teaching that sex is an expression of love for another. If my sexual love for another was not sanctified by marriage, much less by heterosexuality, I never doubted, not for a second, that it was love, and even if I spent only one night with someone, what that person and I had exchanged over the night, in the wholeness of our love-making, was love. I have never, not for a second, felt any guilt about making love. I have always felt that in making love with a body in its wholeness I was also making love with a soul. This idea fills me with the longing to make love, and this idea comes directly from my religion.

The very images of the body my religion gave me that have added to, rather than detracted from, my sexual attraction to the body are images of wholeness, a wholeness that goes beyond the contours of the shoulders, chest, thighs, groin, legs to something else that, in itself, gives wholeness of soul to all the body. Saint Thomas Aquinas said we have a sixth sense, the sense that apprehends wholeness in diversity, and I, since I first heard this teaching, have taken the sixth sense to be as sensual in its apprehension as the eye, the ear, the finger tips, the tongue, the nose. It is the sense that can make one aware, at singular moments during love-making, of a larger, fuller, more erotic body just beyond the body you are holding in your arms, but which gives to the body you are holding in your arms a wholeness that your mere senses of sight, hearing, touch, taste, smell can't in themselves account for. My religion taught me that the body has its largest, fullest sense—its fullest sensuality—in the soul.

And if my religion taught me that the greatest desire one can have is the desire for eternal happiness with God, it taught me that we would experience the fulfillment of his desire in our resurrected and glorified bodies. No image of the body, as conceived of by Catholicism, is more potent than that of the resurrected and glorified body, which would occur at the end of the world, not too far off. We would rise from the dead, from the rot and ruin of death, with bodies made entirely beautiful—we would be aged thirty-three, which was the age of Christ when he died and was the age at which, the Church calculated, we are at our height physically and mentally; and we would shine, in our great beauty, with a bright light; and we would be like this forever and ever and ever, eternally happy with God. What is important to remember is that we would be in, not outside, our bodies, as much in our physical bodies as we were on earth, and there would be no conflict, but total accord, between the body and the soul, so our bodies and souls would be one, and all our desires would be fulfilled.

However separated off from the Church I am, the Church I once belonged to gave me the possibility of such awareness, and I am happy for it. My religion gave to sex its greatest sense—and here once again I insist on the most acute sensuality of a sense that apprehends a whole larger than all its parts, in the same way this sense apprehends the beauty of a naked body as more than skin, hair, bone, blood, in the same way that the Catholic church apprehends itself in all its parts as the living Mystical Body of Christ.

❦ MICHAEL NAVA

# COMING OUT
# AND BORN AGAIN

*I am the Lord your God who brought you out of the land of Egypt, the house of bondage: You shall have no other gods beside me.*

—Exodus 20:2

*No law can be sacred to me but that of my own nature.*

—Ralph Waldo Emerson

My uncle by marriage is a fundamentalist Christian. His father was a Pentecostal minister, who operated out of tents and rented halls. When I was twelve years old, I went with my uncle to one of his father's services. He preached from a stage at the front of the room. On the stage was a child's wading pool filled with water. From time to time, people would come out of wings wearing white gowns to be immersed in this pool by my uncle's father who, simultaneously, screeched nonsense words into a microphone. "He's speaking in tongues," my uncle explained, which amounted to no explanation at all. There was shouting and singing and it got terribly hot and I began to worry that my uncle would make me go up to the front of the room to be dunked in the wading pool. I must have said something to him because before the service was over, we left.

My uncle is one of the kindest men I know. He married my favorite aunt and took her from Sacramento, where her family lived, to San Diego, where he did. My uncle is an Anglo, fair-skinned and blue-eyed, and in marrying him my aunt married out of the Mexican community, the only one of my grandparents' children to do so. They have, by far, the happiest marriage of any of those children. Not only do they have a deep affection for each other, but they also allow each other to be separate human beings, something that's hard to sustain in any marriage. They are working people and it has often been a struggle for them to raise their four sons on my uncle's wages as an electrician, but no one is more generous to strangers. The IRS can attest to that; it once audited them because their charitable contributions seemed to the government grossly out of proportion to their earnings.

My aunt and uncle have also been generous and loving to me. They've met my boyfriends, read my books, and talked to me honestly about a family from which, other than them, I am estranged. I don't remember how it came up, but I was once talking to my aunt about her marriage and she said, "If Edward wasn't a Christian, we would have been divorced a long time ago." Normally, when I hear the word "Christian," my hackles rise, and from that point on, I simply stop listening. In my world, Christianity is not something to be embraced, it's something to be resisted. But because it was my aunt speaking and I know she is without prejudice against gays or anyone for that matter, I had to relax my own prejudice against Christians to hear what she was saying. What she meant, I think, is this: Both she and my uncle grew up poor and rough, without much education or many prospects, and he, particularly, was a hell-raiser, as only perhaps a preacher's son can be. Had my uncle not been "born again," and accepted the moral strictures of Christianity into his life, their marriage would have fallen apart over the first crisis. Instead, they are approaching their fourth decade together.

❧ "Born again." It comes from the Gospel of John, where Jesus says to the Pharisees, "In very truth I tell you, no one can see the kingdom of God unless he has been born again." When one of them sneers, "But how can someone be born when he is old? Can he enter his mother's womb a second time and be born?" Jesus replies, "Flesh can only give birth to the flesh; it is spirit that gives birth to spirit."

❧ I lived with a man named Bill for nine years. One night, not long after we met, we were lying in bed and I looked into his eyes and saw a love and acceptance so deep that I felt forgiven for the fear, shame, anxiety, and confusion I had constructed around being gay. It wasn't Bill by whom I felt forgiven, but by love. In that instant, I understood completely what Paul meant when he wrote to the Corinthians, "There is nothing love cannot face; there is no limit to its faith, its hope, its endurance."

I date my coming out from that night. Although I'd had sex with other men for many years before I met Bill, it wasn't until that moment that I "came out" from behind my fear long enough to risk being loved by another man and to love in return. From that time on, it became clearer and clearer to me that loving and being loved are the true purpose of my sexuality and not the pursuit of sex. As long as I believed that homosexuality was simply sexual activity, it was peripheral to my struggle to define myself and my values. When I understood that my being gay had less to do with sex than with an expression of love that began with the physical but went beyond it, I could accept being gay in a way I never had before. More than that, I could fight for my right to be open in my intimate relationships and to have them accepted and honored. I was able to imagine for myself a whole life, one in which the division between public and private was one that I chose, not one that was imposed on me by a hostile society and my own shame.

What my uncle found in his Bible when he was born again and what I saw in Bill's eyes that allowed me to come out from behind my fear and shame had similar effects on our lives. Being "born again" and "coming out" are transcendent experiences that produce a profound change in perception. You never look at yourself, your life, or your culture in the same way again. Much of what you have been taught is true is revealed to be false. Self-approval becomes infinitely more important than the approval of other people. You feel enormous relief when you surrender the baggage of shame and guilt produced by living a life that was not true to your experience of yourself. You look for a community that will support and reinforce your new direction, your new ideas, and your new identity. These experiences are common to evangelicals and gays and separate them from much of the rest of the culture.

So why is it that we are screaming at each other across police barricades?

The current political struggle between Christian evangelicals, on the one hand, and gay and lesbian activists, on the other, is not, ultimately, about "family values" or sexual practices. It is a struggle between those whose moral lives are guided by an external authority and those whose lives are guided by an inward truth. What makes the struggle so bitter is that both groups believe, on the basis of their personal transcendent experience, that their moral truths are absolute.

Christian evangelicals believe that the Bible is the word of God and every word is literally true. If, therefore, they interpret certain scriptural passages to condemn homosexuality, the condemnation comes from God himself and it must be applied in the civil law because civil law is subservient to divine law. From this position, the gay and lesbian civil rights movements must appear to evangelicals as a war against God. Their view of homosexuality is only part of their larger vision about what the world should be like based on their reading of the Bible. It is also clear, for example, that because Paul, among other biblical sources, commands women to be subject to their husbands "as though to the Lord," evangelicals also perceive the movement for gender equality as an attack on religion. The political order that evangelicals envision in the place of liberal democracy is one based on patriarchal authoritarianism; a culture organized to support the role of men as rulers of their families.

It is a mistake, however, to condemn the religious impulse because of the political agenda of the religious right. Many, perhaps most, people rely on an authoritarian God to develop a moral life. At best, religion teaches people to use self-discipline, self-criticism, and self-control to break the cycle of impulse-action that takes no account of the needs, or even the existence, of other people. Breaking this cycle can be the beginning of the spiritual consciousness of which Jesus spoke when he admonished his followers to "Love your neighbor as yourself." That admonition is a call to people to change their lives, and many people, including my uncle, have heeded that call to their own moral betterment.

Most gays and lesbians, however, have been excluded from Western religious tradition because of its apparent condemnation of homosexuality. For us, the challenge has not been so much to love our neighbors, as to love ourselves, including our homosexuality, in the face of an unrelentingly hostile culture. We have had to defy convention to follow the promptings of an inner truth about who we are, and in the process we have had to change our lives in ways at least as dramatic as those who heed the call of Christianity. This change can involve the development of a spiritual consciousness in which, as Emerson wrote, "no law can be sacred to me but that of my own nature." This kind of spiritual consciousness is firmly rooted in individualism, and it is enshrined, at least in form, in the founding documents of our democracy; in the Declaration's guarantee of life, liberty, and property and the Constitution's promise of individual liberty and equal protection.

But there are limits to the use of individualism as a tool of social organization. If everyone insists on the absolute freedom to do as he or she wishes, it is impossible to achieve any kind of consensus on which to build the community where we must all spend at least part of our time. For example, there exists among many gay men a defensiveness about examining the moral implications of their sexual behavior. This defensiveness is the understandable result of living in a culture that condemns all same-sex intimacy as immoral *per se* whatever its quality or duration on the grounds of religious stricture. It is one thing for gays to reject a particular moral condemnation of homosexuality, however, and quite another to reject all discussion of sexual morality as self-hatred or "sexphobia." The same inner truth that compelled many of us to come out of the closet also lets us know that there are limits to our sexual expression beyond which it becomes destructive, not because it offends someone else's God but because it offends the sacred self.

Both born-agains and gays believe they have a piece of the truth, one they have paid for with their suffering, and neither is willing to surrender that truth because to do so would be tantamount to surrendering the self. What I am saying is that spiritual consciousness is reached by many paths, and one's truth is not less true because not everyone shares it.

There can be no reconciliation of any kind between gays and lesbians and evangelicals until, at the very least, each side recognizes the right of the other side to exist. Evangelicals must realize that the scriptural precepts by which they live their lives cannot be imposed on people who don't share them without fatally compromising the democratic ideal. They don't have to accept homosexuality, but they must accept that part of their responsibility as American citizens is to put up with people they don't like just as people who find their views distasteful must put up with them. Unlike Jesus, our democracy doesn't require people to love their neighbors, but it does draw the line at throwing rocks at them.

Gays will have to accept the fact that, separation of Church and State notwithstanding, most Americans call themselves Christian and do not accept the proposition that homosexuality is the moral equivalent of heterosexuality. This is not to say that gays should give up their struggle for civil equality, but they must recognize that gaining civil rights is not the same as winning moral acceptance. Whether Christianity will ever relax its condemnation of homosexuality is something to be decided within the various sects and denominations of which Christianity is comprised; those debates should have no bearing on the civil rights of gay people. On the other hand, if gays and lesbians want to be included in the polity, they must also realize that issues of personal morality are legitimate areas of public debate and public policy-making and agree to be governed by those decisions so long as they are applied even-handedly. If, for example, gays and lesbians win the right to legal marriage with all its benefits, they must also agree to accept its responsibilities and burdens, because citizenship is a two-way street.

I don't know whether any of this will actually happen. The battle lines seem more fixed and heavily defended every day. If, however, gays and fundamentalists are willing to see the similarities in their experience, they can begin to move toward some acceptance of their differences.

❧ GABRIEL LAMPERT

# BAMIDBAR

*Bamidbar* is Hebrew for "In the wilderness." I live in Las Cruces, New Mexico, deep in the Chihuahuan Desert, so the word fits me. In addition, *Bamidbar* is one of the weekly portions of the Torah, the one, in fact, that I chanted from on my Bar Mitzvah. And *Bamidbar* is the Hebrew name for a whole book of the Torah, which is called Numbers in English because it opens with a census of the Israelite nation in the desert (*bamidbar*), so I lay claim to that meaning as well, since my profession is statistics.

I was not always at ease as a gay Jew living in this desert. Perhaps the turning point was the day in 1980 that I came out to the rabbi. I had lived here from 1968 to 1976, and had come back to town after a year in Santa Fe and two years in Tucson. While I was in Tucson, a friend had moved to Phoenix and been shot outside a gay bar, and that may be what got me to go back to somewhere I felt safer.

I hadn't thought of coming out during my earlier stint in Las Cruces. For one thing, the synagogue was already on my case for being part of the anti-war movement. I remember the apology of one of the synagogue members: In a small town, the Jews are *pareveh,* neither milk nor meat. They don't want to be too visible.

And there's also this: The whole time I was growing up back east in Philadelphia, my looks, voice, and stance told everyone I was Jewish. When I first moved to Las Cruces, where Jews were indeed very few, I was suddenly free in a new way; no one seemed to know. I started hearing the things that people don't say when they know you're Jewish. I remember one older woman telling me, "His eyes lit up like a Jew church," a phrase I've never heard before or since.

So I kept both my Jewishness and my queerness under wraps. By 1979, though, Manny's death was making the difference. He died without coming out to his parents, and their shock was so great that they seemed unable to push the police to find the killer. I knew that I didn't want to end up that way; I didn't want to disappear unnoticed like a stone in the ocean. I came out to my parents, rudely. I told them I didn't want them being ashamed of me if someone gunned me down. Then I moved back to Las Cruces, and I looked around for places to belong.

I began to attend synagogue again, sitting in for just part of a service, then compulsively walking out, proving to myself, I guess, that I didn't *have* to stay if I didn't feel safe. After a few months, I knew I had to come out to the rabbi. If he couldn't accept me, I would not come back; I felt I could not stay unless I knew I could belong. It was a Reform synagogue—in their own words, a temple—and the rabbi was also a Reform rabbi, which should have given me confidence. But he had grown up in an Orthodox home, he often espoused ideas that were more traditional than was common among Reform Jews, he was of an older generation, almost seventy, and, though the Jewish community in town had grown spectacularly over the years, they might still be obsessed with being *pareveh,* so I was not confident at all.

After making an appointment with him, I cycled up to

his house on Pomona Drive. There was a cluster of Jewish homes there and we called it "Kiryat Pomona," a pun on Kiryat Shemona, a town on Israel's northern border. He invited me into his study and, in the expert way a rabbi develops after forty years, got a conversation going, about what I'll never remember. Finally, I said it, "I'm gay." He said, "Well, I don't know anything about homosexuality, but the important thing is that you're here in the temple."

He also put me in touch with a rabbi in Los Angeles who he knew was heading the gay synagogue there, Beth Chayim Chadashim, and I talked a lot with her over the phone, but it was what the first rabbi said, and especially the way he put things into perspective, that mattered to me. The important thing was that I belonged. Yes. And I heard an echo from Pirqe Avot, "Ethics of the Fathers," where the criteria were given for who is tzaddiq, a righteous person. The final one was, "And about what he does not know, he says, 'I don't know.'"

The rabbi was not kidding about belonging, either. When he decided to have the wording changed on the doors to the Ark where the Torah is kept, he told the temple president about my ability at calligraphy, and got me to design and lay out the wording, and ultimately to find and help the workman who cut the letters out of brass. It is still up there on the Ark, where the focus of any religious service is, so I often find myself looking at those doors, and it still feels good.

Since then, I have become more actively involved in synagogue life. I was chairman of the worship committee. The congregation elected me to its board of trustees. I have often led services, have read and chanted the Torah portion, instructed Bar and Bat Mitzvah students, given sermons, and twice sat on the committees to select a new rabbi. I have spoken openly about being gay with probably most of the congregation—we are only two hundred adults or so. Last Yom Kippur, I sang Kol Nidre to a packed house (and my voice did its nervous trick and climbed an octave higher than usual). I am the synagogue's official representative to the city police chief's public meetings. Twice I took my roommate to the community *seder,* and the congregation treated him as my life partner, though our relationship is more accurately a close friendship. The synagogue has grown steadily—people in town are beginning to know what a Jew looks like—and I am now at fifty-one a relatively senior member. In 1993, at my request, the board of trustees and the rabbi sent letters vigorously supporting the effort to enact a gay-rights law in New Mexico.

In a personal, day-to-day sense, then, being gay is not a problem in the synagogue. Yes, there may be some individuals who are not comfortable with me, but they are not many, and are more than balanced out by those who are genuinely supportive. But what about the religion itself? What about non-Reform Jews? What about Leviticus? What about Sodom and Gomorrah? What about the Judeo-Christian tradition?

Well, some of these are easier than others. I, for one, don't think that there is such a thing as a Judeo-Christian tradition. The two religions are so different that one might equally well talk about a Judeo-Islamic or Christo-Islamic tradition. For example: Judaism is a tribal religion for Jews, not a world religion; non-Jews don't need to convert to Judaism to be "saved." Judaism is less concerned with the afterlife than with life here on earth. Et cetera.

And if there really were such a tradition, then Christians would know that Jewish tradition has always held that

Sodom and Gomorrah were destroyed for lack of charity to the poor, lack of hospitality to the stranger, for being too concerned with property rights, for being unwilling to give others the things that would cost the giver nothing. All these are mentioned in the Talmud as examples of *middat Sdom*, the personality of Sodom. Any crime labeled "sodomy," then, would be some crime of selfishness or meanspiritedness. Jesse Helms and Pat Robertson would be in jail for sodomy.

If there really were a Judeo-Christian tradition, then Christians would know that all the occurrences of "sodomite" in the Old Testament of the King James Bible are mistranslations of *qadesh,* a man who acts as a cult prostitute, giving his sex money to whatever (non-Hebrew) god he is employed by.

Still, though Reform Judaism is committed to embracing Jews regardless of their orientations, it is true that not all Jews are accepting of queers. Orthodoxy is still flat-out opposed. Conservative Judaism, however, is waffling its way slowly toward acceptance. In the December 1993 issue of *Bible Review,* mainstream rabbi Jacob Milgrom comments on the Levitical laws about homosexuality. Milgrom is a respected scholar across boundary lines of Jewish belief. In the article, Milgrom says that (1) the Levitical laws were never meant to apply to anyone but Jews—non-Jews are exempt; (2) it is not an accident that lesbian sex is not prohibited—that's exactly what was intended; and (3) gay sex for Jewish males is prohibited because it wastes a life-giving resource (semen), so—hold on to your hats—gay Jewish men should have the duty to adopt children as a way of compensating for spilled seed!

Other commentators on Leviticus have noted that the word that is translated "abomination," *to'evah,* seems to be a technical term. After all, though it appears in the sentences that condemn sex between men, it does not appear in an adjoining sentence that condemns bestiality; that is given a different title. Surely, the Torah does not mean to say that bestiality is not abominable but homosexuality is. . . In fact, in most places where *to'evah* appears in the Hebrew Bible, it has something to do with "foreign ritual." In Genesis, for example, it describes why Egyptians refuse to eat with Hebrews or live among shepherds. Some have proposed that what is being condemned in Leviticus is ritual homosexuality as part of a cult.

What certainly can be said is that the backgrounds of much of Torah are beyond our knowing; some of the words themselves had faded into obscurity even before the rabbis of the Talmud had gotten to them. For example, in Exodus we are told not to make a *pesel* or a *tmunah* of anything. The usual translations are "graven image" and "likeness." Question: Is a crucifix with an image of Jesus *pesel?* Clearly, Christians do not think so. Jews debated the issue over a millenium ago, and came to an uneasy conclusion, "no." It should be clear, however, that the Hebrew prophets Isaiah, Jeremiah, and the others would certainly not have countenanced the kinds of images that are common in churches of even fundamentalist sects. No one thinks that a photograph is a *tmunah*. In a court case, a woman in Iowa who did prefer not to carry a photograph as part of her driver's license was told that she must. The images on our money are strangely close to idolatry, but televangelists still seem to welcome these engraved images gladly.

And that is the most important truth: The Bible is not unchanged. People have changed it, Jews and Christians. People have found ways to interpret the Law so as to live with it. Usually they have done so for their own comfort, of course. I am lucky in that my community has seen my needs as theirs.

So there certainly are intellectual arguments that can be made in our behalf, but even this is not the real question. The real question is, How do I *feel* about these words? How have *I* managed to reach some level of comfort with my tradition? I think that I look at the Hebrew Bible as my family scrapbook, with its sometimes contradictory stories about some rather contradictory men and women. I can't possibly know why some things are written in it. Though I read Hebrew moderately well, much of the language has changed radically. Sometimes an ancient phrase, only half understood, will raise the hair on my neck. Imagine, for example, the four-million-year-old hominid Lucy, the bones found in Africa. Suppose you knew for certain that she was *your* direct ancestor, not in a general sense but that she was the mother of someone whose line came directly down to your own mother or father.

I feel that same awe-filled connection when I read the Bible or when I celebrate holidays that always fall at the full moon (Passover, Sukkot, Tu Bishvat, Purim), aware that the origins of that dating process are older than anything we know. Here in the desert, I am reminded almost every night of where we are in the lunar month. I don't need any other calendar to tell me when the holiday is coming. When Sukkot arrives, I hold the bound cluster of thin slats of palm leaf, the *lulav,* and shake it to the North, then East, South, West, up, and down, hearing the slats slap! slap! against each other. I know I am performing a ritual whose age is beyond our reckoning.

While the English translation of the Bible drones on as a

ceaseless declamatory orator, the original is a colloquial storyteller in Genesis, then a lyric poet in the Psalms, a wailing
keener in Lamentations, and a ribald jokester in Esther. In
the Hebrew, the Twenty-third Psalm has almost no adjectives, relying entirely on verbs and nouns for the strength of
its descriptions, so the Bible is a source of literary inspiration, too, from the terse, limited vocabulary and late grammar of Jonah back to the ancient case endings of the Song of
the Sea in Exodus.

I like knowing that our hero David was sometimes a jerk,
and that Abraham was so scared of Pharaoh that he tried to
pass off his wife as his sister, so that Pharaoh wouldn't have
him killed to get to Sarah. I hear ecologists grumble that our
current lack of respect for the earth is due to the line in
Genesis where Adam is given dominion over all creatures,
but I hear what the ecologists don't—that we must let the
land lie fallow every seventh year, that we must let our animals rest every Sabbath, that we may not defoliate a forest in
a siege, that we may not eat the blood of an animal because
it is the very life of it. Our dominion is not so total after all.

And the later writings, the Talmud, the Midrash, the Aggadah, some of it only eighteen hundred years old, also have
things to tell me that I am happy to be able to find: that the
commandment to "Love your neighbor as yourself" includes
the admonition that we must love ourselves so that we might
love others. We hear this again in *Pirqe Avot*, where we are
told not only, "Do not judge your fellow until you have been
where he's coming from," but also, "Don't count yourself as
evil." Be kind to others, be kind to yourself—these are inseparable parts of a whole. I included these two quotes from
"Ethics of the Fathers" in the calligraphy I put on the cover
of the synagogue's yearly directory a few years back.

❦ I hope I've given some idea of what it is I get out of being a Jew, and how I have managed to find a way to be gay in the Jewish community. I think I must also address the problem of being a Jew in a gay community. That has turned out to be a little harder. It's not that I'm sent away or told not to be so Jewish in public. But I *have* been told, "The Jews don't have to worry about the next Holocaust, because they own the media, so it's just us queers who will get slaughtered."

And it sometimes seems that I am held responsible for whatever evil the government of Israel commits (though I'm not given any congratulations for my presumed part in any peace accords or anti-discrimination laws passed by the Knesset). Once, when the local gay men's group's Sunday evening pot luck coincided with the start of the Jewish New Year, I brought the special round *challah* for the occasion, full of raisins. Three members of the men's group confronted me by crowing about having called their senators to make sure that Israel should not get any loan guarantees until they promised to stop building new settlements in the Occupied Areas. Now, I myself was opposed to settlements and had participated in a joint Jewish-Arab peace demonstration while in Israel, but I was both hurt and angered that these gay men on whom I lean for support chose to make the holiday an occasion to jump me this way, or that somehow I was equally worthy of some kind of punishment.

Such occasions are not that common, though it doesn't take too many of them to set the tone for a dialogue. What I really find difficult to deal with is the insensitivity, ignorance, and lack of interest of my gay community when it comes to my Jewishness. I sometimes want my gay friends to be there when I do have the chance to perform at the synagogue, but I rarely am able to get anyone to go.

There are other ways I feel excluded, too. About four years ago, I remember running into a lesbian sociology professor and her gay student in the parking lot after a local event. They were discussing his upcoming paper for her, titled something like "Religion and Homosexuality," in which the student was interviewing members of the local gay community about how they got along with their congregations. When I suggested myself as a possibility, they said after an embarrassed pause that they were really interested only in the churches. As if Judaism were not a religion.

On the other hand, I *am* invited to participate in Christmas caroling at convalescent homes, though everyone knows that I was forced to participate in hymn singing in elementary school and how I feel about that. Asking a Jew to participate in Christmas is like asking a Native American to march in the Columbus Day Parade. The New Mexico Gay Men's chorus comes down twice a year from Albuquerque to serenade us. The December one is Christmas with Friends, with an amazing array of Christmas songs of other centuries, some in Spanish and even Catalan (a good idea in an area where Spanish can be heard on the streets so frequently), and one tacky inclusion of a *dreidel* in one song. Considering the wealth of *Ladino* songs now in print or on CD—sung in the Spanish dialect of Sephardic Jews—and the wealth of other Jewish music available, I resented having to choose between being "with friends" and feeling alone, or truly being alone. I discovered I had to be alone, and I think that my gay friends don't understand the ramifications of this choice. Why don't they see it? They certainly can gripe from time to time about some heterosexual wedding they're forced to attend (or forced to boycott), or about how the latest movie is just one more boy-meets-girl epic that they don't need another example of. They get as outraged as I do if a television biography of Walt Whitman dances around his homosexuality. But still they don't make that leap to where I am.

We are, of course, a small and relatively inexperienced group of queer women and men in Las Cruces. It has only been since the summer of 1992 that we have had any political organization at all. The Jewish community is more organized and to some extent better educated. I can see how much we have changed in the past two decades.

And Christian insensitivity to Jewish concerns is certainly not limited to gay people. All of the unfortunate interactions I've just listed have happened outside our gay community as well. Yet there is change happening. When a bishop was appointed to the newly created Diocese of Las Cruces, he made it one of his first acts to come to the synagogue and acknowledge, years ahead of the Vatican, the responsibility of Christianity for creating an environment in which the Holocaust could happen. He pledged himself to eradicating anti-Semitism from the Church's teaching. We shall see. I am hopeful. As our small lesbian and gay community grows and matures, I don't doubt that it, too, will move toward a greater awareness of all its members.

# A CHRISTIAN IS SOMEONE WHO'S MET ONE

When I was a baby I wasn't baptized. That summed up my parents' attitude toward religion. My father didn't see any point in churches. My mother felt sentimental about them only as repositories of Easter and Christmas family memories: as pop-up Hallmark cards.

Somewhere around age twelve I talked my mother into taking me to a Presbyterian church she'd attended as a girl. Having seen *The Ten Commandments* five times, I was searching for my own God in a bush of fire. I found him temporarily in the minister of the church. I remember him as tall, with wavy black hair and a deep, steady voice. During his sermons, I was convinced that I could guess what he was going to say before he said it. On the way out, he'd grab my hand in his bigger hand. I was in love. As soon as I arrived home, I'd play church, using my mother's vanity as the altar, propping a Bible on her jewelry box, dressing up in a black robe I'd adapted from a Zorro costume. I soon had the minister baptize me, worrying all the while that the drips of holy water would sprinkle on my good suit.

During that year I began to sense that something was up. Leaving church on Sundays there'd often be a black Thunderbird parked out front with New York plates. Sitting behind its wheel was another handsome young man, his hair slicked back like a gangster on *The Untouchables*. Sometimes the minister's mother would be with him. She dressed in fur coats. If you stuck around long enough you'd see the two, or three, of them drive off, leaving the quaint stone church in their beautiful sleek car's exhaust.

Then came the scandal. I have yet to find out what happened (although I've asked many times over the decades), but there was a hush-hush meeting of the congregation. The next I knew the minister was gone. And so was my interest in attending church. The last I heard of his whereabouts was a newspaper clipping my mother sent reporting that he had been stabbed to death several times by a young man in upstate New York, where he had been hired by a church after leaving ours in Wilkes-Barre, Pennsylvania.

Flash: I'm sitting in the high-school auditorium on a weeknight watching the film *The Cross and the Switchblade,* a presentation of a Billy Graham Crusade. I'm so moved that at the finale when converts are asked to come forward to the extinguished screen, I do. Later I realize I had actually been "sent" by the imagery of leather jackets, knives, sideburns. I got my wires crossed.

Flash: Joining a Methodist Youth Group for a while. I'm particularly fascinated because one of its members is a local hood—he used to both threaten and flirt with me when he visited me at my job as a page at the local library. I always try to ride with him in the cars to our picnics and other whitebread outings. Sometimes he brings a friend whose head has been shaved in jail. One of the Methodist girls' boyfriends is a proto-criminal as well whose look is out of Genet (although I didn't know that yet). "Lick my arm," Mitch once said to me alluringly.

In every case my propulsion into a religious setting was

partly erotic, partly male. I never deduced syllogistically that God was gay. But I do think that for a sensitive little boy whose wires were crossed—for whom violence, love, and prayer seemed similarly charged—the central image of a man nailed to a cross was not exactly a No Trespassing sign.

At Columbia College I felt I had better things to do. Kenneth Koch was teaching me the joys of New York School poetry. Morty Manford invited me to stop by the Gay Lounge in the basement of Furnald, where I met W. H. Auden, among others. After seeing a Reichian analyst on Thursday nights in the Village—she encouraged me to hit a couch with a tennis racket, scream, jerk off—I'd go off, fortified, to try new sexual moves at The Trucks, Ty's, The Eagle's Nest. My I.Q. shot way up.

After graduating in 1973, I moved to Paris. There I began to hear a spiritual tone reasserting itself in my head and resembling in feeling the transcendent Ligeti chorus in *2001*. I was lonely. I was often sick. I was living in a *chambre de bonne* behind the Montparnasse cemetery. I'd walk the streets all night. Paris became my personal phosphorescent desert. I visited cathedrals—Notre Dame, Chartres. I felt in agreement with a selection from Thomas Aquinas's *Summa Theologica* titled "Treatise on Happiness." "Happiness is man's proper good," the saint said. My spiritual impulse was flowering in a soil of medievalism. In that instance, at least my longings were not a matter of personalities, and so weren't particularly erotic. But they were definitely high-concept.

When I came back to New York I began to look for people to talk to about religion and spirituality. Not easy. Finally someone suggested I meet Canon Edward Nason West at the Cathedral of St. John the Divine. He put a face to my inklings that was eccentric, sophisticated, wicked, and infinitely gentle enough for me to fess up. In his sixties at the time, he was quite aware of his own personal glamour. He sported a white beard, a Russian Orthodox cassock, walked with a wooden cane. His apartment in the Cathedral close was a glistening display of Greek icons, Fabergé eggs, Elizabethan painted portraits. A prized possession: the teeny communion cup of the last Russian czarevitch arranged next to a photo of the assassinated tyke.

"A Christian is someone who's met one," Canon West once said to me with that case-closed clip of his.

I'd confer with him in his office every few weeks. He'd send me off with out-of-print books, mostly about Russian spirituality.

I remember running along the beach at Fire Island that summer practicing the famous Orthodox mantra, the Jesus Prayer: "Lord Jesus Christ, Son of God, have mercy on me, a sinner."

I was firm with Canon West that I wasn't interested in Sunday church services or masses. I wanted my religion to be as futuristic as a space shuttle. As I wrote in a poem at the time: "The Cistercians [Trappists] should think about regrouping in space stations." He suggested I spend a week at Holy Cross, an Episcopal monastery on the Hudson River. I did. One afternoon I participated in a mass for the first time in my life. We stood around in a circle. I did feel charged by the drinking of the wine and eating of the bread. I did feel warmed by standing in a small, quiet circle with others. For once I wasn't in an idea. I was in a circle of people in a three-dimensional peaceable kingdom. The lingering hum of the actual experience changed my mind though I couldn't explain why. I wasn't St. Thomas. I found I was temperamentally closer to the medieval author of *The Cloud of Unknowing* and others who felt religious thoughts were in dark orbit around a fixed and brightly illuminated planet of logic and explanation.

I began to go to the Cathedral of St. John the Divine on Sundays, followed always by lunches at Canon West's, at which lots of Glennfiddich was drunk. I also decided I wanted to be a monk. So I went shopping for a monastery. I visited Russian Orthodox monasteries, Episcopal monasteries, Trappist monasteries. Along the way I found lots of gay activity.

At one Episcopal monastery an athletic, blond brother—a sort of prep school fantasy athlete—would knock at my cell door so that we could run five miles together at daybreak. On one of my last days of retreat he made a pass at me while I was still lying in bed. Apologizing a day later he explained that his lover—another brother—was away for a few weeks. "Huh," I thought.

At a Trappist monastery I met a brother who lived in what looked to me like a split-level ranch house. It was his hermitage. He was an icon painter, and the modernist, angular hermitage doubled as his studio. It turned out that he once had a lover brother, too. While helping him to build his hermitage, the lover had fallen from the roof and broken his neck. Now the icon painter claimed he was just staying on to be close to the angel of his departed lover. I heard later that this period of mourning ended. After twenty years, the brother put on Wellington boots and jeans and took a plane to New York City, where he went straight to Christopher Street and Ty's bar. Either on the plane, or at the bar, he met someone from Atlanta, Georgia, moved there, and was living happily at last report.

My conclusion: Why bother with a monastery? It seemed just like living in New York City. After all, this was now the cusp of the 1970s and 1980s when I remember admiring an essay by Edmund White in *The New York Review of Books* describing gay life in New York as a community of brotherly love in which sexual escapades turned over easily into friendships. Going to bed with someone was the equivalent of a handshake. Post-nuclear families were fashioned from communities of guys who had been to bed with each other. Old models of monogamy needn't apply.

I had one last parish experience during the 1980s at a church in New York to which Canon West directed me. The rector was Italian, but again dashing, reminding me of my first juvenile brush with a man of the cloth. His assistant pastor was tall, with big warm hands, a priest who was deeply interested in Buddhism, meditation, and healing. My heart skipped like a pebble to hear Buddhism talked about in this little church with Tiffany windows. Buddhism had always appealed to my spacey, cosmic side. So I settled happily into that parish. Then Canon West died of old age. Then the Buddhist-Christian healer of AIDS. Then the minister, also of AIDS—although he never allowed anyone to say so publicly. When I helped carry his casket out of the church at his funeral, I felt as if a part of my own life was over. I was standing at the edge of a cliff with no one any longer in front to buffer the wind or conceal the extent of the precipitous drop.

These days my religious life is squarely between me and my icon—a nineteenth-century Russian icon of Christ Pantocrator brought to me once from the Maria Andipa Icon Gallery in London by my lover of eleven years, Howard Brookner, who died of AIDS in 1989. I sit on my bed, breathe deeply, look at the Pantocrator's blue eyes, at the way his fingers are bent into shapes such as kids make to cast rabbit shadows on walls, at the globe he holds half in darkness, half in light. We talk without words.

Religious life always seemed to me as natural as breathing, in and out, systole and diastole. Right now I suppose I'm breathing in. I hope someday there will be another period of breathing out, of meeting and making connections with others who've felt a tingle like that emotional heat the disciples felt when Jesus (in disguise) talked to them on the road to Emmaus: "Did not our heart burn within us?" one of them asked. Nothing is more romantic, or perhaps "passionate" would be a better word, than looking for, or hearing, the truth. I do feel that gays have particular promise as a group for cultivating a new orchid of spiritual life, as long as it's planted in the black erotic soil they've tilled so generously over the past few decades. Edmund White was right about the brotherly love part. I think my early monastic fantasies were a wish for a community. And perhaps my sexual ones as well.

Generally I don't have many thoughts on religion. I'm not much of a theologian. Looking back, my variety of religious experiences seem to have come from momentary weaknesses for life. I've always gone on hunches, intuitions. Gay men are a noticeable string I've followed through the labyrinth. That's probably because I'm a gay man. I assume that in an incarnational theology—where God is made flesh and dwells among us—Canon West's comment is a basic truth: "A Christian is someone who's met one." And in an incarnational theology, stories and anecdotes are just as telling as sermons.

❧ ALFRED CORN

# What is the Sexual Orientation of a Christian?

Self-acceptance for those of us described as "minorities" never comes easy. I've worked toward it most of my adult life yet didn't feel fully comfortable as a gay man until after I became a Christian. I should say, "returned to Christianity," because I was brought up in a family in which faith and religious practice were very important. During my teens I was so devout as to decide I had a vocation for Christian ministry. I can still vividly recall the moment when, during a nighttime service at a week-long summer retreat for young Methodists in South Georgia, I looked up at the huge face of a Christ with long flowing hair and a steady loving gaze, projected by a slide machine on a giant screen in a darkened auditorium. Emotion overtook me, and I decided that I was being commanded to surrender my life to Him. Eventually I went down to the altar with a few others and signified that I had accepted the call.

It was also during those years that I became aware that I had sexual feelings for men. This strange discovery—which nothing I had been taught prepared me for—might have made me think I had developed some form of mental illness. I even remember briefly considering suicide. But two providential finds helped me get over the first shock: a book on sexuality, written for teenagers and informing them that "homosexuality" (a new word to me) was a phase experienced by many people and that its opposite, heterosexuality, would emerge in time. The second find was a paperback titled *The Sixth Man,* which maintained that one out of six males had had sexual relations with his own sex, and then went on to describe gay life in America of the fifties. I was fascinated by the portrait, but also frightened by it. The lives described were far removed from anything I knew, and my view of happiness involved settling down and being married.

I was a Christian, so I prayed that the "homosexual phase" would pass away soon. I took young women out on dates and even followed prescribed courting rituals like driving to a secluded spot at the end of an evening and trying a few experimental kisses and caresses. They were pleasant, but nothing like the anxious tingle of affection I felt, for example, when I changed clothes in a locker room with athletic classmates or watched them dive and swim, or, for that matter, just strut around and be themselves. I could see the same excitement function in other boys my age when they looked at pinups of women, pictures that meanwhile had no special appeal to me. How easy it was for my classmates to be themselves—and how difficult for me. I prayed every day for this anxious and painful chapter in my life to end.

Days and years of prayer passed, and the situation remained the same. By now I was in college, a student of science, history, and philosophy, immersed in the secular atmosphere of advanced education. It became clear to me that I preferred this knowledge to the constriction of the fundamentalist environment of my childhood. When I attempted to apply logic to the unflinching credal solemnity of those childhood teachings, the following argument came into sharp focus. God made everything, including me: my sexuality then was God's doing also; but God had declared relationships between persons of the same sex sinful. Therefore, my only choice was to remain celibate or choose sin and damnation. Actually, even celibacy wouldn't really work, because we can sin in our thoughts as well as in our deeds: The man who so much as thinks of committing adultery has already done so "in his heart," according to a well-known passage in Matthew. The orthodox view was that I could repent of such thoughts, seek forgiveness, and emerge with a clean slate. But I had also been taught that repentance was insincere (and therefore insufficient to merit absolution) if the penitent didn't firmly resolve not to sin again. A great disadvantage for me in going through penitential procedures of thought was that I don't have much talent for self-deception. After several hundred efforts at repentance, each followed by a return of thoughts I had promised to forswear, I had to acknowledge that I wasn't going to be able, in all honesty, to promise never to feel an attraction to men, and to desire them. According to the logic just outlined, that meant that I was not making a sincere repentance.

What I saw before me was a long life of continual and unavoidable sin and so of hopeless guilt. Is there anyone who could face that prospect? No doubt some people have, but it struck me as unjust and cruel. Why were some people singled out for this special burden? The comparison with physical disabilities didn't work because, although physical disabilities can be viewed as a result of God's will, no one ever suggested that being disabled was a form of sin. The paradox was that I had been created sinful, was even so required not to sin, and would be eternally damned for that sin. And yet Christianity teaches that God is Love. Was it possible to believe in a God of love who treated his creatures—his children—that way? Maybe it was possible, but, if you did, was it possible to *love* him in return, even as you were being damned by him?

Because there was no one to propose a different narrative of creation and redemption to me in those years, I lost my faith, and along with it, all the guidance it might have brought to me for nearly two formative decades of my life. I will never know how my life might have been different if there had been a more accepting—no, affirming—spirit abroad in the Christian churches of America in the late fifties and early sixties. Nearly twenty years of faith and service (and the happiness they might have brought to me) were lost forever.

❧ The Contributors note in this collection tells that I am a poet, and I know that a note like that is necessary because I don't expect the general reader to be aware of anything I've published. Poetry has few readers in this country. I never expect any new person I meet to have the faintest idea about what contemporary poetry in America is like. When a direct question from a stranger forces me to say what I do "for a living," in response to what I tell them I often hear something like this: "Oh, poetry. I studied that in high school (or college) and the teacher was so terrible and the poetry so boring, I've never read a word of it since." Well, in the contemporary, secular world of the fine arts, being a Christian is like being a poet in the nonliterary environment. When my peers in the arts become aware that I am a churchgoer, they often say, "When I was a teenager, the nuns (or some fundamentalist relative or preacher) made me so angry with their ranting about sin and damnation, as soon as I could get away from religion I did, and I've never set foot in church since." To both groups, those who in their teens were once turned against poetry, and those who were made to despise religion, I offer this suggestion: Since you are no longer seventeen years old, why be content with the version of religion or poetry that was presented to you decades ago, often by insufficiently trained persons or teachers who had no special interest in the subject? Why not spend some time exploring what religion and poetry are now in particular books or particular congregations here in the 1990s? Both religious faith and the art of poetry have always constituted a way of being and a subject that many people who were, after all, not fools have considered supremely important. Of course, looking into them is a large-scale commitment since no one who visited one service at one church or synagogue or read one book of contemporary poetry could fairly say that the subject had been sufficiently investigated and that there was no reason to look further.

It still astonishes me that I found my way back to faith, given who I was. It even seems miraculous. The New Testament records a number of miracles where the blind begin to see and the lame walk. To me, the conferral of vision in the spiritual sense, and the ability to move forward through the difficulties of life with confidence and hope, no longer hindered by a sense of being permanently at odds with God and man, are all analogous miracles. I was the least likely candidate for conversion imaginable. Throughout my twenties and thirties I, like nearly everyone I knew, was atheist (or at best, agnostic) and religion among my friends was a common target for scorn and abuse. And let's be honest: The picture of Christianity that comes to us through the media is awful. There are the TV evangelists, with their calls for contributions and a life of sacrifice, their fancy cars, and million-dollar mansions. Profit like theirs points toward two truths: First, that the general population feels an enormous spiritual hunger, to the point of agreeing to send money they often can't reasonably spare to prove their need and love for God; second, that the television medium is persuasive, almost hypnotic. It's dangerous to watch TV unless you also come prepared with countering influences of reason, faith, and, I believe, the kind of understanding that works of fine art bring.

Also on the negative side is the effort by some Christians to silence debate on pressing issues like birth control, the ordination of women, marriage for priests, and acceptance of lesbian and gay sexuality. I'm relieved that Christian opinion on these issues isn't monolithic. It has been pointed out to me that the Roman church, to take one example, cannot be summed up in the opinions of its hierarchy alone: The priests and laypeople who propose a revision of canon law on the subjects of birth control, women's ordination, and full acknowledgment of gay sexuality are also the Church, that is, the Body of Christ. I admire the heroism of those who want to stay in the Church that is their heritage and work to improve the Church's understanding of these subjects. After all, history demonstrates that the Roman church has modified doctrine over and over again. For a thousand years Roman Catholic priests (though not bishops) had the option of marrying until canon law was modified to forbid it. Meanwhile, marriage was not proclaimed a sacrament until the thirteenth century. Church law permitted the corporal persecution of heretics until the nineteenth century, when it became impermissible. For example, Galileo's proof that the sun stood at the center of the solar system was a heresy punishable by being burned at the stake. Present-day discipline imposed by the Roman church on its university professors or clergy who teach or publish arguments in favor of same-sex relations are mild by comparison: You can only be silenced (and then, if you persist, excommunicated). The dogma of the pope's infallibility when speaking *ex cathedra* about matters of doctrine was only instituted in 1870. So Roman Catholic reformers are not mistaken to continue to debate the topic of sexuality; history shows canon law can be changed. I applaud these faithful people; but it would be very hard for me to imitate them, and I'm relieved not to be confronted with the choice of staying on as an embattled member or leaving the Church that had been mine since childhood.

Fundamentalism, dogmatism, and bigotry are not, of course, the sole property of Christianity. I wonder whether a study of religious typology has ever been done, so that psychological profiles operative in all the world religions could be discovered. Every religion seems to have its scriptural fundamentalists as well as its legal experts, its libertarians, its poets, and its mystics. Wherever the fundamentalist or ultra-orthodox temperament appears, though, trouble follows, as we've seen in Iran, the disputed territories of Israel, and North Africa. Trouble, and sometimes disaster. In mainstream Judaism, and in Buddhism as well, the most venerable tradition has always been to accept people of all nations who are righteous, whose lives embody peacefulness and probity. The world religions might consider adopting this stance instead of a militancy that usually becomes intemperate and sometimes violent.

I have met and talked with people who could be described as fundamentalist and those who accept the theory of biblical inerrancy. They have impressed me by their fervor and dedication. I don't question that they love God and seek to do good. Experience teaches, though, that having good intentions is not always the same as doing good—even

St. Paul admits failure on that score. For anyone considering this topic at length, I think what emerges is the sense that fundamentalism, the theory of scriptural inerrancy, intolerance, and dogmatic militancy all attest to the presence of fear and the lack of faith. The recurrent impression is of a mentality that doesn't trust God to judge and set things right. It is afraid that if so much as one brick in the edifice of orthodox belief and practice is removed, the whole building will fall. In this frightened and rigid mental framework, critical examination of Scripture is impermissible and "inerrancy" the only acceptable view. Meanwhile this new theory, developed only in the twentieth century, is applied to writings that were, after all, produced by human beings two millennia ago, responding to different pressures at different points in history. To be divinely inspired does not mean that a writer is taking dictation, and certainly none of the evangelists says that he is doing so. The simplest refutation of the inerrancy theory is to point out that the genealogies of Jesus as given in Matthew and Luke do not agree: one of them was in error at least, perhaps both, but in any case, the theory of scriptural inerrancy won't account for the difference, no more than it can account for the differences in the story of the Resurrection as reported in the four gospels. Thank goodness Christian faith doesn't depend on something as peripheral as the factual accuracy of differing genealogies. Any time the whole of Christian faith is attached to any single point of fact, interpretation, or practice, a danger is introduced. A larger sense of the central import of Christianity's good news has to be maintained—that God loves us and that we are meant to love God in turn, and our neighbors (including our enemies) as ourselves. Once we realize that, we can be taught to praise God and God's wonderful works, to be persuaded away from resentment and violence even as we are led to serve others and relieve suffering wherever we find it.

If the mission behind fundamentalism is to bring redemption to a world in need of it, then honest observers will have to acknowledge that the theory of inerrancy has failed in that mission. Instead it has raised up powerful opponents everywhere and prejudiced the chances for wide acceptance of Christianity's central content. Fundamentalism and ultra-orthodoxy do not sum up the vast spectrum of human relationships with the divine. But their prevalence and the media coverage they receive have put up a serious obstacle for the person who might otherwise try to find a path toward faith. Meanwhile, those concerned with free inquiry and reason should, in the name of consistency, be wary of falling into a sort of "negative fundamentalism," in which religious truth is a closed book, not worthy of investigation or reflection.

Earlier in this essay I made a connection between faith and poetry. The connection between them is real for me in more than one sense. During the years when I was an atheist, my view of the universe was as a sort of accident whose properties science could describe and operations predict, with no meaning except what one isolated person through his own subjectivity could attribute to it. I was often prey to a metaphysical vertigo: I saw myself alone, suspended, so to speak, out in the vast emptiness of interstellar space, far from any other solid object, surrounded by darkness. I could flail my arms, or kick, or scream, but I couldn't move because there was nothing to push against. Eventually I was going to die in that condition, and then it would be as though I had never existed at all. The universe, the world and all those in it, would come to an end for me, and then they, too, might just as well have never been. Bleak? Yes, and absolutely terrifying. When I tried to counter this negative vision, I would propose to myself the human value of love, and that would help: Since there is no God, let us love one another and forget the inescapable situation that we are in.

It's impossible to live more than three decades, though, and not realize that human love is inevitably flawed and undependable. I wasn't capable of perfect love and neither was anyone else. Love created as many problems as it solved. Even when I loved and was loved in turn, that didn't console me for terrible events in experience—especially the loss of people close to me and the unavoidable approach of my own death. All right then, I still had my work, the poetry I was beginning to write. As long as I felt engaged by it, that meant I hadn't succumbed to the sort of nihilism that says life is meaningless and our brief little span on earth not particularly important. I also discovered that poetry, because it is communication, retained an ineradicable ethical dimension. Arrogance, violence, and pathology make for bad poetry, even though nihilism might say you can write anything you damn well please. Of course you can. But I discovered that I wasn't interested in art that didn't hold out some promise, or point to the possibility of solutions or consolations for our dilemmas—an art that helped us to enjoy life more or better endure it, as Samuel Johnson said. My "official" position might be nihilistic or despairing, but my poems said something different. They attested to a sense of right and wrong and perhaps to a rudimentary spirituality. Once again, the inability to deceive myself for long came into play, and I realized that I was in a state of self-contradiction.

This brooding, unformed spirituality led me to ask friends

of mine who were practicing Christians what they thought they were doing. One was a professor of English and a Dante scholar, gay, Episcopalian, extraordinarily likeable, and the very opposite of the "American Gothic" image of the Christian. He made it clear that his faith belonged to the affirmative side of his life, something he couldn't imagine living without. Another friend of mine who had been brought up a Mennonite, also gay, had been unchurched for many years and then, because a man he was going out with was a believer, began attending Episcopal services with him and was eventually confirmed as a church member. Later, after that relationship ended, he continued to attend and took things a step farther by becoming a novice in the Franciscan order of the Episcopal church. It seemed strange to me at the time, but, on the other hand, whatever your friends do must be all right, so I tried to keep an open mind. We had been close friends for a number of years. In fact, a poem in my first book titled "The Bridge, Palm Sunday, '73," recounted a walk he and I took together across Brooklyn Bridge. In this poem the question of meaningful existence is posed in terms of the imagination alone, but even so it uses Christian symbols in its unfolding, as the title indicates.

By the early '80s I had to face the fact that I no longer felt I had a clear and reliable view of how life should be lived. Nothing I was used to worked any more, neither simple hedonism, nor drink, nor drugs, nor a smug sense of superiority to those who were believers. When I looked ahead toward three or four more decades of such a life, my stomach turned. One day my friend who had become a Franciscan telephoned and invited me to attend a service at St. Mary's Church on 46th Street in the heart of Manhattan. It was February 2, which is celebrated as the Feast of the Presentation, commemorating the moment in the gospel narrative when Jesus is taken to the rabbis and elders at the Temple and is proclaimed by Simeon and the prophetess Anna to be the Messiah. I remember that the organist began the service with Bach's extraordinarily beautiful "Schmücke dich, meine Seele" chorale prelude. The composer Schumann once played this work for Brahms and then said, "If a man were not a believer, he would become one after hearing this." (In the interval since those days, the essential connection between religion and the arts has become clearer and clearer to me.) The priest and his assistants moved through their liturgy slowly and reverently, the altar grew dim with incense, eloquent words were spoken. I was, as John Wesley once said about a parallel instance in his life, "strangely moved." When the Eucharist was offered to the people, my friend asked me to come up to the altar, but I refused because I wasn't certain that I should participate. That showed at least that I took the meaning of the ceremony seriously, otherwise I might as well please my friend and go through the motions with him without attributing  any significance to it. I said no, but when I left the church the experience followed me.

And so it did the following week. Eventually, I called my friend and asked him what I ought to do if I wanted to look further into the question of religion. He suggested I call and make an appointment with the assistant vicar at St. Peter's Church in Chelsea, not far from where I lived. I did so. This man was a young priest and, as I eventually realized, gay. I explained my doubts to him and was assured that I was entitled to them. As for the question of my sexuality, it was no barrier. He suggested that I come to services and see how I felt about them. This was Lenten season, so over the next several weeks I visited St. Peter's and other churches in the neighborhood. Finally, on Palm Sunday, I went out to meet my Franciscan friend at St. Ann's in Brooklyn Heights, where he was employed part-time. We were joined by another friend of his, a woman seminarian who was also Native American, and who turned out to be one of the most brilliant students of theology I've ever met. (It came as news to me that ordination of women as priests had become part of the Episcopal church's canon law, news I received with a great sense of relief.) The sun shone, music swelled, and so did my heart. This time, when the Host was offered to the people, I went up with my old and new friend, stood between them, and accepted the Body of Christ.

During the following week I attended Tenebrae, Maundy Thursday, and Good Friday services. Finally on Saturday night I attended the Great Vigil of Easter, which begins late at night with the congregation taking a single lighted Paschal Candle into a dark church. Once inside, worshippers light their own candle from it and pass it on to each other in turn. The service included an infant baptism, the liturgy of which summons the faithful to repeat their own baptismal vows. I did so haltingly but willingly. My throat went dry at the words "You are sealed as Christ's own forever." When I left the church, I felt as though I had been launched on an extraordinary adventure. And so it has been. As the fervent aria from Handel's *Messiah* says, echoing Job, "I know that my redeemer liveth."

The decade since these events occurred has had its share of ups and downs, of error and recovery, of sadness and joy. I believe I have learned an enormous amount about faith and the practice of faith, about myself and about others—though not as much as I still hope to learn. One of the high points was marching in the annual Gay Pride parade under the banner of Integrity, the Episcopal gay organization, along with my vicar (who is not gay) and other parishioners gay and straight. The self-acceptance mentioned at the beginning of this essay has at last come, partly through my own efforts, partly through becoming open to God's love, and partly through the support and love of a particular congregation. I now know that I am myself because God wanted me to be who I am, and that God rejoices with me in my life as a gay man. Of course I have my griefs and disappointments as all people do, with the new difference that I don't have to rely on myself alone in working through them. Actually, there is one sorrow that I would like to report here. When going through my daily round through the streets of my neighborhood in Greenwich Village, I will often see a gay man or group of gay men, and, through a proudly displayed pose of insouciance and bravado, I will sense a deep, hidden wound, a wound with consequences for the lives involved. I recognize that look of concealed desperation from remembered moments of my own more than a decade ago. Of course I could risk being thought mentally ill and go up to these strollers and tell them what I know. Even if I didn't frighten them, though, would they readily believe that there was a place for them in today's Church after what they have read in the newspaper? It saddens me to see people just like me, people who might be my co-religionists and friends, left to lead their lives without the sanctions of faith, with almost no guidance except what the media offer them. And I think to myself, Oh if they knew that there was a place they could come to where they would be welcomed as brothers and helped toward a basic sense of joy, how wonderful it would be for them—and for that place! This isn't idle speculation or wishful thinking: I've seen gay men brought into my home parish and slowly come to life under the influence of active concern and love. What next happens is that they begain to give back that devotion; they bring all their energy and talents to the project of adding to parish life and work. If the gay and lesbian members of my congregation (vestry members, sacristans, subdeacons, chairpersons of committees, outreach workers) were suddenly to disappear overnight, I wonder how the parish would manage. These members have become "indispensable." Apart from the question of acquiring useful new members, can we avoid admitting that the Christian mandate of telling good news to a world of suffering and despair calls on the churches of America to make it known to gay men and lesbians that the Church does not vilify them or think they are monsters; that they want these brothers and sisters to come home and receive the love available there?

If we base our attitudes about family life on several prominent scriptural admonitions, we would come to negative conclusions. For example, Jesus, during the marriage at Cana, speaks abruptly to Mary, saying, "Woman, what have I to do with thee?" which echoes the same sense of a separate duty heard in the boy Jesus' statement when his family discovered he was no longer in their party on the return to Nazareth from Jerusalem during the Passover. Jesus expresses surprise at their concern and says, "Why did you look for me? Did you not know that I had to be in my Father's house?" (meaning, of course, the Temple). The twelfth chapter of Matthew concludes with an incident in which Mary and Jesus' brothers are waiting outside the house where Jesus is preaching. When Jesus is told that they want to speak to him, he says, "Who is my mother? and who are my brethren?" Then he stretches out his hand toward his disciples and says, "Behold, my mother and my brethren. For whosoever shall do the will of my Father who is in heaven, that person is my brother, and sister, and mother." The eighth chapter of Matthew also tells of a young scribe who told Jesus he wanted to become a disciple but that he had first to bury his father. To which Jesus answered, "Follow me; and let the dead bury the dead."

St. Paul made his disapproval of marriage plain not only by refusing to marry but also by stating that disapproval outright, allowing for marriage only as a last resort: "It is better to marry than to burn." Of course he did not tell those who were already married to separate. On the contrary, he had constructive suggestions for them, and he saw that Christ intervenes in human life, among other ways, through marriage. For, even though many scriptural teachings contradict any complacent reliance on the family as a substitute for righteousness, I believe that we find support for family values in Christianity if we consider the Christian ethos as a whole, rather than citing particular passages. It may be that individual vocations will demand celibacy for some believers and even sometimes estrangement from a given family, but not in most cases. The family can be one of the strongest instruments in society for the dispensation of divine love and teaching. And so it's not wrong for contemporary congregations to think of the familial model in forming their self-conception and program of action. The spread of the Kingdom is also a spread of Kindom, where all are our brothers and sisters. By the same token, Christian kinship must not be extended to heterosexuals alone.

For three years now, I've been living with my life partner, Christopher, who joined the church after we settled down together and who eventually accepted to serve on the vestry of our parish. We are looking into the possibility of having a ceremony of union, perhaps based on one of the texts given in John Boswell's recent book *Same-Sex Unions in Premodern Europe*, which recounts the history of these unions in the Roman church from the eighth century up to the twentieth.

I realize that the prospect of same-sex unions is a cause of great distress to many Christians. For them, all same-sex relations are sinful, and consecration thereof heinous. I know that they will turn to isolated verses in Leviticus and Paul to prove to me that I have broken God's law. I will in turn ask them why they consider only this proscription in Leviticus binding and no others—for example, avoiding even so much as touching women during menstrual periods, or meals that include both milk and meat. These laws are interesting to study, but they belong to an earlier era in our history and cannot reasonably govern contemporary Christian behavior.

If critics of same-sex relations turn to the writings of St. Paul, I will remind them that Jesus never made any statements about those relationships, for or against. Jesus did speak out firmly against divorce, but most Protestant churches nevertheless accept it, as does the Eastern Orthodox church, and even the Roman church if conditions permitting annulment are satisfied. If despite Scripture Christians do accept divorce, it must be because the Holy Spirit has given different instructions, reminding us of the sacred inviolability of individual human lives and warning us not to make a universal policy depend on a single verse from the Bible. Fundamentalism is strange to me, but selective fundamentalism is stranger still. And I ask those who use scriptural arguments as the basis for prohibiting same-sex relationships whether they may not simply be using the Bible to enforce their own personal dislikes. To say you dislike same-sex couples is one thing; to assert that God considers them automatically sinful is quite another and not something to be undertaken lightly by anyone who remembers Jesus' admonition, "Judge not, that you be not judged."

Of course St. Paul made a number of recommendations that the contemporary church does not follow; for example, he urged slaves to submit to bondage without resistance, and he told women to obey their husbands, not to attend church without covering their heads, and to be silent while there. He said all these things, and yet the weight of his theological argument is opposed to the spirit of law and in favor of grace. Paul was a man of contradictions, then—human, susceptible to error, but, even so, a great saint whose writings are foundational for Christianity. We have to put his assertions within the larger context of a gospel that tells us that God loves us and sent Jesus to us that we might have life and have it more abundantly.

If we believe this, we cannot refuse the blessing of full acceptance into the Christian family to those of variant sexual orientation. We are all God's children; God chooses our brothers and sisters, not we. But I want to conclude by saying as firmly as possible that, if I have a different opinion from some of my orthodox or fundamentalist brothers and sisters, that doesn't entitle me to hate them or treat them with violence or disrespect. God loves all of us equally. For that very reason I trust that the Holy Spirit will move opponents on this issue closer to understanding each other. I can see that I have written much of this essay in a spirit of persuasion, but the truth is, it isn't up to me to persuade anyone. God is doing what I could never do. For the justice and unity that is certain to come I give thanks, as I do for the truth and grace that has made me free.

🕸 PHILIP GAMBONE

# SEARCHING FOR REAL WORDS

Squeezed onto a parcel of prime real estate in the midst of the retail and financial district of downtown Boston is the Franciscan Shrine of St. Anthony. Except for the enormous bronze crucifix that hangs above the entrance, St. Anthony's Shrine—also known by its address, Arch Street—is a fairly unremarkable building, typical of so much Catholic architecture built during that heyday of Boston Catholicism, the reign of Cardinal Cushing. From the outside, it has the look and feel of fifties functionalism: a flat sandstone facade, a bank of aluminum, and glass fire doors. Even the wall of frosted glass windows that fronts the sidewalk, each window depicting one of the saints, is bland and unobtrusive.

During my boyhood, services at St. Anthony's were unobtrusively functional, too. Arch Street specialized in "quickie" masses: in and out in under half an hour. Because of its two chapels, "upstairs" and "downstairs," a person could be sure of finding at least one mass in progress at any time of the day and well into the evening.

It was to Arch Street that my parents would sometimes take the family when, for one reason or another, we had missed mass at our own parish in a suburb north of the city. This most often happened during the spring and summer.

Having spent the weekend at our cottage on Cape Cod, we would race back up to Boston to catch the last mass at Arch Street, thereby fulfilling our Sunday obligation. It must have been during those years that I learned that a mass didn't "count" unless you were present by the time the Gospel was read.

This kind of obligatory, letter-of-the-law Catholicism pretty much describes the religion I grew up with. As a boy, I went along with it unquestioningly; and why not, since, as the nuns had taught us in Sunday school, Roman Catholicism was the "true religion," the religion Christ had established once and for all for His people on earth.

There were, of course, many comforts to be had in this kind of thinking, not the least of which was that it removed most—if not all—of the ambiguity about who one was and how one needed to behave in this world. I grew up with a clear understanding that God wanted me to be a "good boy," which pretty much meant that I should not transgress His laws and the laws of His Holy Catholic church. Although I was not particularly pious or devoted, I did my best to learn my Baltimore Catechism (I can still picture its dark blue cover), to obey my parents, and to "love God with my whole heart and soul and mind and strength."


With the onset of puberty, all this began to change. I was still, publicly, a "good boy," but the demands of the flesh and the fantasies of my imagination led me into carnal temptations and "sins." Catholics grow up with a clear understanding of the difference between love and lust. We hear countless exemplary stories of the many virgin saints who willingly suffered martyrdom for Christ rather than submit to the lascivious importunities of some pagan Roman soldier. As a young adolescent, I extrapolated a harsh personal code from these tales: Erotic pleasure of any kind violated the true purpose of the body, which was to be a "temple of Christ." And so, while no one ever officially taught me that masturbation was a sin, by the time I was twelve, I was dutifully including in my Saturday confessions the "impure thoughts and actions" I'd committed that week.

"Alone or with others?" the priest would ask.

At first, I masturbated alone, thinking about other boys in my junior-high class, or in one case, the older, football-playing brother of a junior-high friend. But by eighth grade, I'd found a jerk-off buddy, a boy in my Confirmation class. Every Tuesday, after we had sat through another lesson about the sacrament the bishop would confer upon us that spring, we'd go to my house or his and "mess around."

I soon became aware of the fact that these sessions meant very different things to each of us. For "Timmy," our mutual masturbation was just a way of getting off, a convenience, a buddy-buddy kind of thing. "Well of course," my friend David, an ex-Catholic himself, recently told me. "Pulling it is one of the major activities of all Catholic adolescent boys."

But for me, "pulling it" with Timmy meant something more. At least I wanted it to mean something more. And although I didn't have the words to describe what I was feeling, for me there was a dimension to our weekly clandestine get-togethers that went beyond the casual. In some unverbalized way, I understood that erotically touching another boy—being with a boy that way—was going to be a fundamental, inescapable aspect of who I was.

Timmy's and my jerk-off sessions came to an abrupt demise when, toward the end of that eighth-grade year, he announced that he thought we were getting too old for "that sort of thing." Awkwardly, hesitantly, inarticulately, I tried to dissuade him from his line of reasoning, but he wouldn't hear of it. I heard panic in his voice—maybe even some disgust. The fact that he was an altar boy (and I wasn't) made it worse: Clearly he was a better Catholic than I, one who had mustered the moral fortitude to turn away from such sins. We remained friends throughout high school but were never as close as we'd been that year of our Confirmation. There was always an edgy tone to the spirit of friendship he tried to show me, as if too much chumminess on his part would be misinterpreted by me.

For the next five years, I managed to sublimate my erotic feelings for boys by busying myself in school work and a host of after-school activities. If there's a simple explanation as to why lots of gay teenagers (at least in those days, the late sixties) got so involved in drama, music, student government, and the like, I think it's this: that "extracurriculars" were a good distraction from the yearnings we were trying to cope with, feelings that had no name and no foreseeable outlet.

Of course, I still thought about boys, and continued to jerk off, and continued to confess my sin.

"Five times, Father."

"Alone or with others?"

"Alone."

"It's the seed, wanting to come out, the seed that God has planted in you, whose proper use is for the procreation of children with your wife after marriage."

"Yes, Father."

Early on the morning of June 5, 1968, at the end of my sophomore year at Harvard, after working all night on a term paper, I turned on the radio to take a break and listen to some music. The paper, like so many of my assignments that year, was long overdue: the result of procrastination, self-doubt and the increasingly unavoidable distractions of my unrequited homosexual inclination. My two roommates had already left for summer vacation. The suite of rooms we occupied was empty and quiet, as was the entire dorm. I was lonely, exhausted, feeling lost. How appropriate that the paper I'd been trying to finish was on the second book of Dante's *Divine Comedy,* the "Purgatorio."

The radio program was interrupted by an emergency bulletin. Robert Kennedy, the leading candidate for the Democratic Party's nomination for President, had been shot and gravely wounded shortly after making a victory speech in the California primary. He was not expected to live.

I was stunned. Though I did not take a great interest in politics, it had been impossible to ignore Kennedy's candidacy and what it stood for. Since my sophomore year in high school, when John F. Kennedy had been assassinated, I'd witnessed a series of national and international crises that had challenged the cozy, suburban world view I'd grown up with. The escalation of the Vietnam War, the race riots in Watts and Newark, the assassination of Martin Luther King, Jr., and student unrest at colleges across the country—all of these events made it increasingly difficult for me to see the world as a place that made sense, that could be relied on for comfort and joy and justice. Bobby Kennedy's run for the presidency had promised to bring some peace and sanity back into the American—and into *my*—psyche.

The next thing I remember I was on the subway headed for Boston. It must have been one of the first trains out of Harvard Square that morning. Early commuters filled the car. They looked somber, but I couldn't tell whether their expressions were full of grief over the attack on Kennedy or grimness about another work day looming ahead. Tears were streaming down my face. I remember wondering if anyone would notice and what they would think, though I didn't care. My sorrow was too intense.

I got off at Park Street and, still in a daze, wandered through the shopping district, until I came to Arch Street. It was the only place where I knew I could find a mass being said so early in the morning.

I prayed for Kennedy's recovery. But I was praying for myself, too. It had been six years since I had had sex with another boy. In all that time, I had not been able to put an end to my many feverish, hopeless, secret crushes on guys. As so many of us who came out during those pre-Stonewall years, I thought I was alone. I did not know any other gay people. I did not know about gay bars. I did not know about gay newspapers or organizations. What I did know is that I could not stop my feelings.

I had certainly tried to stop them: with good resolves, and acts of contrition, and immersion into school work. By that spring, I'd even begun to hang out with students affiliated with Opus Dei, the arch-conservative Catholic lay organization. Harvard had inculcated enough liberal secularism in me that I never completely bought into Opus Dei's agenda. Nevertheless, the spiritual and intellectual camaraderie of the fellows I met at Opus Dei, many of whom lived in an elegantly appointed residence a few blocks from Harvard Square, seduced me sufficiently that, for most of my sophomore year, I'd been trying to model myself after them.

Lonely, confused, and feeling utterly disenfranchised from the kinds of pleasures—romantic love, marriage, family—that straight men enjoyed and that were sanctioned by the Church, I rediscovered through Opus Dei the promise of an even better enfranchisement. "I have come that ye may have life and have it more abundantly," Christ said. Yes, that was it! There was something *far more real* than my sexual desire, something that would deliver me out of the pain of my loneliness and frustration and heartache. The abundant life Christ offered, the life that was available through adherence to the doctrines of the Church, was the true life I had been longing for all along. The pleasures a boy could offer were nothing in comparison to the Life that was Christ.

In retrospect, my attraction to Opus Dei had as much to do with the physical attractiveness of several of its members (one of whom, a doe-eyed boy with a beautiful smile, I was in love with) as it did with their theology. I tried to be just like the doe-eyed boy—calm, scholarly, ascetic, chaste. Without being aware of it, I was trying to seduce him with the only seductive quality I thought I had: virtue.

By the time of Bobby Kennedy's assassination, I had driven myself nearly crazy with ascetic practices—praying the rosary with the Opus Dei boys, going to mass, refraining from masturbation—yet none of these things had put a stop to the sexual urges that kept churning within me. The distraught feelings I brought to St. Anthony's Shrine that June morning were, in fact, more about my failure to become like the Opus Dei students than about the impending death of another American hero.

Something shifted for me that sad June morning, a subtle change that, at first, I couldn't possibly have recognized or named. It began with the fact that I felt no consolation from the mass that I'd sped to in such pain and need. The Holy Mysteries remained just that, mysteries—cold, inscrutable, unyielding—a bunch of overly familiar words that, to my senses, had no power to change anything. Kennedy died the following day, my feelings for boys would not leave me alone, and the urgent call of masturbation kept insinuating itself during all my waking hours. All my efforts to turn my life around during that lonely, distracted sophomore year had been for naught.

And so, a few days later, with Bobby Kennedy dead and my Dante paper finally completed and joylessly turned in, I packed up the accumulation of my second year at Harvard—books, notes, clothes, good intentions, and saintly resolutions—and returned home. Three weeks later, I was on my way across the state, to Lenox, where I had a small administrative job at Tanglewood, the summer home of the Boston Symphony Orchestra. It was to be the summer that changed my life.

As soon as I arrived at Tanglewood, I knew I had made the right decision: an entire summer in the bucolic loveliness of the Berkshire hills, my first real paying job, a chance to live on my own. I needed this respite from the intense self-criticism I'd put myself through in Cambridge.

I shared an apartment with a guy I'll call "Andrew." Three years older than I, he was someone I had known briefly in college, before he graduated during my freshman year. Now, like me, he had been hired as a kind of factotum for the Tanglewood administration. Blond, blue-eyed, and boyishly lanky, Andrew was exactly the body type that turned me on. He was also the kind of person who turned me on: smart, witty, talented. Andrew was a pianist, an organist, a conductor, a composer, and a gourmet cook. Although he'd majored in music, he knew more about literature than I, an English major. It's not an exaggeration to say he seemed godlike to me.

I soon learned that come September Andrew would start

graduate studies at the Episcopal Theological School in Cambridge. When our conversations weren't about music, they were about religion. We talked about the Church, about the differences between Catholicism and Episcopalianism, which Andrew claimed *was* Catholicism, the English—as opposed to the Roman—branch of Catholicism. We talked about transubstantiation, papal infallibility, the sacraments.

Eventually, we got to talking about the Church's attitude toward sex. Andrew took a scornful view of the "Roman" Church's teachings on matters of sex. All those strictures against contraception, masturbation, premarital sex, sex for pleasure—"they're silly, antiquated, medieval," he said. "Homosexuality, too."

All of this talk was academic, but my heart was pounding with excitement. If Andrew was sending signals in my direction, I didn't know it (after all, I had no context in which to read any signals), but his words were enough to set me dreaming about the possibility of living with permission—*theological* permission, no less!—to accept and enjoy my homosexuality. Here was someone I admired and respected (not to mention someone I found very cute), a guy who was about to study for the priesthood, who was telling me it might be all right, at least in the context of deep and abiding affection, to make love to another man.

From the hindsight of over twenty-five years, I now realize that Tanglewood was full of gay men that summer, including our boss, a man in his late thirties who used to invite Andrew and me to boozy, late-night parties at his summer home on a lake in a neighboring village. There were always lots of young men at these parties—musicians, singers, other office staffers—and eventually a suggestion would arise that we all go skinny-dipping in the lake. The pagan sensuality of those mild Berkshire evenings—the conviviality of the parties, the dark, starry sky, the naked swimming, the beautiful young men—worked their magic. I was utterly happy. The parties would break up late and Andrew and I would tipsily drive the mountain roads in his VW bug back to our apartment, where we'd fall into our respective beds (we had side-by-side twin beds) to sleep off the white Russians or rusty nails or whatever else we'd been drinking.

And then one warm July night, as Andrew and I were returning home from one of these parties, our talk once again turned to religion and sex. Even after we got to the apartment and were changing for bed, we kept talking. Even after Andrew turned off the light. It was then that I had an inkling that our conversation wasn't entirely academic. Giddy with alcohol and horniness, I embraced my pillow, hugging it close to my chest, imagining what it would be like to be holding Andrew that close.

"So you're saying that if two men really love each other—I mean, like with a holy, selfless love—then it wouldn't be a sin for them to sleep together?" I asked.

"Yes."

I think I was quiet for a while. And then I must have giggled, because Andrew asked me what was the matter.

"Andrew," I asked tremulously, "can I crawl into bed with you?"

"Sure," he said.

To paraphrase Dante, that night we talked no more.

Idyllic is the only word to describe the rest of our summer. Each morning Andrew and I would get up, muss the bed we hadn't slept in (just in case someone came by while we were out!), and go to our office jobs in the Victorian Main House on the Tanglewood grounds. Music from the BSO rehearsals across the Great Lawn came over the intercom system, and there I'd sit, enveloped in glorious music and the tingling sensations of first love, typing program notes or tabulating the results of an audience survey, all the while trying not to show how in love I was. In the afternoons or on weekends, Andrew and I would drive out into the country—sometimes as far away as Vermont—for picnics and al fresco love-making.

It was impossible for me not to find a religious dimension in that first love affair. I felt blessed, graced, smiled upon with divine permission to love this man. Nothing in my Catholic education had prepared me to feel that way. Indeed, it should have been otherwise. So many other Catholic gay men I know agonized through their first homosexual experiences, repressed them, fought them, sublimated them, repented of them. Why was I so lucky as to escape all that? In part, I'm sure, it was the idyllic context in which Andrew and I conducted our affair. More so, it was the fact that I could trust him: his intellect and his comfort with his religion. To be able to *relax* with one's faith—especially, to be a gay man and relax with one's faith—seemed extraordinary to me. Rather than guilt, I had found God.

🦋 We were together, on and off, for about five years. During that time, Andrew earned his degree at the Theological School and I finished my undergraduate education at Harvard. There was still no possibility of our being open about our love, but increasingly I was invited into his circle of friends, most of whom were serious Episcopalians. Under the circumstances, it was only a matter of time before I fell in love with his church, too.

What attracted me to the Episcopal church, at least that small segment of it that I found in Cambridge during those final years of the sixties, was its comfort with—indeed its celebration of—the physicality of the world. I remember Andrew showing me a cookbook by an Episcopal priest, Father Robert Capon, called *The Supper of the Lamb*. The very fact that a priest—whom I had always thought of as pious and ascetic—would write a cookbook astounded me. Father Capon's message thrilled me all the more. The "theology" of the cookbook was that food is another kind of sacrament, another mediator of God's grace and love.

Everywhere I turned in Andrew's Episcopal world, I found more of the same: permission to be fully in my body, fully in the material world. The sensual stuff of the world—music, food, nature, and (at least privately) sex—all of it was part of God's creation, God's "plan" for His world. It was *good*. More to the point, there was an *incarnational* aspect to all this: the world and all its pleasures were good, not in some hedonistic, pagan sense but because it was the physical manifestation of Christ. *Deus caro factus est*. As God had become flesh, so too the world's delights—especially sex— were the "enfleshment" of the Divine.

I needed this divine permission. It was the only way I could come to accept my homosexuality.

By the time Andrew and I left Cambridge and moved to the Midwest (he to teach music, I to teach English), I was thinking of myself as an Episcopalian and, sometime around 1972, I agreed to being admitted into the Church, at a ceremony that took place one Sunday in the Episcopal Cathedral in Kansas City. Becoming an Episcopalian, which technically made me an apostate Catholic in danger of ex-communication, was not a difficult step. I did not think of myself as leaving the Church but only of entering into a different (only *slightly* different, I reminded myself) "communion"—the Anglican communion. In an era of radical politics and cultural rebellion, in an era when gay people were beginning to fight for enormous changes, joining the Episcopal church was my squeaky little rebellion, a rebellion that I had convinced myself had a sound theological basis.

This need to understand and explain my homosexual self in a theological context was the only way I could accept the feelings and behaviors I found myself trying to deal with. There was a kind of elaborate strategem involved here—an almost Jesuitical circumvention of the plain truth. In the eyes of the Church in which I had grown up, what I was doing—this homosexual life I was leading with Andrew—was wrong. But, by the neat trick of replacing my childhood Catholicism with a Catholicism that I had convinced myself was as legitimate, if not more so (even if it was somewhat unorthodox), I could have my cake and eat it too.

After Andrew and I split up, I continued to be an Episcopalian. In fact, a year after we separated, in the fall of 1974, I began my own formal theological studies at the very school that Andrew had graduated from a few years before, now rechristened the Episcopal Divinity School. But already the rosy glow of my first years as an Episcopalian had begun to fade. These were years of intense controversy in the Episcopal church. The ordination of women and homosexuals was being hotly debated. The church that I thought I had entered—a church that supposedly was about love and tolerance—was showing its true colors. And while the spirit on the EDS campus was liberal, the institution as a whole was decidedly more conservative.

Nevertheless, my two years in divinity school gave me a chance to refine my thinking about homosexuality and the Church. There were several theologians then writing—in particular, I remember Norman Pittenger and Malcolm Boyd—whose work was an attempt to reconcile Christian faith and homosexuality. Inspired by such writers and encouraged by my professors, I wrote most of my course papers on various aspects of gay life and the Church. I doubt that there were many seminaries in those days that would have allowed me such freedom of thought.

There was also a significant gay and lesbian population among the student body at EDS, some out of the closet, some painfully in for fear that their bishops would never ordain them. As a group, we met fairly regularly for conversation and socializing. Boston is a theologian's paradise: There are over a dozen schools of theology in the area, loosely affiliated through an umbrella organization called the Boston Theological Institute. Gay seminarians from several of the schools in the BTI also used to meet for support and discussion. I think most of us were looking for boyfriends, too.

All of this was heady and wonderful. I saw myself participating in what the Brazilian theologian Paolo Friere called "the pedagogy of the oppressed." It was about this time, too, that I started writing for a gay newspaper in Boston, *Gay Community News*. By default, I became their unofficial reporter on religion, contributing pieces on gay Jesuits fighting for ordination and other such topics. By the time I graduated from EDS, with a Master of Theological Studies, I was something of an expert on matters of homosexuality and the Church. At the same time, I was very much *not* an expert in the nitty-gritty of sex and dating and relationships. My preoccupation with religious studies had kept me from knowing myself—my feelings, my needs—in some basic and fundamental ways.

It would be easy to be dismissive of this period in my life. It would be easy to say that I was indulging in elaborate "mind games," games that began way back on that first night when, trembling with excitement and fear, I crawled into bed with Andrew and told myself, "God wants this." It would be easy to say that my pilgrimage through Catholicism and Episcopalianism was just a way to avoid asking myself what it was that I really wanted. It would be easy to say that what I really wanted was just a boyfriend, or sex, or a way to feel acceptable. It would be easy to say all this, but I'm not sure it would sum up everything that I was struggling with. I'm not sure I wouldn't be leaving out part of the story.

 I remained an Episcopalian for several more years, encouraged in part by the fact that my second lover, a man I'll call "Alfred," was another practicing Episcopalian. (It would be easy to come up with a psychological explanation for this, too.)

Alfred and I lived on Beacon Hill, just a few blocks from one of the most famous Anglo-Catholic churches in the country, the Church of the Advent. In those days, the late seventies and early eighties, the Advent's congregation was made up almost exclusively of gay men and Boston Brahmins, a strange and tenuous coalition at best. What brought these unlikely factions together was a shared passion for the Mass—for the mystery of the Mass, and for its high church aesthetic. The Advent knew how to "do it right." Every genuflection, every reverencing of the altar, every swish of the thurible was done with utmost style and taste and dignified seriousness. There was, in so much of this fastidious attention to the choreography of the Mass, a preciousness that bordered on the ludicrous. But we told ourselves—and I suppose there was truth in this—that all of the pomp and circumstance, the "smells and bells," as we called it, was for the "greater glory of God." The same could be said of my "marriage" to Alfred: it was a scenario of domestic decorum and utter tastefulness that, more often than not, substituted for an intimacy we never managed to achieve.

It still amazes and embarrasses me that I took so long to see how precious and silly and stiff my religious life had become. Or how stiff my marriage had become. It still amazes me that I could tolerate the stultifying atmosphere of either for as long as I did. But the truth is, I was still looking to Catholicism (Anglo-Catholicism in this case) to keep me in check, to speak my life for me.

Why did I feel I needed that kind of reining in? What was I afraid I would lose if I cut loose from either the Church or Alfred? What did I think I was getting from them that was so absolutely necessary?

Eventually I drifted away from the Advent—a drifting away that paralleled the start of my drifting away from Alfred. *Mirabile dictu,* I drifted back into the arms of Holy Mother Church once again!

At first, I went to the Paulist Center on Park Street (whose congregation was mainly comprised of disaffected Catholics); then back to the Franciscans at Arch Street; to the Jesuits in the South End; thence to Harvard Square, to St. Paul's, the parish that serves the considerable Catholic student population at Harvard; and finally to Dignity, the gay Catholic organization. Each move felt like a step closer to something more "authentic," closer into a community that was struggling with the same spiritual issues I was. For by now I was beginning to understand that my search was not so much a search for the right denomination or parish as it was for a mode of spirituality that would clear away all the bullshit and let God truly speak.

"I want real words, not this rhetoric of inane piety," Richard Gilman writes in his memoir *Faith, Sex, Mystery.* That's what I was looking for, too—real words from myself, real words from God. How ironic that the realest words I had to speak in those days were words I needed to tell Alfred, but couldn't: "I want out of this relationship!"

By the time Alfred and I split up (it took my having an affair with another man, my current lover, Bill, to pull it off), I was again feeling the old restlessness with regard to religion. Dignity, where I'd been going for about three years, seemed bogged down in the same kind of stuff that had turned me off to the Advent: debates about how "Catholic" the organization should be. I drifted away once more, and have been free-floating ever since.

Free-floating, but with summer sojourns at the largely gay Unitarian-Universalist Meeting House in Provincetown, where Bill and I have spent the past four summers. At first the services at the Meeting House were some of the most exhilarating religious experiences I'd ever had. Here, finally, was what I'd been looking for all along: a place where "real words" were spoken. Most of all, I was deeply moved by that part of the service called the "congregational response," when anyone could get up and speak. And speak they did: about joys and sorrows, struggles and accomplishments, about the most personal and intimate moments of their lives. Many times I was moved to tears.

But gradually even that exhilaration wore off, and by the summer of 1993, when Bill and I took a house quite a distance from the Meeting House and AIDS left him too sick to attend most Sundays, we both just stopped going.

I'm not the kind of person who needs a religious "high" every Sunday. In fact, if anything, what I missed during my three-summer sojourn with the Unitarians was the "ordinariness" of the Mass, its predictability, and the opportunity it presents for someone to be with his or her own thoughts and prayers. I missed the idea that my participation, or lack thereof, did not affect the profound mystery that takes place at every Eucharist. Yes, I missed that sense of mystery—that sense of the universe as a place that cannot be taken at face value—which seems to be at the heart of what is best in Catholicism.

※ Toward the end of his great Catholic novel, *Brideshead Revisited,* Evelyn Waugh inserts the story of the final days of Sebastian Flyte, "the joyful youth with the teddy bear" who had been the best friend of the novel's narrator-protagonist, Charles Ryder. Sebastian, a homosexual, and his German friend Kurt go to Greece, where, for a while, they lead a happy life—"bathing in the Mediterranean, sitting about in cafés"—until the Nazis round up Kurt and ship him home. Unable to rescue Kurt, Sebastian resumes his former dissolute bouts of heavy drinking. Eventually he makes his way to Tunis. Drunk and ill, he's taken in by the Superior of a monastery and allowed to hang on as a kind of under-porter, "a familiar figure pottering round with his broom and his bunch of keys."

Cordelia, Sebastian's sister, who is telling the story, ends by speculating about Sebastian's death: "Then one morning, after one of his drinking bouts, he'll be picked up at the gate dying, and show by a mere flicker of the eyelid that he is conscious when they give him the last sacraments. It's not such a bad way of getting through one's life."

Cordelia is Waugh's spokesperson for the Catholic interpretation of life's meaning. Her point is that, in the eyes of the Church, Sebastian is not a tragic figure, for in his degradation and abject humility he has achieved a kind of holiness. His final acceptance of the sacrament, which rescues him from eternal perdition, epitomizes this.

This scene has always struck me as one of the most stunning moments in this stunning novel. With great dramatic economy, Waugh manages to get at the essence of the Catholic message: that "salvation" (our ultimate reality and destination) does not hang on worldly or personal achievements of any kind. There is another factor, another dimension, operating in our lives that means more. Catholicism is gloriously clear about the fact that he who has the most toys at the end is not necessarily the real winner.

I want to be rigorously unsentimental about this. I want to say that my nostalgia for a sacramental religion is just that, a piece of nostalgia that I must get big enough to overcome. I want to say that the Church as I know it today—the Church of papal encyclicals against homosexuality, the Church of an all-male celibate clergy, the Church in whose name all manner of oppression and intolerance continues to be practiced—that that Church is an irrelevancy in my life. I want to say that I wish it a swift death.

And yet . . .

❧ A little while ago, I returned to Arch Street. I hadn't been there in years. Ostensibly, I went just to check on a few architectural details for the opening paragraph of this essay. Yes, the doors were just as I had remembered them—as plain and functional as the doors to a post office or an elementary school.

But as it happened, it was Holy Saturday, and the Great Easter Vigil was in progress in the upstairs chapel. I decided to go in. I'll just stand in the back and have a look for a minute or two, I told myself. I arrived in time for the Gospel. (Whimsically, I noted to myself that this mass would "count," if I wanted it to.) When the officiant invited us to join in the renewal of the baptismal vows and asked, "Do you reject the glamour of evil," something opened my voice and I joined the congregation in declaring, "I do." I took Communion, too, and, at the end, sang the final hymn, "Vigiles et Sancti," with gusto. It was all very familiar.

I don't think I'm about to become a practicing Catholic again. As much as I enjoyed reliving the Mass, a lot of it left me cold. I could not assent to all the words—I did not say the Creed—but something was happening at that Vigil that would have seemed almost sacrilegious to ignore. I do not know what that "something" is. I can't even say I felt it. And yet . . .


   "Do you think God will throw you away?" Gilman is asked by his French confessor. "You know," the confessor continues, "it is such a mystery how belief of the kind you describe comes and goes. We cannot know why we have it—except that it comes through grace—or why we can lose it. But really it is never lost, it only makes itself unknown for a while . . . although I admit it can be a long while."

As far as religion goes, I do not know what my next step will be. Even to say that I am "waiting" to take that step seems like a more deliberate posture than I feel I am taking. But if there is a God—and even that is up for grabs with me these days—then I firmly believe that She is not about to throw me away.

This is why, I suppose, when Bill (who is also a lapsed Catholic) got even sicker this winter, he and I both thought it might be a good idea to talk to a Catholic priest. Not for confession, not for absolution or the sacrament, but because—and now this is my understanding, not necessarily

Bill's—because if there is a God who does not throw us away, then a priest seemed like the kind of person who might help us (me?) to be open to that presence again. With a little calling around, I found a gay Jesuit, and, as of this writing, he has been to visit us a few times.

The first time they met, Bill wanted some questions answered about Heaven and Hell, about sins he'd committed or thought he had committed, about what his homosexuality meant in the scheme of eternity. It's hard for me to know how anxious he was about these things—issues that don't concern me at all now—but I know he was satisfied with their conversation. The second time they got together, Bill was ready to talk about his funeral, the music he wanted, the kind of casket, the reception afterwards back at the house.

"I want it to be the biggest and best party I've ever given," he told the priest. "I have to make sure it's all planned the way I want it, because"—he chuckled—"I won't be there to check up on things!"

At their most recent visit, the priest, whose name is John, gingerly brought up the idea that Bill might like to take the sacrament some time. I have no idea whether Bill will follow up on this, whether it will be important to him. I have no idea if it would be important to me. I have no idea if the Eucharist will ever be as important to me as it once was.

But there is something about John's presence in Bill's— and my—life right now that does seem important.

On the last page of his memoir, after he has been away from the Church for twenty-five years, Gilman writes, "[I]t isn't quite the power of repentance I'm hoping for, nor, whatever my distress, do I anguish over my possible damnation. I want to be 'saved' (who would wish to be lost?), but outside the temple I don't know what that means anymore. I only know that I don't want to die as an act purely of nature, of this world."

Perhaps this is why I have asked John to be with Bill during these final weeks and months, why I have asked him to be in my life, too. I don't want Bill to die as an act purely of nature. I want to believe that none of us dies that way.

And right now, those are the realest words I can say about my religious life as a gay man.

**❀** FENTON JOHNSON

# GOD, GAYS, AND THE GEOGRAPHY OF DESIRE

After eight children my parents had run out of ideas for names, so they gave me over for naming to the monks at the nearby Trappist monastery of Our Lady of Gethsemani, the rural Kentucky abbey where Thomas Merton wrote. In the 1950s, the Trappists more rigidly observed the rule of silence and mortification of the flesh. They spoke only at prayer or in emergency; they slept on pallets in unheated rooms; they fasted on not much more than bread and water throughout Lent and on all Fridays. My father, a maintenance worker at a local distillery, delivered to the monastery the bourbon the monks used in the fruitcakes they baked and sold to raise money. The monks appreciated my father's studied casualness in counting the bottles; for his part, my father preferred their company to the responsibilities of parenting his sprawling brood.

Within months of their acquaintance, some of those monks became regulars at our dining table. Through various subterfuges they slipped from the abbey to make their ways to our house, managing to arrive just before supper. *They* got the pork chops, *we* got fried baloney, but still as children we adored their company. For the most part they were educated men, Yankees from impossibly exotic places (Cleveland, Detroit, Trenton), who stayed late into the evening drinking beer, smoking cigarettes, watching football on television, and talking, talking, talking.

Brother A. was fond of a fake grass skirt someone had sent my mother from Hawaii. When the moon was right and the whiskey flowing, he donned the skirt and some hot pink plastic leis, then hoisted my mother to the tabletop and climbed up after. There she sang "Hard-Hearted Hannah" ("the vamp of Savannah, G-A!"), while Brother A. swayed his hips and waved his hands in mock hula. Later he launched into Broadway tunes, warbling in falsetto with his arms thrown around one or more of his brother monks.

Brother Fintan, my namesake, was a baker who made elaborate cakes for each of my birthdays until I was five, around which time he left the monastery for never-explained reasons. Years later he returned for a New Year's visit, accompanied by a handsome young man.

I was sixteen years old. I'd understood since earliest consciousness my own attraction to men, but in this I thought myself alone. Growing up gay in an isolated hill town, I had never encountered so much as a hint that others might share my particular landscape in the geography of desire. I understood this as the defining fact of my life: the utter invisibility of any resonant construct of passionate adult love. As a gay teenager, I found nowhere a model for the love that most profoundly elevates; the love that so often fuels art; the love that finally underscores our notion of God itself, love whose nurturing and dissemination forms (along with familial and platonic love) the literal and spiritual heart of contemporary religion. As far as I was concerned, passionate love was something other people felt. In my quiet way, I considered the books I'd read, the television shows and commercials I'd seen, my classmates' vocal heterosexuality, the models offered by my religion. I concluded that I was an aberration, one of a kind, an emotional eunuch with a heart of stone.

Then Fintan and his companion appeared.

My family received them with their customary hospitality and enthusiasm and food and drink. More monks arrived to visit their old companion—there was dancing on the table; we trotted out the skirt and leis for Brother A., now in need of a stool to climb to the tabletop but otherwise as sinuous and campy as ever.

Afterwards I listened for the customary post-party gossip. Had Fintan arrived with a woman, the household would have been abuzz: *Who is she? Might they get married?* Had he brought a mere friend, there would have been idle chatter: *Nice man. Needs a haircut.* But: Nothing. My namesake and his companion might never have sat at our table.

In my small town among garrulous Southerners, only one subject invoked a silence so vast and deliberate. That night I went to bed understanding that Fintan and his companion were lovers. Which meant that I was perhaps not the freak of nature I had until then believed myself to be; I was not alone.

I find something poignant and fiercely right in my owing, to my namesake and (in a manner of speaking) to the Church, my discovery that this essential fact of myself—my sexuality; more than that, my capacity for passionate love—had a correspondent in the outside world; maybe even a name. Those who have survived adolescence: Consider what it might mean at sixteen years old, suddenly to be snatched into the light, the rabbit jerked from the dark hat of profound loneliness into an understanding that one is not alone; that one might love and be loved, in fact, in the ways that one's heart, soul, and body have already imagined.

❧ All this, of course, has nothing to do with religion. Or has it? For a thousand years and more the Church had reserved a place for me. Youngest son of a large family, introspective, intellectual, gay, I was the perfect candidate for what the French call *"le donné"*—the youngest child given over to the religious orders, the family's gift to God. The turbulent 1960s changed all that—instead of aspiring to the priesthood, I aspired to be a hippie (arguably a similar profession in different costume). Still: I was marked by the role, even as I evaded it.

I want to make emphatically clear that my rather extensive experience with the religious orders lends no support to the notion of cloisters or convents where sexuality runs rampant. I have no idea and do not care whether the monks and nuns of my childhood were sexually active. I know only that, by any reasonable standard, many were gay men and lesbians, drawn to the institution that historically had provided them a place to retreat.

We're surrounded these days by folks who look back with vocal nostalgia to what they imagine as times of religious harmony, which lacked the fractious dissension and doubt that plague contemporary Christianity. The harmony was a sham, of course, built on the mutual and collective participation in a lie. Everyone knew, had they stopped to think, that some of the monks, and the Baptist church organist, and the spinster librarian, and the close-cropped phys. ed. teacher were gay. But no one stopped to think—society and religion depended on and enforced that thoughtlessness. (Having witnessed both, I can point out its analogue—the complacent paternalism white Southerners so often exercised toward "our blacks.")

The emergence of lesbians and gay men into the light faces contemporary organized religion with the challenge, never easy, of accommodating truth. This is what makes it so exciting to be gay *and* out in the 1990s—the simple fact of declaring oneself advances the cause of truth, so crucial to what George Eliot called "the growing good of the world." Well into the age of technology, who would have thought it possible to be a kind of Galileo? Yet here we are, living, omnipresent evidence of a fact of life far more obvious than the heliocentric planetary system—with Brother Fintan and his handsome companion, who needed a telescope?—but apparently just as difficult for Christianity to accept.

In looking at gays' and lesbians' place in Christianity, I want to make clear my concerns: not the overpublicized arguments over public sex, or promiscuous sex, or the purported decline in morality, sexual or otherwise. Whether or not these issues warrant discussion, they apply to and ought properly to consider heterosexual as well as homosexual conduct. Throughout what follows I will limit myself to writing on Christianity—the only religion I know in depth. And, though Christianity provides individual spiritual guidance, I will limit myself to considering the public stance its organized, collective institutions preach toward sexually active gays and lesbians.

Along the way I will write as much of love as of religion. This is not confusion on my part but a deliberate focusing of attention where it belongs. For what is (or ought to be) contemporary, institutionalized Christianity but the communal celebration of love in its multitude of manifestations? Religion serves as the collective repository and arbiter of community morality, yes, but in Judeo-Christian history this has been marked by a progression from preoccupation with ritual and social custom (e.g., dietary laws, circumcision) to a more general concern with the importance of love as the foundation of human community.

What I am writing about—what organized religion properly concerns itself with—is the collective acknowledgment and encouragement of the ways through which we express love for another, and our collective awe at the mystery that has brought us together. What I am writing about is the institutionalized exclusion of men and women, gays and lesbians, from the religious community on the basis of one of those means of expressing love and awe. What I am writing about is not sex but love.

❧ Like many lesbians and gays, I do not attend church, in part because I actively abhor the notion that any person might be expected to lower his or her self-respect to meet standards set by an external agency. I take no pleasure in writing this—my life, and by extension that of my community, is poorer for my lack of a collective acknowledgment of spirituality. But I am a Southern boy, raised with manners. I have no interest in crashing a party to which I have been so expressly disinvited. More to the point, through hard trial and labor I have earned my right to passionate love and to be loved passionately in return. I have, in fact, arrived at the heterosexual take on passionate love, which is to say that I have integrated that love so wholly and completely into who I am that to deny it would be to deny my whole being.

As one who has decided to explore and express his spirituality apart from organized religion, I admit to some discomfort at finding myself arguing that organized Christianity must accept sexually active lesbians and gays, and that lesbians and gays should make that acceptance a priority in our struggle for equality. Why, finally, should it matter whether institutionalized Christianity accepts us as we are? We have our own churches, after all, for those who wish to worship, where our worth is assumed (as it should be) rather than considered something we must prove. The question is more than incidental, and broader in its application than to lesbians and gays. It engages at the most profound level the purpose of organized religion in all its forms.

Every day of my childhood the Roman Catholic church set those questions before me: Where do we come from? What are we? Where are we going? (Their precise articulation I owe to Paul Gauguin, himself no stranger to Christianity.) Transmogrified cannibalism, mortification, exaltation—these were re-enacted according to a routine as dependable as sunrise and nearly (it seemed) as old. The Church calendar was the literal expression of the cycling seasons. Lent: interminable Fridays kneeling, while the black-garbed priest prostrated himself before each station of the Cross, *Stabat Mater.* Easter: transformation, rebirth, renewal, acted out in golden costume at midnight rituals, *Pange, lingua, gloriosi.* May, Mary's month: processions of girls in white, boys in blue, strewing flowers before a plaster Virgin, *Salve Regina.* Corpus Christi: massive assembly in the high heat of summer to sing the praises of Christ's bloody wounds, *Tantum ergo sacramentum.* For the feast of St. Blaise: the cool touch of candlesticks, beeswax against the throat. The gritty rub of ashes on the forehead. Clouds of cloying myrrh ascending to the high-domed ceiling. Mind-numbing mantras mouthed in a tongue at once centuries dead and more evocative than our quotidian English, *ora pro nobis, ora pro nobis, miserere nobis.* Ours was a sensual church, the Opera of Faith, and we were its captive patrons.

I acknowledge the shaping hand with gratefulness. Because of it I grasp in some way the incomprehensible magnitude of the mystery of being. Because of it I appreciate the importance of parable and ritual, storytelling and metaphor as our most appropriate means to the invocation and expression of mystery. We cannot know the answers to the questions which Gauguin so eloquently poses; we can only ask. The history of religion in all cultures is the ongoing expression of that asking.

In my small, backwoods hometown, religion was not mere social exercise but the necessary response, evolved over time, to the paradox of the human condition: our collective attempt at reconciling our place as self-conscious beings with an incomprehensible universe. Human beings are the animals that must ask why; organized religion is our most democratic means of bridging the gap between that imperative and the void that lies on the other side of asking.

To observe that institutionalized religion has historically preoccupied itself with exclusion ("you may not belong to our church unless . . .") is only to point up the greatest of its failings. Even now, religion continues to be one of the many ways (among them skin color, nationality, gender, sexuality) through which human beings categorize and discriminate; one of our ways of defining the Other.

The last several centuries of secular history have been an evolution toward an at least official acknowledgment that such discrimination is harmful to individual and communal well-being. I am arguing that religion, too, may evolve, from an earlier preoccupation with particularized theology to a place where its appropriate and necessary role is to celebrate diversity—to establish, then strive for an ideal in which we acknowledge our various ways of being "other" *within* community. Religion should define a moral structure which acknowledges and promotes this yin and yang of the human condition: our place within larger community structures; our uniqueness as individuals.

With its ages-old roots in collective experiences and wisdom, religion is better suited than any other institution for this arduous and time-consuming task. For it to exclude any person of whatever sexual identity, or race, or gender, or nationality from participation in this collective expression of love and awe is to deny that person's humanity—to exclude her or him from the religious covenant. As the Catholic church acknowledges, no more significant exclusion exists. The application of that exclusion to whole categories of peoples reduces religion to a social circle exercise, a country club with hymns and history, of no more significance than any secular institution embroiled in the politics of the accumulation and hoarding of temporal power and wealth.

❧ For many years I described myself as having left the Church, but I understand now that I misspoke. These days I say more accurately: The Church left me. Rather than acknowledge the existence of lesbians and gays, it promptly tossed my brothers and sisters and me out on our collective ears.

In this the Vatican is hardly alone. Organized Christianity has failed lesbians and gays, at a time when we need access to the accumulated moral and spiritual wisdom of humanity as much or more than any segment of society. We are in the earliest stages still of creating a community, which is to say a stable set of values against which we may measure and reward or correct our conduct. Many of us are in the midst of battling to stay alive, or taking care of those engaged in that battle. Like all great religions, Christianity at its best can offer wisdom, lessons learned from the testing and tempering of values over time, which wisdom could be of priceless value to many lesbians and gays in facing our challenges.

Yet organized Christianity persists in its preoccupation

with exclusion rather than inclusion. Churches (including those located in the heart of urban areas, where so many gays and lesbians live) turn their backs on us, even as they bemoan their declining congregations and participation. A gay friend—a longtime, devoted communicant—wonders aloud: What is wrong with this picture?

For our part, gays and lesbians have alienated potential allies in the churches by allowing ourselves to be defined not by how we love but by how we have sex. Gay publications, largely supported by advertising from bars, phone sex lines, and sex clubs, focus (surprise!) on bars, phone sex lines, and sex clubs. I write this not by way of denigrating those establishments—my family ran a tavern, and I'm a happy patron of many a well-run juke joint. But they have dominated our community's public persona, set the terms of our definitions of self-respect, and shaped our community morality, simply because until recently we have had no other institutions to fill those needs.

This is not the place for an extensive exploration of the relationship between morality and sexuality, except to say that they are intimately related. One has, finally, no more precious gift than that of one's body, and while some may give that gift more often and to more people than others, one loses sight of the connection between morality and sexuality at peril of one's self-respect, and by extension one's ability to love oneself and others. Not least among the arguments for welcoming lesbians and gays into mainstream religion is that such religions are, or ought to be, the appropriate institutions for the development and nurturing of individual and community values based on rituals, assumptions, and manners other than those formulated in bars and sex clubs.

Several years ago I wrote of the contradictions and rewards of being reared in a flamboyant, Old World religion in the midst of the New World, Protestant South. I tried then to grapple with issues of sexual identity, but each time I turned to the subject I was consumed with bitterness and anger by the thought of the time wasted and lives ruined in the name of Christianity in general, Catholicism in particular. Finally I set issues of sexuality and religion aside, hoping time would bring me to some more forgiving place.

I have not yet found that place, but more than bitterness and anger at organized Christianity I now feel a consummate sadness that the wisdom it has to offer is lost to so many because of the ends to which it has been turned by the unscrupulous, the ignorant, and those confused and corrupted by power. Speaking of his symphony "Jeremiah," Leonard Bernstein argued that the great crisis of the twentieth century is the crisis of faith. The dominance of Christianity by exclusionary, narrow-hearted men is the direct cause of whole segments of America (hardly limited to gays and lesbians) dismissing one of the cornerstones of faith and spirituality in Western culture. This is a great tragedy, acted out throughout gay and lesbian life. Taught to hate ourselves, denied the ability to love fully and openly and with social approbation, we turn to self-abuse (especially through drugs and alcohol) and inevitably to abusing others.

I sympathize mightily with gays and lesbians who dismiss organized Christianity as at best a lost cause, at worst irredeemably pernicious. I do not dismiss so-called "fringe," "New Age" religions, or the growing number of gay and lesbian converts to Eastern religions. In these trends I see a legitimate effort to satisfy—for people whom Christianity has failed—our elemental hunger for a spiritual expression which celebrates our self-respect.

But for any foreseeable future, organized Christianity will continue to provide most American children with what moral instruction they receive, and to shape American social policy, morality, and lives. It will continue to provide the majority of Americans, regardless of their sexual orientation, their most readily available institutional expression of spirituality. If nothing else, realism demands that gays and lesbians engage it actively, if not in the churches at least in secular forums. And that requires not sit-down, shout-down activism—however necessary and effective that has been and continues to be in other struggles—but informed, enlightened discourse from open gays and lesbians who invoke the past only and always in the spirit of forgiveness. For we cannot make peace with ourselves unless we make peace with our pasts, and we cannot make peace with our pasts unless we forgive (without forgetting) what religion has done to us.

I have not abandoned organized Christianity (though it has abandoned me) because I understand the power of religion to ennoble and elevate to a degree perhaps greater than that offered by any secular institution. I understand and appreciate its democratic appeal to our interior seat of mystery, which it touches and for which it offers expression. I want access to this experience for my people—I want it for all people.

❧ In 1990 I helped my lover through his death from AIDS. From our first meeting I knew that he was HIV-positive; not long after our meeting I learned that I was (as I remain) HIV-negative. The disparity of our situations was the source of great anguish, much of it centering around the possibility, however remote, that he might infect me. Among my friends and family many never understood and still do not understand how I could have subjected myself to such risk; one straight friend accused me of having "a romantic deathwish."

I can only answer that I was in love. I had been uplifted, transformed. Had I refused this love—the most profound yet given to me—I would be a vastly poorer man. I think of Chekhov's wife, the famous Russian actress Olga Knipper, who chose to live with and marry him when it was clear he was dying of tuberculosis, a disease more contagious than AIDS and at that time both more mysterious and nearly as fatal.

In caring for my lover I came to understand the tautological relationship between God and love. My lover's love for me and mine for him made me into something better, braver, more noble than I had imagined myself capable of being. I was touched by the literal hand of God, for this is what love is, in a way as real as I expect to encounter in this life. I may be forgiven some impatience with those who would ascribe to that sacred experience anything less than spiritual dimensions of the highest sort—the domain, in a word, of religion.

In various essays and in a *New York Times Magazine* profile, Lewis Thomas suggests that humanity may evolve spiritually as well as physically, adapting (he hopes) to an understanding of the world that makes more room for community virtues and values. Is it so farfetched to see the struggle of gays and lesbians for acceptance in mainstream churches as another step in the maturation of Christianity? As anyone who opens him- or herself to humankind's multiplicity of ways of being learns, engaging other cultures and communities benefits oneself as much or more than they. What gays and lesbians have to teach the larger religious community is a profound understanding of the necessity of love, in all its infinite permutations and manifestations.

I like to think that gays and lesbians may perform for organized Christianity our customary role of defining the cutting edge. In this case, agitating for acceptance in mainstream denominations pushes further the historical shift in Christianity's concerns away from the particular and toward the general—away from concern with (for example) theologically correct methods of baptism, and toward a focus on the preservation and propagation of love, which is to say the manifestation of God in our time.

Why do I suppose that gay men and lesbians may have some special access to understanding the nature and importance of love? Because no one knows the value of something better than those who have struggled to achieve it. Denied love from without, our challenge has been to create it from within. This is no easy task, and is not accomplished by the simple declaration of the wish that it come true. Like all struggles of any significance, the fight for the right to love and be loved is ongoing and omnipresent, and manifests itself in every act of every day. Our reward is, or may be, a fuller understanding and appreciation of what others so often take for granted.

❧ The monks of my childhood are almost all gone now, drawn away by marriage, secular careers, other religious orders, death. But their presence remains with me and my family, evidence of the rippling effect of human goodness; the best argument for virtue that I know.

My sister sends a black and white photograph taken on

my fourth birthday. In it I'm seated before a vast cake made in the shape of the head of Mickey Mouse. Rendered with painstaking verisimilitude in vanilla and chocolate icing, Mickey Mouse is nearly as large as I. Chin resting on one fist, I preside over it with the contemplative air of a young mystic. Along with the photo my sister sends a saucer-sized medallion made from wheat paste, the centerpiece of my first birthday cake, which has survived the depredations of time and insects. On it there's painted in pale blue and ochres an elaborate Virgin and Child, one of Christianity's most potent symbols of love.

These works of culinary art came from the hand of Brother Fintan. They are evidence of his greatness of heart, the boundlessness of his love, large enough to encompass me and my immense family and the young man whom he brought to the Kentucky hills to meet us that New Year's Eve.

Gays and lesbians, brothers and sisters, are finding our ways to spirituality; we are making communities across America and around the world. That we would do so sooner and more effectively with the assistance of organized Christianity I do not doubt, but we live in the here and now, we do not have time for the women and (mostly) men of Rome and the various Protestant denominations to open their hearts to the community of love. I write in celebration of what I see happening in meetings and community actions and hospices and service organizations and yes, churches. I write in celebration of the spirituality I see explored and expressed in its multiplicity of ways, in a community to which I am proud to belong. I open my arms to it and through it to the world, an act of faith in life and in love.

In Sophocles' "Oedipus at Colonus," Oedipus speaks to his daughters:

I know it was hard, my children—and yet one word
Frees us of all the weight and pain of life:
That word is love.

Over two thousand years later Oscar Wilde wrote, "God's
law is only love."

Religion's proper concern is the preservation and propagation of love, which is to say the manifestation of God in
our time.

# MICHAEL LOWENTHAL

# SAYING KADDISH
# FOR PETER

There was an angel in my grandfather's obituary. He was there, crouched between the lines of the *Boston Globe* clipping my father had sent, waiting for me to discover him.

Reading this utterly public recounting of my grandfather's life seemed a violation of his trust, when in the privacy of our home so little had ever been told. My father's father was a storyteller, but his tales were Talmudic, intellectual word games, never anything about his own life. He and my grandmother had escaped Hitler's Germany miraculously late, and they refused to speak about their lives before America.

Although almost all of the obituary's facts were news to me, most fit snugly within the image I had of my Papa Eric, a formidable, white-goateed rabbi with a severe accent. But one brief, chillingly matter-of-fact paragraph stunned me to a halt: "Rabbi Lowenthal and his wife, Suzanne (Moos), fled to New York in July 1939, escaping the Nazi purge of the Jews. However, a son, Peter, from an earlier marriage, was a victim of the Holocaust."

A son? Peter? Why had nobody ever told me about this man? The fact of the earlier marriage had been alluded to vaguely but never discussed, even when a daughter from that marriage visited one holiday. But nobody had ever mentioned Peter.

I was midway through my fifteenth year. Like most boys that age, I was struggling with raging hormones, but there was the confusing twist that my crushes were on other boys. Since my parents' divorce four years earlier, I had been living with my mother and sister, a life nearly devoid of older male figures. I yearned for a big brother or uncle, someone I could trust with my secret.

Now, with a single line of the newspaper's cold black type, I was in one staggering instant granted and then deprived of an Uncle Peter.

I asked a few tentative questions about this mystery relative, but nobody in my family wanted to talk. The person who would know the most—even though Peter was not her son—was my grandmother. But her own father had been killed at Thereisenstadt, and I couldn't ask her to dredge up those painful memories.

So, knowing nothing more than the single sentence in the *Boston Globe,* I developed my own stories about Uncle Peter.

From the start I felt a strange, visceral connection to this gift of a relative. Sometimes a child will be born with red hair or green eyes, some trait exhibited by neither parent, and it will only be an uncle or cousin with the same features who proves that the new child is one of the tribe. Peter, as I conjured him in the following years, was precisely such a genetic match. Like identical twins separated at birth and then reunited as adults on "Unsolved Mysteries," a miraculously revived Peter and I would discover amazing similarities: we both drove 1974 Volkswagens, we were both jazz trumpet players, we parted our hair on the same side. In my most private moments I was sure that he, too, was gay.

I never told anybody about my feelings for Peter, embarrassed by what might be taken as desperate wish-fulfillment. I distrusted the feelings myself; they seemed too easy, the convenient fantasies of a lonely teenager. But in synagogue, when we recited the mourner's Kaddish, I always said it for him. I would see him sitting on the edge of the bimah, dangling his legs awkwardly as if embarrassed that I would call his name.

❧ Then at this year's seder, the tenth Passover since my grandfather's death, I learned that in his final months, Papa Eric had recorded a cassette of his memories. I asked for a copy of the tape, and when my grandmother gave me one on my next visit I rushed home to listen. I was eager to glean any details I could about my grandfather's sketchy biography. My secret, desperate hope was that he would say something about Peter.

I pressed Play and suddenly the room was filled with the gravelly, cigar-stained sound that had haunted my dreams for a decade. In his painfully direct manner, still mixing Germanisms into his stiff English after forty-five years in America, Papa Eric recounts his devout childhood and his studies at university. He explains his rejection of Orthodox Judaism, choosing to become a merchant instead of a rabbi like his father and grandfather before him.

Fifteen minutes into the monologue, I knew I was getting close. Papa Eric tells of marrying his first wife, then of going to Palestine during the depression of the 1920s. Finally, the payoff: "My former wife arrived . . . giving birth to our son Peter, born in Tel Aviv, February 17, 1924."

I moved to the tape recorder, slid the volume control up to high. There is a sentence about the baby boy's bris. Then, with no particular emotion: "On April 9, 1924, we returned to Berlin with our son Peter, who died in Bergen-Belsen concentration camp on March 13, 1945." Without so much as a pause, Papa Eric resumes his account of the Hebrew-character typewriters, flower-pot lamps, and mother-of-pearl jewelry he sold back in Germany.

This is all? I thought. A first-born son, reduced to a couple of dates?

I continued to listen to my grandfather's memories but with only half an ear, distracted by my disappointment. He recounts more of his merchant's life and eventually comes to the sudden death of his father, one of the most prominent Orthodox rabbis in Germany. Papa Eric says that he loved his father and knew it was to the old man's "deep sorrow that I had alienated myself from the Jewish tradition."

He describes the large funeral and then sitting shivah, the traditional week-long mourning vigil in the dead man's house. "On about the fourth day," he says, "our son Peter led me into the study."

Subtracting dates in my head, I determined that Peter would have been only four years old. I pictured a tiny dark-haired boy in late 1920s European garb.

"On the huge table he had spread opened books from the bookshelves and told me, 'Study them!' That was like a voice from heaven. At that moment I decided to become a rabbi myself."

I stopped the tape, rewound, and listened again, memorizing instantly the cadence of the sentences and the sound of Papa Eric saying "heaven," a word he never once uttered in my presence.

My grandfather was probably the most anti-mystical person I've ever met. One of my clearest memories is of him at the head of the seder table, quizzing us grandkids on the

Pythagorean theorem as if this geometric formula were the Eleventh Commandment. Yet here was his confession of a profound spiritual conversion—and the direct catalyst was Peter.

I have listened to Papa Eric's cassette over and over in the past few months. Strangely, each time I hear the story of Peter and the books—the only account I have of an actual event from his life—he becomes less and less real to me. Did a four-year-old's commandment really change the course of my grandfather's life? Did the actual Peter bear any resemblance to my fantasy uncle sitting before me in synagogue?

But Peter has never been about reality, he has been about possibility: The possibility of a merchant becoming a rabbi, the possibility of a confused gay teenager having somebody to turn to.

I am already three years older than Peter was ever allowed to be. Yet I still think of him as my protecting uncle, my benevolent guardian angel. I know that he waits for me in all the unexpected places.

# AIDS: THE NEW CRUCIBLE OF FAITH

It's almost three years since I stood in the Intensive Care Ward of Cabrini Medical Center on Manhattan's East Side, my hands wrapped around the feverish, limp, familiar hand of my friend and companion of the past sixteen years as he lay, twisted in sheets, encircled by tubes and apparatus, barely alive, barely conscious, hearing myself say these words: "I promise, if there is another life, another time in which we exist, I will find you and we'll be together again. I'll find you if I have to spend my entire life looking. I promise." Sensing some tiny response from him—real or imagined, voluntary or perhaps strictly autonomic and instinctual—I stopped speaking.

Seconds later bells and lights went off on one of the many machines monitoring him, and I was pushed out as a group of interns and nurses flooded in. Within hours he was brain dead and completely gone, the man I'd awaited for the first thirty-one years of life and from whom, ever since the day we'd met, I'd seldom been parted from physically, and then only with at least two telephone calls daily, even if one of us was halfway around the world.

What was I thinking as I stood there, saying those words? Was I, a professed Buddhist, believing my words? Finding calm solace in the realization that indeed life was smoke, a bubble, a breath, a mist, all illusion, and some time soon I'd be testing that theory myself and the other one of reincarnation? Was I facing the ultimate question of life and confirming those tenets I'd come to accept when all others had failed?

The truth is I don't remember a great deal what I was thinking and feeling at that moment. I do recall I wanted him to know I'd never abandon him. I wanted to comfort him one final time, he who'd altered my life and viewpoint with his affection. I'd known for years that when he couldn't sleep and we were apart, I could sometimes calm him even via telephone just by talking to him. Talking about anything, anything at all: my voice calmed him and he would sleep.

To myself, relegated into the bleak hallway waiting area outside the Intensive Care Unit, even as I was saying them, my words had seemed melodramatic and hollow. They carried no conviction. I didn't that moment believe in reincarnation, even though it is one of the bedrock foundational tenets of the system of belief I'd come to identify with myself. In the past decade I'd lost my mother, my favorite brother, my sister-in-law, my eight closest friends, another hundred or so less close friends, going back to Nick Rock, who'd died in 1979 of an unknown cause, and whose death had shocked me to the core. Nick had been the first of a quarter million people in this country known to have died of AIDS complications. Did I actually believe I'd meet all of them again? No, what I felt now was my greatest to date impending loss, mixed with shock and disbelief. How could this happen? How could this happen to us? How could this happen to me?

In the months and now years after my Friend's death, I still have no answer. I also no longer profess even what little and loose belief in Buddhism I used to have. People have given me books, people have sent me to psychics and spiritualists. None has helped, although each has said things, written things, that may or may not be right. Laeh Maggie Garfield, in *How the Universe Works,* a book given to another dying friend, writes, "Death came first. Then life. Death is the pre-existent state. We come into life." It's Buddhist and New Age at the same time. And whatever it really means, it certainly is the only thing that makes sense in my own experience, now that eighty percent of the people I've ever known are dead, and I just turned fifty. Not eighty, not ninety.

❧ Religion, we are told, and possibly all human culture and thought itself, derives from the question of how to deal with the undealable: i.e., death. Anthropologists and archaelogists have discovered that those most maligned of all early peoples, the Neanderthals, seem to have been the first to consciously bury their dead—and to memorialize them. Fragments of flowers and seeds have been found arranged in certain patterns in their primitive gravesites. And their bodies appear to have been handled and moved such as to place the limbs in specific positions. Naturally, we have no idea what they thought of what happened to their dead.

The first historical cultures we do know seem to have had mixed responses to death. The Sumerians and Indus Valley peoples appear to have simply put most of their dead out of the way, concentrating on a handful of tombs for especially great rulers. In contrast, the Egyptians were completely obsessed by their dead and what went on with them; food and household supplies and elaborate boats for the underworld journey, an entire landscape of death, a Judgment God on the other side, you name it, virtually all of our beliefs have come somewhere or other from the Egyptians' speculations. But it wasn't only the Pharaohs who were buried with their living entourages. Shang Chinese rulers were, too, if sometimes only statuary representations of their court, their army, their entire former life.

The Greeks provided us with the first literature of the dead. Who doesn't know the story of how Orpheus went to the underworld to reclaim his dead Eurydice? (And when he returned without her, he allegedly swore off women forever, thus becoming the first homosexual, for which he was torn apart by a group of females.) Who hasn't read Homer and Virgil and heard the words spoken by the ghost of Achilles to Ulysses: "Better to be the lowest servant, beaten and abused and yet alive, than to be the greatest king and hero of the dead"? No, the Greeks and Romans didn't think much of death. Yet when they devised a geography of their Elysian Fields, it included a new, psychologically interesting touch: a three-river system to the underworld: Styx, Nepenthe, and Lethe. One river gets you there, one causes the "surcease of sorrow," and the third allows you to forget all that happened while you were alive.

For the Hindus, with their enormous and complex religious system, the dead returned corporeally to Brahma, the vast universe-sized god, who would periodically breathe Atman, the breath of life, into some specific cell-spirit until it lived again. Christianity derived a lot of its mythology from its nearest middle eastern competitors, among them Judaism and the dramatic myths of Zoroastrianism and Manichaeism. As a result, Christians have two markedly different places—a heaven and a hell—after death: and, conveniently, a reason to behave in certain proscribed ways during life.

Buddhism wasn't ever very exact about its own afterlife. Its hell is reserved for demons. Those who in life do evil deeds don't burn and suffer eternally as they do in Christianity but instead are reincarnated, born again, into a much lower state of existence, a work animal, a wild beast, a crocodile. All humans die and are reborn in the Hindu and Buddhist system, but according to Buddhism you can earn rebirth into successively higher states of consciousness until you reach *satori* and no longer need to be born. It's from reincarnation that the strong Buddhist strictures against killing any living creature derive (and thus vegetarianism)— and if you absolutely must kill that charging lion or mosquito or cockroach, you say *"Na Amida Mitsu,"* which in effect wishes it to be reborn to a higher state.

"All creatures fear death" is the third sentence of the *Dhammapada,* the Buddhist text which purports most closely to report the teachings of Siddhartha Gautama, the fifth-century B.C. Indian princeling who found enlightenment and thus became the Buddha, the Enlightened One. His story is a simple one. A pampered royal, he was kept from the horrors of the world by doting parents. But once exposed to the great suffering of life, the young man renounced his former life and searched the countryside looking for an answer to the universal pain and suffering he saw around him. What he eventually found, he could only really hint at. Words—as the Zen branch of Buddhism points out so wittily (what is the sound of one hand clapping?)—cannot really convey these truths. So, unlike virtually every other religion, Buddhism is at its roots democratic. Its prophet-God invites each person to emulate him, indeed to become exactly like him: to experience suffering and to find enlightenment.

❧ That democratic, emulative element was what initially attracted me to Buddhism. It seemed far less dogmatic than the religions I'd known as a child—Catholicism, Protestantism, Judaism—and far less value-oriented than many I'd read about and studied in high school and college. Hinduism might be a lovely religion to grow up and live with, were I living in India or another Hindu country. Ditto Shintoism if I were living in Japan. For outsiders they weren't easy to really get into. Yes, there were elements to mystical Judaism—Buber, Kafka, and the stories of the Hassidim—which I found extremely attractive. And elements of contemporary, philosophical Protestantism—Bonhoeffer especially—struck me, as did what I learned of the rigorous belief training systems of Loyola and the Jesuits. And the Sufi sect of Islam had produced wonderful poetry, song and dance: a life-affirming mysticism different from the more dour aspects of that rigid religion.

In a sense, Islam shared an aspect of both Protestantism and Catholicism which I found was the most difficult to deal with: Its underpinnings completely revolved around the acceptance of everything that happened. "It is the will of Allah," the four World Trade Center bombers declared just the other day in a loud voice after the jury sentenced them to life imprisonment. "Allah is Great." To me, that equals the Calvinists declaring that one is "saved"—i.e., going to heaven after death—whether one does good deeds or not, and "damned," i.e., going to hell, whether one does evil deeds or not, such is the literal acceptance of the concept of "original" or Edenic (Adam and Eve) Sin. It was the same whenever I would hear a Catholic friend of mine complain to her mother of some injustice and the unswerving mother would reply "Offer it up to Jesus." In all three cases, my instant, instinctual reaction is to haul off and slug the believer.

For being a believer? No. For being dumb, animal-like, unthinking. For so easily giving up what has always seemed to me the essence of being human, i.e., the ability to think, to work it out, to see injustice and to complain of it. That's the *least* we can do.

How did I reach this, to many, completely rebellious point of view? And so early? As with many things in life, it was taught to me by my parents. Not that they *meant* to teach me to be irreligious. I don't think my siblings are. Except for my younger brother, now deceased, who like me, questioned everything he ever heard—and ultimately found it wanting. In fact, if you look at the externals of my early life, you'll find a younger son in a family that seemed as religious as the next. For many years, we went to church every Sunday morning. We were all baptized (to clean off that "original sin"), went to Sunday school afterward and thus learned enough so that we'd know what we were doing when we went through the rite of First Communion ("eating the body of Christ" turned into a sticky flour wafer), then went to weekly instruction every Friday or Wednesday afternoon until we'd learned our Bible stories and been catechized so we could know what we were doing when we were confirmed (as "Soldiers of Christ" for some unnamed battle to come).

Of course, when my sister Cathy-Ann died suddenly four days after being brought home from the hospital, my mother never joined us at church again. And my father was by then keeping his business, a deli-grocery in Richmond Hill, open on Sunday mornings until lunchtime, so he didn't go either. But we children were old enough to go ourselves and we did. Except that it seemed after a while that my older brother was attending another church, the Lutheran one, because his friends and his Boy Scout troop were all connected with that church. Then I went to junior high school and discovered that my closest new friends were all Jewish, and they attended a synagogue, on Saturday, not Sunday.

I looked into that, got my parents' approval to join David and Michael every Saturday and even to go to the Yeshiva, where they'd all begun to study Hebrew, or at any rate, enough Hebrew to be able to get through their Bar Mitzvahs. I was considered "an interested party" by the young Reform rabbi—possibly a convert. He treated me like everyone else in the class and I even learned a few words of Hebrew—but many more words and phrases of Yiddish, which was spoken by the older two generations in my friends' homes, where through junior high and my first years of high school I spent a lot of time.

What made this religion class different from any I'd attended or sat in on before (like my elder brother's Lutheran one) was that it was as much a discussion as a catechism. One could ask questions. Why? Why did God do all that to Job when he was such a good man? Why did God let Cain kill Abel? Why did God allow Deborah the Judge to rule Israel? The Sunday School teachers and nuns and priests had all answered, "Because that's the way it happened. God's God. It's true. Just learn it." But the young rabbi would say, "I wondered about that myself. And this is what I concluded," and would then tell us his opinion. Or the opinion of some other Hebrew scholar who'd studied the matter. Often, one of the boys would speak up. His father—or uncle or grandfather—said something else about the question and he'd tell us. And we'd discuss it, not always reaching a conclusion. When we left these classes we'd still be discussing it. I didn't feel forced to learn by rote, but as though I'd been intellectually engaged, challenged. I came to understand how this was an important training ground for the young and why my Jewish friends were so intelligent. They were being *taught* to think.

On holidays, especially on Christmas, my family, sometimes even both parents, would attend church. By this time, I had no compunction about not joining them. By my last years of high school, I'd already begun reading philosophy and about other, Eastern, religions, and all thoughts of converting to Judaism were gone, especially since most of my friends had stopped going to *shul* and only attended the synagogue on the "High Holy Days," Yom Kippur, Rosh Hashanah, and Purim, and then usually only with and because of their families.

I'd been investigating religion in a leisurely, even a desultory manner, thinking it wouldn't have much influence on my everyday life. All that changed during my early twenties when all the inchoate feelings I'd been having, mixed with all the physical sex I'd been having, suddenly came to a head: I'd concluded that I was homosexual and felt I had to do something about deciding whether or not I was going to lead a homosexual life. Religion could wait.

❧ But of course, religion became a factor in this decision, too. And once again, my parents' example, especially that of my mother, turned out to be important.

I'd never forgotten that tall, slender, red-headed young man with a turned-around collar who'd spent an entire afternoon in my mother's bedroom talking to her the day after my sister Cathy-Ann had died. Never forgotten how drawn and tense he'd looked when he'd come downstairs at last and smiled wanly as my sister and I offered him cake and coffee.

My sister and I had both heard the outbursts from upstairs: My mother, crying unceasingly for the past day and a
half, had suddenly shouted "*No! No! I can't stand any more! I
want to die! Let me die with her!*" We could still hear—and
more, *feel*—her crying upstairs as he took a sip of the coffee
and bit an edge off the cake, and said simply, "She'll sleep
soon." Failure covered the poor young man. My sister and I
were thirteen and eleven, old enough to know my mother
had not expected this child, had been ill when she'd conceived but had been talked out of aborting it. She'd suffered
nine months of illness throughout the pregnancy, had then
undergone a three-day birth ordeal—only to lose the child.
And with it, whatever tatters of belief in religion she'd possessed.

A decade later, she mentioned to me that she'd been at
church with a friend. I must have looked startled because
she immediately defended herself by saying, "Of course, it's
only *social* for me, now. You know, my women friends, they
still *buy* all that . . . " In other words, what I'd suspected,
what had gone unspoken in our house, in our family, for
years, was true. At the moment of Cathy-Ann's death, my
mother had had a severe crisis of faith, and had lost her belief.

Several years after that when we were both adults and
friends, when I spoke about the difficulty I'd had reconciling being gay with any of the religious teachings of my
childhood, she said, "You know that was the first time I ever
questioned religion." She explained that it had occurred at
some sort of religious instruction she'd had as a young
woman, where after meeting as a group, each person would
meet with their pastor individually.

"I was young and stupid, then," my mother said, "so it
took me a while to figure out what he was saying when he

kept asking me what I did with my hands at night." To better understand his question as well as her answer, it should be noted that my mother was an athlete and runway model when young—and very attractive. Explaining it years later, she said, "I was *so mad* when I realized what he was asking me, so I told him I wrapped my hands in waxed paper and rubber bands to keep them from being damaged." She laughed. "And I never went back to that church again. Except to get married. I saw him after that and I said, 'Ask me *now* what I do with my hands at night.'"

About my father, I only knew that while treating Catholicism—in which he'd supposedly been raised—and all other religions with respect, he professed no particular belief. At first I thought this was the result of his being a great reader of science, of fact, an intellectual, a scoffer. Later, I somehow or other overheard adults talking about a death early on in my father's life which had changed everything, including his beliefs. Could it have been his father's death in the great Spanish Influenza of 1921? I wondered. No one would say, and it would be decades until I discovered the truth. Clearly, however, whatever faith he'd had as a child had also been shaken by death.

Nowhere was this attitude of my parents toward religion seen more clearly than when we went to visit my father's aunts and uncles and cousins, the people he'd grown up among in South Ozone Park. Their homes weren't as large or handsome or expensive as ours, they weren't on curving, tree-lined streets, surrounded by tended flower gardens with sloping, perfect expanses of lawn. Instead, their homes were a chunk out of a long attached block of buildings, and consisted of back rooms and upstairs apartments connected to some business—floor coverings or furniture. Yet on every wall of every room was a crucifix, a Saints'-Day calendar, some gaudily beribboned little rendering of St. Christopher, a larger print or oil copy of some Old Master's Virgin and Child, Marriage at Cana, or Miracle of the Loaves and Fishes. Every bureau or chest contained a handful of ornate Mass Cards for the recently dead. We had none of these things in our suburban split level home, and they were fascinating to us children, but I accepted them, as I accepted the tiny sweetened cups of black coffee and the lemon and anise and almond-flavored cookies and cakes with funny names I would get to eat only at their homes, as I accepted the fact that my cousin Anna-Marie was already planning to become a nun, while another cousin, Theresa, would be a lay teacher in a parochial school. For me, it was all exotic, *Italian, New York City!* It had nothing to do with my life.

🐚 Because I was already in such complete rebellion by the time I came to accept my homosexuality, I missed a great deal of the specific angst that many of my gay friends went through. I was politicized early. Long before Oliver Stone's movie, I was convinced that the death of the Kennedy brothers and Martin Luther King, Jr., was a coup d'état and conspiracy. I marched and sat in for Black rights in the South and for students' rights when I was still in college. By the time I graduated in 1964, Paul Krasner's supremely cynical newsletter, *The Realist,* was my Bible. I questioned everything, doubted all, used drugs to explore my consciousness, and sex to explore my body. I was a hippie. I wore a pirate earring in 1967. People would yell, "Get a hair cut!" I became part of an urban commune with rural extensions in Massachusetts and California.

This was the time I began to investigate Buddhism most seriously. At first I was attracted to Zen, the more elegant

Japanese version. But after learning meditation and the Zen art of calligraphy, it felt a bit too attenuated for me, and I went back to origins. The Western idea of either/or was replaced by the Eastern idea of both/and. That simple renegotiation of reality changed a lot; everything, really. And I now looked into all of the Eastern religions and began putting together elements of belief for my own construct. Among them came the "pagan" aspects called spiritualism, Tarot cards from Zoroastrianism and its Gypsy descendants, The *I Ching* from China's early Taoism, astrology from the Mesopotamians, *Book of the Dead* from the Tibetans, *Seven Arrows* from the American Indians, *Maya Codices* from Central America.

What struck me about all of these systems was how adult and sophisticated they were about life in a way that made the religions I'd grown up with seem childish and incomplete. I was now a young man finding myself, and these belief systems were able to point me and encourage me and give me examples from the past in a way those other, far less inclusive religions hadn't. Those had excluded the religious from the material life. Not Taoism or Tarot. Those had all spoken only to selected days and moments of worship. These alternative systems integrated worship into everything else in life.

Certain ideas from these unconventional systems seemed to be greatly similar across their many differences: ideas like *dharma* and *karma*, ideas like destiny and fate. The more I'd read, the longer I lived, the more aware I'd become of people's lives being astonishingly individual and strange, worked out according to some unknown system that appeared to have nothing at all to do with the simpler "sin and atone" religions of my youth. Yet, these alternate belief systems had detailed, in often difficult to understand expressions, forms and terminology. Some claimed to be predictive; others to be instructional. All of them connected this current life with some longer chain of lives. In all of them, one carried material from life to life (*karma*) and one discharged the bad and created the good as one lived and learned. One also had certain work or tasks (*dharma*) to perform in this life, sometimes via one's career, sometimes as a hobby or vocation, often unconsciously, as with great heroes and heroines who became a symbol to people, a rallying point for their nation.

In my twenties, I wanted answers to real, not metaphysical, questions. Firstly, I felt drawn to writing as a career, yet I was always being pushed into commerce, bookselling, and publishing instead of writing, and succeeding there quite well, usually in exactly such a way as to keep me *away* from writing. Could I ever succeed as a writer? So few ever did! And would I ever write anything worthwhile if I ever did manage to get past the endless, seemingly ceilingless obstacles that faced me? Secondly, I knew I could live comfortably as a heterosexual. I liked women and they often loved me. I knew I could probably have a long-term marriage, a family, if I decided to quash my truer feelings. But shouldn't I try relationships with men, where I really loved the sex and felt far more emotionally stimulated—even though there was so much danger, psychically, socially, personally, and to my career?

Neither of these—to me burning questions—would ever be answered by Catholicism or Judaism or Protestantism. They simply wouldn't take the second one in any way seriously, and the first question didn't matter, so long as I attended on the sabbath and paid tithes.

Eventually I cobbled together my own religion, with Buddhism as the basic system of belief, the similar but even more objective Taoist *I Ching* as my daily teacher and action guide, and astrology as my general life guide. This, despite the fact that using horoscopes had shown me not only difficulties and pain in the past but those still to come.

One of the most unmistakeable of those predictions was the death of a partner, a specifically male partner. It couldn't be any clearer from my birth chart. Another was the eventual transformation of my life through separation from my former connections. But how could I possibly know these two predictions would be worked as a result of my nearness to the beginning of one of the worst epidemics in history? And how could I know that going ahead with writing despite the obstacles shown in my chart and then allowing myself early on to be the homosexual I actually was, despite what society told me, would meld into something unexpectedly large and fine—in on the ground floor, present at the creation, as it were, of gay literature?

❧ So much known, so much still to know about something as small and meaningless as this particular single life. Yet what else is religion for but to explain our life—and death?

That, I suspect, is long off. My ancestry is filled with the long-lived. If you make it to sixty-five on either side of my family, you generally make it to ninety, or a hundred. My father is eighty-two years old and still going strong and he abused his body far more and far longer than I ever did. Is that what I want, I ask myself, to live another forty or fifty years without my Friend? I know I won't consciously seek another companion ever again.

Can I bear another entire lifetime, equal to what I've already lived, without him? Often I think not. After almost three years, I've still not felt any return of the light that left my life when he died. And though several family members and friends have since sickened and died and are now sick and are about to die, I'm no longer strongly affected by it.

I've tried to ask those people who still profess one of the more standard religions how they've dealt with all this death and disease and loss. It's a difficult question to ask even those you know well. I'm either stopped at the onset by my own embarrassment as I bring up the subject or stopped by their unwillingness to speak if I do manage to get it out. Somehow, I feel they're coping about as poorly as I am, while publicly forced to show a much more placid demeanor. Early on, a few tried comforting me with platitudes—"For every door Christ closes, He opens a window"—which earned my withering response, "Maybe, but I *hate* what's outside the window He opened." One acquaintance, a devout and practicing Catholic, asked what I thought of the problems gays are having getting the approval of the Church. I hesitated a long time, knowing I would end up sounding superior, but after he'd badgered me a while, I finally admitted, "It seems utterly irrelevant to any of the larger issues of life. To me, it's like needing approval from the witch doctor of some cargo cult."

Of course anyone who was close enough to discuss those larger issues with me is now dead. Several spiritual-minded people have spoken of the karmic past of those who've died of AIDS. How they're reincarnated from the millions who died in Hitler's gas ovens and concentration camps, and are living out the rest of their lives, which had been cut short by the Nazis. How am I to respond to that? And a few others into New Age matters speak of how gay men dying of AIDS are the new Priests and Mediators of humanity. How they're spreading understanding and tolerance and eventually how all of this will integrate homosexuality into the World Consciousness. I sure hope so.

In a strangely oblique way, I've achieved something akin to that balance the *I Ching* speaks of as required for the Superior Man, that objective compassion Buddhists seek for enlightenment. Yet oddly enough, I don't feel any peace. Most days I feel irritated and sad. If there *is* a deity, I now know that She/He/It is *not* my particular friend; too often has She/He/It been my enemy, thwarted my wishes and needs for some other ends She/He/It required. In truth I've felt manipulated, pushed around. And I'll say it, I don't really care for my life any more. It's lost its value to me. I'd throw it away on a whim . . .

Still, I sometimes wonder if in that time of crisis I can never forget, those last moments of my Friend's partial, imperfect consciousness, if I truly *believed* what I said—as adolescent children still believe in the so-called Magic of Christmas long after knowing there's no such thing as Santa Claus—and if that frayed tatter, that broken fragment of belief in the face of everything else, is somehow, ultimately, what counts.

## ANTONIO FELIZ

# PERSONAL DICHOTOMIES

"Holiness to the Lord." The familiar words greeted me as I prepared to enter the temple in Los Angeles, California. It was the autumn of 1973 and the temple was solemn and majestic against the blue California sky. This holy edifice truly was for me a place where heaven and earth met, a window through which I personally could step into heaven. A young couple would kneel before me today at one of the altars in this place that was so sacred to me, and with the power that had been given to me through a Prophet of God, I would seal them to each other for the rest of their eternal lives.

I had the power spoken of in the Scriptures. According to the belief of my Church, I had been given that power to bind on earth in such a way that those I sealed to each other could be together not only in this place and time but in all places and times: Marriage for Eternity, unique to our belief in some respects, but so common a desire throughout the human family. I was the agent. As always, the weight of it was heavy on me. But today, somehow that weight was even heavier than usual.

What presumption is it in us that lets us think we can act for God? Who was I to exercise such a power as this? To speak for God? To act in God's place? I knew I had the power. It wasn't that. I had stood often enough in that place and had my mind opened to know exactly what it was a particular man and woman needed to hear, needed to know and remember as they began their life together. I knew how close heaven and earth really were. But today, I felt strangely unworthy to use that power. I sought assurance. I needed to feel again, as I'd felt before, that I really was worthy to do what I was going into the House of the Lord to do.

I changed to my white clothing. It was some time before the ceremony was to begin. The carpeted hallways softened my steps as the noise of the world began to recede. These walls protected me. The distractions, the rush, were left behind. I checked the necessary paper work. Everything was in order. I needed to be alone. I climbed the massive circular staircase to the upper chambers of the temple. It encircled the huge chandelier around which this spiral took my steps. At the top, I stopped and looked down at the brightness of the thousands of lights in the chandelier. Beauty filled the hollow shaft which I'd just climbed. I went on.

Where could I go to be alone? The serenity of this place was around me as I passed the Terrestrial Room, a wonderful place of light and growing things, where a large group of people was gathered. I entered the Celestial Room of the temple. Here was our effort to create a place that was as much like heaven as we mortals could imagine. A place where God could come. The large room was empty. I walked slowly around it. The adjoining hallways and sealing rooms were likewise unoccupied. I chose a chair and sat down, trying to focus my troubled thoughts. In this beautiful and sacred place of peace, my mind was not at rest. The more I tried to clear my mind, the worse it was. I couldn't.

Today especially, I needed to feel that God heard me. In my mind, I addressed him as one would speak to another person: "God, Father, let me know you hear me." I still felt very much alone. I took a deep breath and clasped my hands in my lap, and I tried to let go of my connection to earth.

I had tried all my life to do what God wanted me to do. I'd consecrated my time and talents and all I'd been blessed with to the building up of the Kingdom of God on earth. I'd been a missionary in South America, preaching for two years at my own expense, because I wanted others, everyone, in fact, to know what I knew and feel what I felt. I'd been a Bishopric Counselor and High Councilor. I'd blessed many people through those callings. Somehow I felt the need to remind God of that now. Why should I be feeling what I was feeling today when I had tried so hard to do what I felt God wanted me to do? I'd tried to be the man God wanted me to be.

The room was quiet. The peace of the place began to filter into me. I felt a gentle reminder that, as the Branch President of the Spanish-speaking branch in Los Angeles, I had the right to seek guidance concerning the needs of those saints. But it was I who needed guidance today.

Three days before, I had been required to hold a Church court for a young man in my congregation who had been accused of living in a homosexual relationship with his roommate. "No unclean thing can enter into the Kingdom of God," we'd been taught. It was my responsibility to determine if Sergio would be allowed to remain a part of the Church, or be cast out. The memory of the "trial," as ominous and weighty as any physical burden, would not leave me . . .

❦ "Sergio," I'd asked gently in Spanish, "do you understand the seriousness of the charge against you?"

He shrugged his bent shoulders but didn't look up at me. I tried again. "We want to hear your side, Sergio. Tell us what happened."

He raised his gaze hesitantly to meet mine and I saw how his dark eyes were full of the tears he was struggling to hold back. I waited for him to speak.

"Yes," he said at last. "It's true what you say of me. I do love another man. And I know you say it's wrong for me to love him in this way." He paused. "I want to do what's right, President." He said it as if he were afraid we wouldn't believe him. I believed him.

"But it doesn't feel wrong to me! Aren't you supposed to be able to feel it when things are wrong? Can't we tell?"

"Then tell us how it did make you feel," I prompted.

"Sometimes I'm afraid," he said. "Sometimes I feel so alone. Sometimes I think no one will ever love me. Then he puts his arms around me. He holds my body close to his. He makes me part of him." We waited until he was ready to go on. "Then, then it's all right. He loves me. He holds me. We love each other. How can it be wrong to love someone?" He was pleading with us to see it his way. I wanted to. I didn't want to condemn him. I felt the same need to be loved, to be held, to be made whole. He had faced us with courage. A courage I lacked. He'd shared his deepest feelings. Mine remained unspoken.

I had to ask the next question. The part of me that loved my Church and my God wanted to ask it sincerely, but the words did not come easily. "You've taken the first step, Sergio, in coming to us and confessing your sins. Are you now willing to forsake them and make your life right with the Lord?"

He looked at me steadily without answering, and though there was no condemnation in his look, I felt he somehow knew more about me than almost anyone else. That he knew exactly what I'd been feeling as he described his lover's touch and the warmth of his friend's body close to his. Finally, his eyes still locked to mine, he shook his head slowly. "No," he said. "No, I guess I'm not willing to do that."

We invited him to leave the room for a few minutes and I asked my two counselors for their impressions. "He's not sorry," one said. "He's not the least bit repentant. For his own good, we have no option but excommunication." I knew they were right, but I didn't want them to be right. Why should people be condemned because they were honest? I was the one who had sat there in silence. I felt torn.

Sergio rejoined us. I pronounced the verdict. At the word "excommunication," a kind of stubborn defiance replaced the hesitancy with which he'd spoken before. With his hands outstretched, as if he would grab me and shake the truth into me if he had to, he said, almost spitting out the words in his anger and frustration, "President Feliz, aren't you ever going to learn that there are other ways of looking at things? I tell you, the Church is wrong on this one! Why can't you see that?"

I had no answer.

    What would it be like to be touched intimately by a man? In the quiet of the temple, my turbulent thoughts would not be still. To be hugged sensually, even kissed tenderly by another man, and to return those intimate sensual approaches?

I forced the thought away. No! It was wrong to feel that

way. It was wrong to want that. It was a sin even to think about it. I knew that. I tried to pray again.

"Heavenly Father," I began silently. "I'm married to a beautiful and sweet woman who loves me and loves you . . . " Laura's face came into my mind. So serious, so sincere, so concerned whenever she sensed a strain between us. How I'd prayed and fasted and prayed again before I'd proposed to her, begging the Lord to bless me with the ability to love a woman so that I could marry and have children and learn to fill the measure of my creation. And what wonder it had been when I'd finally felt it. And I did love her. Didn't I? I'd been sealed to her. We'd knelt across from each other at the altar, our hands clasped, and had been promised that if we were true and faithful, we would be companions in Eternity. But then why, why couldn't I feel for her what I'd felt for . . . other faces blurred with hers . . .

Terry. When I was near him in the early morning seminary class we'd shared as teenagers, the strength of my incomprehensible desire to touch him and be close to him had simply bewildered me. I remembered the morning after class when Terry looked at me with that same desire, how he'd touched me and how that had called out yearnings for him from deep within me. I remembered how much I'd wanted his look, his touch.

Then Ken. He'd pulled me innocently into his sleeping bag one freezing night so we could keep each other warm as we tried to fall asleep in the back of his pickup on our way to Salt Lake City for Conference. He'd been so warm next to me. I'd felt so guilty enjoying the closeness of his warm body.

Other faces came to my memory, faces of other guys to whom I'd felt attracted in my teen years. Were they all infatuations, a stage, a part of youth?

I tried to repeat the prayer I'd prayed then. The prayer I sometimes felt I'd been praying ever since: "Please, God, take these feelings away from me. I want to love my wife. Keep me strong. Don't let me do anything I shouldn't. Please."

But I felt totally alone. Abandoned even. Pulled and stretched in too many directions. Laura. Terry. Ken. Sergio and others. Unanswered questions hammered at me, relentless and demanding. "Please, God. Please." I realized I was crying. I reached for my handkerchief to dry my face.

Just like Sergio, I wanted to do what was right. I wanted desperately to do what was right. I knew that the men who led the Church were inspired. And if they said that what I was feeling was wrong, then it must be. I wanted to follow them.

I had decided when I was sixteen that I needed to know for myself if David O. McKay, then President of the Church, really was a Prophet of God. Somehow I knew that if I went to Salt Lake City for a General Conference of the Church, I'd find some way to meet this man and, when I did, I'd know if he really did speak for God.

The memory of that experience has never left me; it probably never will . . .


Temple Square glowed in the spring sunshine. Ken's parents were saving our seats in the Tabernacle balcony as he and I went out to get a newspaper before the Conference session started. In the warmth of the sunlit April morning, it was hard to believe that only two days before Ken and I had been caught in a snowstorm in central Utah and had spent the night huddled together in one sleeping bag in the back of his truck, trying to keep warm. We hadn't done anything but hold each other to keep warm, but the guilt surrounded me like a dark cloud, blocking out the glory of the morning.

As Ken and I walked around the Tabernacle, a large, gray limousine drove past us and parked near the west doors of the Tabernacle. For some reason, I froze at the sight of it, but Ken ran right up to the rear door of the car. We both knew it could only be one person—the President of the Church.

Part of me wanted to do just what Ken was doing—to get as close to the car as I could and shake the Prophet's hand and look into his eyes. But the memory of what I'd felt in the back of that pickup was still too vivid. I couldn't move. I stood by the west gate to Temple Square. Ken waved for me to come over and join him, but I stayed where I was.

Through the open doors of the Tabernacle I could hear the choir rehearsing their songs for the next session of Conference. I could hear the excited voices of the crowd that had gathered around the limousine. On the other side of the wall around Temple Square, a police siren blared. But louder than any of the other sounds was the voice in my head: "If you go over there, and if he really is a true Prophet of God, he'll look right through you and he'll know you're queer!" What would his reaction be if he could tell? I didn't want to be queer, but I knew that somehow, I was.

The limousine door opened. There he was. From my earliest memory I'd been taught he was a Prophet. Was he? Did he communicate with God in the same way that Moses and Jeremiah and Isaiah had? I wanted to know, but at the same time I was afraid to find out. The spring breeze fluttered his white hair. His smile looked just like the pictures of him I'd seen in Sunday school. He seemed taller than I'd imagined he'd be. Ken stepped forward from the crowd to talk to him. They both looked toward me. I wished I could simply disappear, fade invisibly into the wall. Ken pointed at me. President McKay looked in my direction and gave me the warmest look I'd ever received from anyone in my whole life. But I couldn't feel any joy in it. I was terrified. He beckoned me to come over to them, and I found myself walking slowly over to where they stood.

The man I had come so far to meet grabbed my right hand in both of his and looked right into my eyes. "It's beautiful weather for Conference, isn't it?" he asked me. I just nodded, still unable to speak.

Ken introduced me and told President McKay how we'd driven from California to be at General Conference for the first time in our lives. As the Prophet listened, his clear eyes were framed by what seemed to be a steady and irrepressible glow. I rubbed my eyes to soften the sudden brightness. It must have been the sunlight, I thought to myself.

Back inside the Tabernacle again, Ken told his parents about what had happened. Was he really a Prophet? It had felt good to shake his hand. Could he see through me? Did he know what I really was? What if he weren't a true Prophet?

The Tabernacle was crowded. We'd come early in order to get seats, and we were standing and talking in the balcony so we wouldn't be tired of sitting by the time the meeting was finally ready to start. A few of the General Authorities of the Church were already in their seats. To Mormons, these men were holy men, what popes and archbishops are to Roman Catholics. Others were shaking hands with one another and greeting the members seated near the front of the hall. The organ played a soft prelude.

Suddenly, I knew he was in the room. Nothing appeared to be any different than it had been just a minute before, but a powerful feeling of warmth and peace surrounded me and filled me. I turned to Ken. "The Prophet is in the Tabernacle," I told him.

He looked at me strangely, then glanced toward the stand where the First Presidency and Apostles sat. "No, he isn't. Look, his chair is empty."

I couldn't see him, but still I knew he was in the room. Ken looked all around, and finally leaned over the balcony railing so he could see the doors beneath us. He turned to me in surprise. "You're right! He just came in through the doorway right below us. How did you know?"

My eyes filled with tears. I watched my Prophet make his way slowly toward the front of the Tabernacle. His whole body seemed to radiate light. He was filled with light. I could not stop looking at him. It seemed almost too much to believe. I realized that the glow from his face I'd seen as we stood shaking hands outside the Tabernacle must not have been the sunlight, after all. I couldn't hold back the tears of joy and Ken's mother hugged me as I stood there. Then, I felt a voice declare, "Behold, your Prophet." For the first time in my life, God had shown me a sign. I'd asked, and God had given me an answer.

I wouldn't speak of this experience until years later in an address at a BYU student devotional assembly.


❧ As I sat in the temple reminiscing about that experience, I knew God knew how I felt about his Prophets. He knew that after that experience in the Tabernacle in Salt Lake, I'd tried to read every word President McKay spoke or wrote. He knew I'd committed myself, seriously and solemnly, to obey the teachings of this Prophet and of every other Prophet that would follow him in the leadership of the Church.

God had shown me personally that I should follow this man and I had done my best to do that. For me, he was no different than Moses or Elijah or any of the other men of the Bible who walked and talked with God. I became known as a defender of the Prophets. People had told me, after hearing me speak, that the strength of my conviction was enough to make them want to believe.

God knew that. He knew my heart. He knew how much I wanted to do what was right. But I just didn't know any more what that was. The Prophets said it was wrong for me to want to be close to another man in the way that I had always inwardly and irrepressibly desired to be. Their sermons left no room for any discussion whatsoever on the subject. I'd heard them many times. Homosexuality was a sin, a despicable, degrading, awful sin, one of the "unholy and impure practices" spoken of in the temple.

Because I supported the Prophets in all they'd taught since the time that I'd received my personal witness of David O. McKay's call, I had sustained the Prophets in all they taught, including their teachings on homosexuality. I could not control what I felt, but I could control what I did. I'd vowed to myself that, no matter how strong my desires were for another man, I would never act on those impulses.

And God knew I'd been true to that commitment. But if I was doing what I was supposed to be doing, if I was doing what the Prophets taught, then why did I feel so . . . so unhappy? So frustrated? Why did I feel that what we'd done to Sergio was very wrong? My tears seemed to increase.

No comfort came. God, who, in this place above all others, should have been close to me, had left me totally alone. He wouldn't hear me. Why? So many times before this, I'd received answers to my prayers in the temple. What was wrong this time? Was it Sergio?

I remembered pondering homosexuality as a missionary
in Peru many years earlier . . .

❧ Elder Hatch, my missionary companion, knocked half-
heartedly on the next door in the small apartment complex
where we'd been "tracting" most of the afternoon without
much success. Tracting was our method of going door to
door in an effort to meet prospective converts for our
Church. We were both very tired.

"Let's go after this one," he suggested. I agreed. A door
opened across the way and a young woman called out to us
to come over and talk to her.

"What are you doing here?" she asked as we approached
her front step.

"We're missionaries," I answered. "And we have a very
important message for you." As she listened, I recited the
carefully memorized story of Joseph Smith, the founder of
Mormonism, who as a young boy had wanted to know the
truth about God and religion. "He read in the Bible," I told
her, "'if any you lack wisdom, let him ask of God,' and then
he decided that that's just what he would do."

"¿Y . . . qué pasó?" she asked. "What happened?"

I told the familiar story. "Joseph went to a grove of trees
near his home. He knelt down and began to pray to God, to
ask which of all the many churches he should join. As he
prayed, he felt overcome by an overpowering darkness; it
pushed him to the ground. When he came to himself, he
saw two heavenly beings standing above him in the air. One
spoke to Joseph and said, pointing to the other, 'This is my
beloved son. Hear him.'"

She wanted us to come in and tell her more. We asked if

her husband was home. "No, but he'll be here later. Come back and eat with us tonight."

She was pleased when we called her "Hermana Griego." She said she'd like to be our sister. We assured her we'd be back in the evening.

When we returned, Mr. Griego wasn't home, but another man was there. He had an interest in our message. This man was Sister Griego's brother, and he introduced himself to us as Pepe Gomez. He indicated to us that his wife was in the back of the house.

"Why doesn't she come out and join us too?" Elder Hatch asked.

"No," her husband answered, shrugging his shoulders uncomfortably. "You see, she's not able to speak and her noises would be too distracting."

We persisted and finally he went to the curtain separating the rooms and called, "Ven, Chica." A thin, pleasant woman ducked nervously into the room and sat down by her husband. Though she was unable to speak, she sat and listened as Elder Hatch and I taught her, her husband, and Sister Griego about the gospel.

Through the next two weeks, we continued to teach the two couples. They were eager to learn and listened earnestly as we taught of the apostasy that had followed Christ's crucifixion, and then of the promised restoration that had brought the full sealing blessings of the Holy Priesthood power back to the earth.

One afternoon, as I was speaking on the power the Priesthood has, I felt a gentle pull on the sleeve of my shirt. Chica had come silently up beside me. She put her hands out together in front of her and moved them in a small tenatative circle, her eyes all the time watching mine to see if

I understood. I shook my head to show my confusion, and she repeated the gesture, this time making a small, definite downward motion with her two hands as if she were laying hands on someone's head.

"She wants to be healed by your Priesthood, Elder Feliz," her husband told me. "She's already told me she knows she'll be healed."

I looked at Elder Hatch. He gave me a small scared half-smile that let me know he'd support me in whatever I decided. But I couldn't tell her no. I'd blessed others, of course, and I'd seen healings, but this was the first time I'd been asked to anoint and lay hands on someone who was totally unable to speak. Would she be healed?

Elder Hatch poured the holy oil on the crown of Chica's head. I then put my hands over his and, after sealing his holy anointing on her head as one from a servant of God, I waited for the Spirit to give me the words. Through me, God then commended her faith, and blessed her that if she had sufficient faith, her affliction would be lifted from her. She was also told that her healing was not for her alone, but in order that this might be a witness of the power of the Priesthood which we had brought with us to bless them.

After the blessing, she thanked me in the only way she could, grasping my hands in hers, and smiling her happiness as she made the small awkward noises that were her only form of communication.

We left to attend to our other appointments. By late afternoon, we'd finished all we'd planned for the day and were returning to our apartment for dinner. As we walked down the main commercial street of the downtown area, I heard someone calling me from the bottom of the hill.

"Elder Feliz! Elder Feliz!" I turned to see who it was. Chica and Pepe were running up the hill and she was shouting my name! They had been scouring the town all afternoon to find me and tell me that right after we'd left their home, her speech had come. We laughed and shouted, cavorting like fools in the street, sharing her joy in her wonderful, newfound power.

It did not take Chica long to learn that she had much to say to everyone. Sometimes it seemed she was trying to make up for a lifetime of not being able to speak. She talked and talked. And of course we let her.

A few days after the healing, however, as we sat around the Griegos' dinner table, Chica broke into the conversation and said, "I need to clear something up."

"Oh, no, don't listen to her, Elders," her sister-in-law warned. She turned to Chica. "You hush now. That's enough of that."

Elder Hatch glanced at me. We both stood at the same time. It seemed best for us to leave, and let the family resolve this problem, whatever it was. But she was not going to let us leave without saying what was on her mind. "El es maricón!" she shouted as we made our way toward the door.

Maricón? Homosexual? Who? She couldn't possibly be talking about me, could she?

Hermana Griego tried to smooth things over. "Don't believe it, Elder," she reassured us. "No es verdad."

Gradually we learned what the truth was. Hermano Gomez, our gentle Pepe, was not really Chica's husband at all. They were living together and Chica had just discovered that he was having an affair with a man he'd met at the casino where he worked.

I set up an appointment to meet with Brother Gomez privately. Elder Hatch and I left the house in turmoil. I knew we couldn't baptize him if he was a homosexual. As missionaries, we had been specifically instructed by our area leaders not to teach the gospel to anyone whom we knew to be homosexual. Homosexuals were not included in our call.

At our interview, Pepe begged me to hear his side of the story. He wanted to be baptized. "Sí, Elder Feliz," he admitted, "I am a homosexual. But I am also living with a woman and she has my child. Shouldn't I be baptized so I can raise my boy in the Church?" This man was my brother. I didn't want to be the one to have to make this kind of decision about his future. "I've known it for a long time," he went on. "I started to live with Chica so no one would know. Your Church has so much truth. I thought maybe you'd understand."

I didn't understand. It would be a long time before I'd understand.


    I glanced toward the sealing room where shortly the young bride and groom and their families would be joining me. I had been entrusted with the sacred sealing power of Elijah, the Keys of Holy Priesthood. Why, then, wouldn't God take these feelings from me? I couldn't imagine how I could pray any more earnestly. Why had God refused to hear me?

My tears became more constant.

A faint but now familiar sound came into me. My pain lifted, separating itself from me, layer by layer. Very slowly, in one of those ways wherein things take place almost imperceptibly, the suffering I was experiencing left. A oneness with the Divine filled me, starting at my very core and spreading out until even the tips of my fingers knew the sense of expansion.

God did hear me!

A hushed murmur filled the room—the same sound I had heard many, many times before when upwards of three hundred people had filled this room and joyously greeted each other in happy whispers. The sound of hundreds of whispered voices communicating their joy in being together. I had always been moved by that sound; it was the same sound I was now hearing.

But I was alone! No one was anywhere in sight. I looked up. Three shimmering crystal chandeliers hung above me, representing the three glories of the highest plane of existence. Each prism caught the light and reflected it until the whole room was filled with light. I was myself, but more than myself. I was one with all that is. Love, as warm and protective as something tangible, wrapped itself around me, enfolding me, encircling me, holding me safe in its glow. It surrounded me, held me, lifted me. I saw it all. Love IS Priesthood power. The creative force, the strength that saves us, changes us, exalts us. I was bathed in it. The whispering sound became a rush.

God loved me! The whispering rush became louder and louder. The power in the love God had for me surpassed any other power I had ever known, or could even imagine.

The sound was so loud that I found myself looking toward the north and south doors. It seemed that others might hear it too and come to see what was happening. Then, as suddenly as it had begun, the sound faded. The room was quiet again.

Peace . . . such peace.

The south door opened and a temple ordinance worker walked into the room and started toward me. I dried the tears I'd been unable to hold back, nodded to him, and started for the sealing room, where I would perform the sealing.

Yes, God loved me! The knowledge of it rang through me. Everything in the Church told me that I was evil, that my desires were sinful. But how could that be? How could anyone experience what I'd just experienced and be "bad" or "evil"? It wasn't possible. I knew it.

I was worthy of God's love. Somehow, what I'd been taught in the Church about people like me no longer seemed to fit. I didn't understand how it all could make sense. I just knew what I needed to know. I'd come to know I was not evil and God did love me as I was.

The members of the wedding party began to enter the room where I waited. Proud parents. Friends. The young bride and groom, holding hands, nervous, but excited. They looked at me with something a little like awe and I knew they trusted me. There was still so much I didn't understand, but somehow it was all right. I was worthy of their trust. I only needed to trust God the way this young couple trusted me. God loved me.

# The exorcism of
# mother and son

My mother is dying. On the phone at Kennedy Airport, I see my distorted reflection in the coin box when she asks me, unexpectedly, to please come home as soon as I can.

"I'm in trouble," she says.

◈ I'd rather not be *flying* to Frankfurt. Two weeks ago, a friend returning from Germany had everybody's worst nightmare when her plane fell three thousand feet in the air. Cocktails flew, stewardesses screamed, passengers got concussions and crawled in the aisles. "We're going to die!" wailed the Muslim lady in the next seat. "No," my friend said, chanting her Buddhist mantra, trying to be fearless.

When the pilot came on the intercom, sounding terribly shaken himself, he said they hit an air pocket. "They come out of nowhere, there's no way to predict them," he explained. Terrific. I fasten my seatbelt and when the handsome steward comes by, take a warm towel off his tongs. The terry cloth feels good on my face—I'm worn to the bone. Tomorrow night, I'll be in Thalheim, kneeling in front of Mother Meera. She'll take my tired head in her hands and bless me with her silence. I close my eyes and try to rest.

✿ My mother cried when I was born. The nurses laid me across her breast and hearing "boy" through her twilight sleep, a woman who never did anything right felt, for a second, that she had. This is a weird phenomenon among the Jews, that even when a woman hates men, when her life has been twisted and fucked by them, she still feels atavistic pride when one comes wriggling out of her. Maybe she thought my father would stay, maybe she thought that a son would heal them, or maybe it wasn't that at all; but joy filled my mother that night when they spanked my ass and announced my gender. Maybe Ida could feel joy then. Maybe she could hold us kids the way that we were meant to be held, lovingly against warm skin.

I can't remember such a time, not because my mother was a bad person but because she'd had no love herself and was starved for a type of intimacy she shouldn't have gotten from me. The images that haunt me arise from that hunger: her legs clutching me too hard in the bath, the feel of her pussy against my back; her breasts swinging down to her waist through a see-through nightie, eyes begging me to look; seductive questions, too loose and explicit not to be alarming. The night of my Bar Mitzvah, she leaned across the checked tablecloth at Dino's Pizzeria and asked me, over sausage heros, how I compared to the other boys.

At first, I didn't catch her drift. "What do you mean, compare?" I asked.

She narrowed her eyes. "How big is it?"

I felt like she'd stuck her hands down my pants. "What does it matter?"

"Because your father was e-nor-mous," she said, mouthing out the syllables. Ida sucked on her Pall Mall, the hint of a smile crossed her face. "Till the last time we did it, it hurt me."

She didn't know that I knew what she meant. Even then, at thirteen, I was no stranger to men and their weapons. Rudy was the best of all; in seventh grade, we couldn't be parted. Those afternoons when I wasn't inside him, he was heftily inside me. Even though it hurt, I liked it, which is why on the day that Ida found us, I was yelping. She opened the door to see what was wrong, then slammed it fast. Rudy dressed quickly and never came back. Ida wouldn't look at me except to say, "Lock the door next time."

That was generous—she knew there'd be a next time—and extremely sad. My mother had been defeated again. Her only trophy became, in an instant, her worst embarrassment, and though she defended my queerness later, she despised it with all her heart.

🌸 "Chicken or beef?" the steward is asking.

"Does it matter?"

"Hardly," he says, leaning down to whisper, "they both suck, sir."

The way he says it opens the door. I smile, he winks, and rolls his food cart down the aisle.

I didn't know I'd become my mother. For twenty years, running from Ida around the globe, I didn't know that I'd swallowed her whole.

You learn the world from your mother's face. Looking around through Ida's eyes, all I could see were pornographies, dog eating dog, souls being torn, the weak being maimed and the devoted abandoned; a nightmare world where nothing was sacred or sublime. The downward pull of her mouth told me that God was dead; that the world I found so thrilling was doomed; that I, who sat for hours in front of the mirror (Who are you? WHAT are you?) feeling like a miracle, was just as orphaned in hell as she was.

By an act of grace, I unwound this lie, began—with innumerable circlings back—to rehabilitate my soul. The lighter I grew, the darker Ida seemed till her shadow stretched like an abyss between us. I saw it once when her sister said that though she wasn't religious at all, she knew in her heart that God exists. I said that I'd come to know that, too. Ida looked at us both and shrugged. "It must be nice to believe in something." Hearing the depth of her loneliness made me so sad I could hardly breathe.

❧ The plane starts rocking over Iceland. Bells ring, signs light up, the steward steals a look between my legs on the pretext of finding my seatbelt. The captain's voice reassures us from the cockpit that this is only minor turbulence, and that we shouldn't be alarmed. I start my pranayama breathing—in with courage, out with terror—conjuring, in spite of my good intentions, chasms of sky breaking open around us, dragging us down, nose first, into flames and carnage.

The rocking stops; the lights go out. I reach for a book of Mother Meera's, open haphazardly to this quote:

"Ask for everything—like a child asks its mother for everything, without shame. Do not stop at peace of mind or purity of heart or surrender. Demand everything. If you ask, you will receive. If you receive, you will have to bear."

❧ The notion of "guru" is misunderstood. Hearing this loaded word in the West, we tend to think of tyrants and slaves, orange robes and affectation. We think of Rajneesh running guns, collecting Porsches, snorting laughing gas at ashram orgies. We lose the beauty of what guru means, literally, in Sanskrit, "dark to light." Guru is anyone who enlightens, and since we are not trained in this science, we don't realize that despite their various styles and shapes—from guide and teacher, to mahatma, saint and incarnation—all gurus share the timeless goal of drawing us closer into God, awakening us to who we are: children in a sacred realm. There was a time not long ago when I believed that this was a fairy tale, that holy love was impossible. I knew nothing at all about the spectrum of consciousness, or what an enlightened master was like.

Then I met her. We were en route to India in 1986, when my ex-lover suggested stopping in Germany to visit a woman that he knew. He didn't tell me anything about her, which is why, when I first saw Mother Meera, I was so unprepared and stunned.

She was sitting with her eyes closed—swarthy and small in a vermillion sari—holding the head of a kneeling child in her hands. Something about her stillness, a mountainous silence that surrounded her, told me in an instant that this woman, whoever she was, was unlike anyone I'd encountered before. Her otherness was unmistakable, though as hard to describe as a scent or a taste, and grew more intense when she released the child's head and stared fiercely into his eyes, like someone boring through a wall.

I sat on the stairs, closed my eyes, and sank into a spontaneous trance. I knew nothing then about meditation—my mind simply stopped—my inner vision went golden-orange and my body felt as if it were dipped in a vat of warm honey. I don't know how long this rapture lasted, but the next thing I knew, my lover was touching my shoulder, telling me to go ahead. Feeling awkward and embarrassed, I knelt in front of Mother Meera and received the blessing. I felt nothing extraordinary when her fingers clamped around my temples, and when I leaned back to meet her gaze, I wondered what she could possibly be seeing as her black eyes darted back and forth.

She haunted me in my dreams that night, ruthlessly, with fangs and piercing eyes, clawing at my guts like a buzzard, ripping me to shreds. I woke up fourteen hours later bawling hysterically, and wept for a long time in my lover's arms. It felt as if a lifetime of pain, hardened like a cyst in my belly, had been lanced, and when the crying finally stopped, the sadness no therapist had come close to touching had mysteriously begun to lift. I felt clear, free, and light as a child.

I could not explain how this had happened; eight years later, I still can't. I only know that from that day forward, my life has taken a new direction, knowing such love as this exists. In time of crisis, confusion, dryness, I travel to this drab town near Frankfurt where a woman younger than myself sits in silence and offers refuge to whoever needs it, asking nothing in return. I've watched Christians, Buddhists, Hindus, Jews, atheists, plumbers, drag queens, poets, princesses, and bishops come by the thousands to take what gift she has to offer before she sends them on their way. I've never met a single person, however skeptical, who was not changed by sitting in her presence. It's uncanny, but true, that regardless of how lost I am myself, how dark and rigid and doubting and sad, the sight of her never fails to renew me, or remind me who I really am.

Tonight, I desperately need to remember.


🐚 Two hundred kilometers west of London, the sky is getting yellow. I give up trying to sleep with my feet around my ears, take my antiviral drugs, and pace the length of the DC-10.

🐚 When I told Ida I'd been infected, she said, "No child of mine will have to die alone." I was standing at another phone booth, on a bison preserve in Minnesota. My lover of another time was waiting in his van. It touched me when she said this, though I knew it wasn't true. My big sister had died alone already, and by her own hand; Ida stood by, confused and blaming.

I said, "Thanks, Mom, but my bloodwork is fine. I'm asymptomatic."

"What does that mean?"

"I'll let you know if I ever need you."

She never brought up the subject again.

It's just as well; my mother has little wisdom to offer. This is why I've always been desperate to learn, looking for answers, looking for God. Her emptiness sent me fleeing. It screamed, Don't get stuck where I am; know yourself before it's too late.

Now it is too late for her, and though I'm in pain to be losing her, there's a blessing here as well. My mother won't live to see me die, should I be taken by this virus. I won't have to see her face when she walks into the hospital room, looks down, and sees me there. I won't have to run interference, become her hero, lover, dad; or pretend—as she's always forced me to—that life wasn't really happening. I won't have to tutor my mother in death, at a time when I will need teaching myself, or explain to an atheist why, despite discomfort and loss, I am truly not afraid.

🌀 Touchdown is smooth. As I leave the plane, the hand-some steward winks and pauses. There was a time I'd have slipped him my number, played with him in an airport ho-tel, promised to call when our cities crossed and know that this would never happen. Today, I wouldn't have the heart.

On the Autobahn to Limburg, I think how strange it is that I've grown so serious. Life has pulled my stuffing out; everything hits me too hard now, lifts me higher, and throws me down. This virus made me a human being, opened my eyes, opened my heart, made me look beneath the skin, be-yond this world, for what could not be taken away.

You hear people say this all the time, for their own rea-sons. Life has gotten out of hand, it's all too much, it never stops, there's GOT to be a better way. Friends who were satisfied once with muscles and big jobs and summers in Cannes are jumping like lemmings into the quest, throw-ing themselves on the fast track to God, reaching for a higher love. We're howling in the nineties, not just be-cause of this virus but over a far more painful disease, an epidemic of godlessness, a hunger for light and meaning and home.

Pulling off the road in Thalheim, I think—for the hun-dredth time—how bizarre it is that I found mine. It amazes me still that a hard-headed nihilist should have been lucky enough to have his window cracked with enough time left to enjoy the view. Ringing Mother Meera's doorbell, I see my reflection in her mailbox, smiling like an old woman.


🌀 I learned the world from my mother's face.

In my favorite Buddhist parable, the unawakened man is compared to an infant sobbing in its mother's lap. She

strokes the baby's head, rocks him against her breast with infinite love and infinite patience. Finally, when he can cry no
more, the child begins to quiet down and, wiping his eyes,
looks up to see the luminous face of the woman holding
him. He feels the softness of her belly and knows, for the first
time, who and what he has always been, progeny of this
great mother, joined to her in body and spirit, never abandoned and never alone. When the baby sees her, the mother
smiles, and seeing her grin, the child learns to smile, too.

In the last picture taken of us together, Ida is sitting at the
kitchen table and I'm standing behind her, my head lowered
on her shoulder. I'm asking her to touch the stubble. I want
her to know how strange my head feels now that I've shaven
it, but she can't bear to touch me. Her face is turned away
with disgust, her hand pushing me out of sight.


❧ I'm thinking of this when the church bells strike seven
and Mother Meera enters the room, eyes lowered to the
ground.

Silence descends on the room as she takes her seat and the
first disciples come forward. An old blind woman, shabbily
dressed, is helped to the carpet and when Mother takes her
head, she begins to weep. I close my eyes and picture Ida in
her place, being blessed for the first time. I imagine her having a moment's peace, a glimpse of faith, a touch of grace before she dies. I imagine the darkness lifting, her nightmare
coming to an end. She would know in that instant that she
had been seen, that I forgive her every mistake, that it is too
late in the day for regret, for anything but love.

I take my mother inside my body, and place her, broken,
at Meera's feet. The delicate hands reach out to take us.

Both of us are free.

# CONTRIBUTORS

MARK DOTY'S third book of poems, *My Alexandria,* won the National Book Critics Circle Award and the *Los Angeles Times* Book Award for 1993, and was a finalist for the National Book Award. A recent fellow of the Ingram Merrill and Guggenheim Foundations, he has taught at Sarah Lawrence College, Brandeis University, and the MFA Writing Program at Vermont College.

DON BELTON is the author of the novel *Almost Midnight.* His fiction has appeared in *Breaking Ice: Contemporary African-American Fiction* and *Calling the Wind: The Twentieth Century African-American Short Story.* He is currently editing an anthology about African-American men's identity and legacy, forthcoming from Beacon Press. He lives in St. Paul, Minnesota, where he teaches literature and writing at Macalester College.

LEV RAPHAEL is the author of *Dancing on Tisha B'Av,* a short story collection which won a 1990 Lambda Literary Award; *Winter Eyes,* and *Edith Wharton's Prisoners of Shame.* He has published dozens of short stories in magazines, from *Redbook* to *Genre* and *Christopher Street.* His fiction and prose have appeared in many American and English anthologies, including *Men on Men 2, The Faber Book of Gay Short Fiction,* and *Hometowns.*

VESTAL MCINTYRE was raised in Idaho and recently graduated from Tufts University. His fiction has appeared in *Christopher Street*. He is currently living, working, and writing in Boston.

JAMES MORRISON was born in Detroit, and now lives in Raleigh, North Carolina, teaching film and English at North Carolina State University. His fiction and non-fiction appear most recently in *New Orleans Review, PRISM International,* and *Other Voices.* He is currently completing a collection of short fiction and working on a novel.

ANDREW HOLLERAN is the author of two novels, *Dancer from the Dance* and *Nights in Aruba,* and a book of essays, *Ground Zero.* He currently writes a column for *Christopher Street* magazine and lives in Florida.

FRANK BROWNING is the author of *The Culture of Desire.* He has worked for National Public Radio, reporting on the Iran-Contra scandal and gay rights, among other things.

KEVIN KILLIAN is a poet and the author of a novel, *Shy* and a book of memoirs, *Bedrooms Have Windows.* His work has appeared in *Men on Men, Best American Poetry 1988,* and *Discontents.* He lives in San Francisco, where he co-edits the writing/art zine "Mirage #4/Period[ical]" and works with the SF Poets' Theater.

D. G. MILLER is a poet and essayist. His poetry has appeared in many publications, including *The Paris Review, The Threepenny Review, Verse,* and *Agni.*

PETER M. KRASK is a contributor to *1 in 10,* the gay and lesbian magazine of *The Boston Phoenix.* He received his masters degree in Music Criticism at the Peabody Institute of the Johns Hopkins University in 1991. He has written for *The Baltimore Evening Sun,* and *The City Paper.* Also an opera librettist, Mr. Krask has written the texts for the prize-winning opera *With Blood, With Ink,* music by Daniel Crozier, premiered by the Peabody Opera Theatre in 1993, as well as the theater piece *Rendezvous of Light.*

DAVID PLANTE is the author of several novels, including, most recently, *Annunciation, The Francouer Trilogy,* and *The Catholic.* He lives and writes in London.

MICHAEL NAVA is a lawyer and a novelist. He is the author of the Henry Rios mysteries, for which he has won four Lambda Literary Awards. His most recent work is *The Hidden Law,* the fourth in the Rios series, and, with Robert Dawidoff, *Created Equal: Why Gay Rights Matter to America.* His autobiographical essays have appeared in John Preston's anthologies, *Hometowns,* and *A Member of the Family.* He lives in West Hollywood.

GABRIEL LAMPERT was born and raised in Philadelphia, and has lived in the Southwest for most of the past twenty-five years. He teaches mathematics at New Mexico State University where he completed a master's degree in creative writing in 1993.

BRAD GOOCH is the author of *City Poet: The Life and Times of Frank O'Hara* as well as the novel *Scary Kisses.* His work appears regularly in *The New Yorker, Vanity Fair, Out,* and *Harper's Bazaar.* He is currently working on a novel set in New York City in the 1970s.

ALFRED CORN has published seven volumes of poetry, the most recent titled *Autobiographies.* He has also edited a collection of essays titled *Incarnation: Contemporary Authors on the New Testament,* and a book of literary criticism titled *The Metamorphoses of Metaphor.* He is a member of the Episcopal Church and lives in New York City.

PHILIP GAMBONE is the author of a collection of stories, *The Language We Use Up Here.* His essays have appeared in *Hometowns, A Member of the Family, Sister and Brother,* and other publications. A frequent book reviewer in the gay and straight press, Philip teaches at the Park School in Brookline, Massachusetts, and in the expository writing program at Harvard.

FENTON JOHNSON is a novelist—*Crossing the River and Scissors, Paper, Rock,* essayist, and frequent contributor to the *New York Times*

*Magazine.* He wishes to thank Steve Palmer and Howard Tharsing for their help with "God, Gays, and the Geography of Desire."

MICHAEL LOWENTHAL'S writing stems from a search to reconcile his various identities: rich white kid from the suburbs, rural-minded gay man living in a city, Jewish grandson of German WW II refugees, Ivy League valedictorian, editor of erotica. His stories and essays have appeared in *Men on Men 5, Sister and Brother, Flesh and the Word 2,* and *Best American Erotica 1994.* He lives in Boston and is an editor for University Press of New England.

FELICE PICANO is the author of several books, including *Ambidextrous: The Secret Lives of Children, To the Seventh Power, Late in the Season,* and *Men Who Loved Me.* Most recently, he co-authored *The Joy of Gay Sex* and he is featured in a book tracing the history of gay writing after Stonewall entitled *The Violet Quill.*

ANTONIO FELIZ was ordained a High Priest in the Melchizedek Priesthood at age twenty-four, served in three state high councils and as a counselor in three bishoprics of The Church of Jesus Christ of Latter-day Saints. He was made a bishop in 1978. After this title was taken away from him, Feliz published *Out of the Bishop's Closet.*

MARK MATOUSEK has written for *The Utne Reader, Common Boundary, Vogue, Details, Yoga Journal,* and countless other publications. He is working on *Sex, Death, Enlightenment,* a spiritual memoir, which Riverhead Books will be publishing in January 1995.